Table Of Contents

Table Of Contents (Continued)

DETERMINING WHICH CLASS OF LICENSE YOU NEED

CLASS OF LICENSE	If you want to get a license to drive this type of vehicle or a similar tank vehicle	Special endorsement may also be needed
A • Combination vehicles • GCWR over 26,000 lbs. • Towed vehicle(s) over 10,000 lbs.		
B • Trucks or buses over 26,000 lbs. GVWR • Any such vehicle towing a vehicle not in excess of 10,000 lbs. GVWR		**ENDORSEMENTS** **N** Tanks 1,000 gallons or greater **H** Hazardous materials **X** Tanks and Haz Mat **T** Double/triple trailers **P** Greater than 15 passengers including driver **S** School bus
C • Vehicles weighing 26,000 lbs. GVWR or less: – Placarded for hazardous materials – Designed to seat more than 15 people including driver OR –Used as a school bus		
D • Generally, all passenger vehicles, except vehicle in Classes A, B, C, or M		**F For Hire** When a Class D vehicle is operated by a person employed for the principal purpose of driving, and used as a public or common carrier of persons or property
H • Hardship license for drivers between the ages of 14 & 16 in special hardship cases		SPECIAL RESTRICTIONS MAY APPLY
M • Motorcycles and motor-driven cycles		SPECIAL RESTRICTIONS MAY APPLY
P • Issued as an instructional permit for a Class A, B, C, D, and M license PD = "Learner Permit"	SPECIAL RESTRICTIONS APPLY DEPENDING UPON THE PARTICULAR CLASS	

This chapter explains who needs a Tennessee driver license, as well as how to decide which class of license you need and whether or not you qualify. It also covers ID-Only licenses and the new Certificate for Driving (CFD) documents that Tennessee began issuing in July of 2004.

Who Needs a Tennessee Driver License?

If you live in Tennessee and want to drive a motor vehicle, you must have a valid Tennessee driver license or Certificate for Driving.

Anyone who moves to Tennessee and has a valid driver license from another state or country must apply for a Tennessee driver license (or CFD) if they:

- live in the state longer than 30 days
- have taken employment, or
- would otherwise qualify as a registered voter.

What Class of License Do You Need?

In Tennessee, driver licenses (or CFD's) are issued specifically for the class and type of vehicle you operate. Therefore, the class of license you should have depends specifically upon the type of vehicle you operate and for what purpose you use your vehicle.

The chart on the facing page and the discussion which follows should help you determine which class of driver license you need, as well as whether or not you need any special endorsements.

Class D Licenses

Generally speaking, the majority of applicants for a Tennessee driver license (or CFD) will be operators of regular passenger vehicles, pick-up trucks, or vans. This handbook is designed to provide the information you need to get a Class D license.

A Class D vehicle is defined as any vehicle, or any combination of vehicles, with a gross vehicle weight rating of 26,000 pounds or less, as long as:

1. The vehicle is not used for the purpose of transporting hazardous materials which are required by law to be placarded.

2. The vehicle is not used to transport more than fifteen passengers **including** the driver, or

3. The vehicle is not a school bus used to transport children to and from school.

If the vehicle is used for any of these purposes, the driver is required to obtain a Commercial Driver License. CFD's are NOT available for commercial classes.

To qualify for a Class D license, you must be at least sixteen (16) years of age, and must pass a vision test, knowledge test, and driving test. If you are under age 18, you must also meet special qualifications described in the next chapter.

Class D With F (For-Hire Endorsement)

If a person's main job is to drive or transport people in a Class D vehicle, a For Hire endorsement must be added to the Class D license. This endorsement replaces what formerly was called a "chauffeur" or "special chauffeur" license.

The Class D license with a For Hire endorsement (Class D with F) serves as a bridge between the regular driver license required for private transportation and the commercial license required for tractor-trailers, large trucks, buses and the like. Examples of people whose job requires them to have the For Hire endorsement include:

- Taxi, shuttle service drivers
- Couriers, delivery services (flowers, pizza, etc.)
- Ambulance drivers

People hired for some purpose other than driving who drive in the course of doing their job, generally do not need this endorsement. For example, plumbers, meter readers and engineers do not need the For Hire endorsement. Volunteers driving Class D vehicles also do not need this endorsement.

NOTE: Although you may not be required by law to have the For Hire endorsement your employer may require you to obtain this endorsement for insurance or safety requirements.

To add the For Hire endorsement, drivers must meet the eligibility requirements, pass the appropriate tests, and pay a fee of $4.50. Applicants are eligible to apply for this endorsement if:

- They are at least eighteen years old,
- No challenge exists concerning their good character, competency and fitness to be so employed, and
- They will be operating a Class D vehicle.

TESTS REQUIRED — Applicants must pass a vision test, and a knowledge test designed specifically for the For-Hire Endorsement. To prepare for the knowledge test, you should carefully study this entire driver handbook.

Class M (Motorcycle)

The operator of a motorcycle, motor-driven cycle, or motorized bicycle will need to apply for a Class M license. These two and three-wheeled vehicles are categorized by cylinder capacity and other design features. Generally, if the vehicle is over 125 cubic centimeters, a Class M license is issued; under 125cc, a Class M limited license is issued.

Class M licenses may be issued as a single license, or along with another primary class. For example, if a driver wishes to be able to operate both a motorcycle and a Class D vehicle, he or she should apply for a Class DM license.

Applicants wishing to apply for a Class M license should obtain and read the Motorcycle Operator Manual in addition to this manual. "Off-road" motor vehicles are not allowed to be used for the road test.

Class A, B, or C (Commercial)

Operators of larger and more complex vehicles will need to apply for a Commercial Driver License (CDL). These licenses include Class A, B, and C depending upon the Gross Vehicle Weight Rating (GVWR), Gross Combination Weight Rating (GCWR), and what is being transported.

In general, state law defines a commercial motor vehicle (CMV) as any vehicle or combination of vehicles weighing more than 26,000 pounds. If hazardous materials are transported, or if the vehicle is designed to transport more than fifteen (15) passengers including the driver, or if the vehicle is used as a school bus, a CDL would also be required, regardless of the weight of the vehicle.

Drivers who need a CDL should obtain the Commercial Driver License Manual which contains detailed information necessary to prepare for the tests. These manuals are available at all driver license stations.

NOTE: If a person holds a valid commercial driver license (Class A, B, or C license), this license is also valid for operating a Class D vehicle. No separate Class D license is required. A Class M license would be needed, however, if a commercial driver also wanted to operate a motorcycle.

Learner Permit (Class PD)

Instructional permits are issued in conjunction with another class of license, indicating the class of vehicle which the operator is legally entitled to drive. For example, the Class PD license allows drivers to learn how to drive Class D vehicles.

To obtain a Class PD license, you must have reached your fifteenth birthday and pass the written and vision tests. You will be permitted to operate an automobile only when accompanied by a licensed driver who is at least 21 years old and who must occupy the seat beside the driver.

To exchange your Class PD license for a Class D license, you are required to take a driving test and another vision test.

If you are less than 18 years old, you must have held a valid Class PD for 180 days and abide by all the requirements of the Graduated Driver License law as outlined in Chapter 3 of this handbook.

No matter how old you are, we suggest that you take adequate time to practice your driving skills and return only when you have mastered these skills. You will not need to repeat your knowledge test unless you let it expire over 12 months.

Class H (Hardship)

A hardship license (Class H) may be issued to a minor who is fourteen or fifteen years old to operate passenger vehicles or motorcycles. These licenses are issued only in cases of family hardship and are limited to specific needs. Proof of hardship must be submitted with a Hardship Application (SF-0263). Each application is reviewed and evaluated on an individual basis. Less than one percent of all licenses issued to minors are hardship licenses.

Applicants who qualify to apply for a hardship license must pass a vision test, knowledge test, and road test. The Class H license is valid only for daylight hours and for travel to authorized locations as specified on an attachment.

Those with a hardship (Class H) license who are at least fifteen (15) years old are extended the same privileges as those holding a Class PD license, when they are accompanied by any of the responsible adults listed for the Class PD.

Regardless of age at time of approval, a Hardship License will expire on the applicant's 16th birthday.

NOTE: If you are approved for a Hardship License and it is less than 6 months till your 16th birthday, you will be required to renew a Class PD upon expiration of your Hardship License. You will need to hold this learner permit until you have attained a total of 180 days driving experience between the <u>two</u> license types and meet the GDL Requirements as outlined in the next chapter.

Identification Licenses ("ID Only")

There are two types of identification licenses which may be obtained for identification purposes only. No testing is required, but all require the applicant to meet the same standards for proof of identity and residency as are required for any driver license. None are valid for any vehicular operation. If an applicant is under the age of eighteen (18) a responsible adult must complete a portion of the Minor/Teen-age Affidavit  and Cancellation form (available at any driver license station) at the time of application.

1. The first type is an "Expiring Identification License" that may be issued to any person not currently holding a valid driver license who presents positive proof of identification and all other requirements detailed in the next chapter.

NOTE: At age sixty-five (65) or older, the ID does not expire.

- Any applicant who does not have a social security number shall complete an affidavit, under penalty of perjury, affirming that the applicant has <u>never</u> been issued a SSN, and must provide either an original or certified copy of one of the following:

    (a) Birth Certificate issued by Tennessee or another state, possession, territory or commonwealth of the USA - OR

    (b) Documentation issued by the United States Immigration and Naturalization Service acceptable to the Department of Safety.

2. The second type is a "permanent identification license" that any person who is mentally retarded or physically handicapped may obtain. In addition to presenting positive proof of identification, they must submit a certified statement from a licensed doctor stating they are unable to operate a vehicle. Those who qualify for this ID may receive it free of charge. ID licenses issued in this manner do not expire.

As a service to Tennessee residents, families with children, including infants, may obtain these identification-only licenses for their children.

Who Is Not Required To Have A Driver License?

- Any member of the armed forces while operating a motor vehicle owned or leased by any branch of the armed services of the United States, including the National Guard.

- Operators of any road machinery, farm tractor, or implement of husbandry which is temporarily operated or moved on a highway.

- Non-residents who have in their immediate possession a valid driver license issued by their home state or country, equivalent to the appropriate class or type of Tennessee license.

- Individuals who are not U.S. citizens and who, in connection with their employment in managerial or technical positions in Tennessee, may operate vehicles with a valid driver license issued by another state, country, or international body for a period of six (6) months.

- Students pursuing an approved driver training course in a public or private secondary school, or in a licensed commercial driver training school for passenger vehicles, when accompanied by a certified instructor.

Who Is Not Eligible?

- Anyone whose license is currently suspended or revoked in this, or any other state

- Anyone the Commissioner has reason to believe would not be able to operate a motor vehicle safely because of mental or physical disabilities

- Anyone who has been proven to be a habitual drunkard or who is addicted to the use of narcotics.

- Anyone required to show proof of financial responsibility who has not done so.

- Anyone under the age of eighteen who has dropped out of school before graduating, or who does not make "satisfactory progress" in school.

- Anyone who cannot provide the required proof of U.S. Citizenship or Lawful Permanent Resident (LPR) status will not qualify for a driver license or identification license (ID Only), HOWEVER they may be eligible for a CERTIFICATE FOR DRIVING (CFD).

Certificate for Driving (CFD)

If an individual is unable to provide proof of U.S. citizenship or lawful permanent residency, they will not qualify for the issuance <u>or renewal</u> of a driver license or identification only license. These individuals may qualify for a Certificate for Driving.

The Certificate for Driving is a certificate issued to persons whose presence in the United States has been authorized by the federal government for a specific purpose and for a specific period of time or to persons who do not satisfy Tennessee requirements for proof of U.S. citizenship or lawful permanent residency, but can meet all other requirements established by the Department of Safety. The Certificate for Driving will clearly state it is For Driving Purposes Only, Not Valid For Identification.

<u>In order to qualify for the Certificate for Driving</u> the applicant will be required to provide the department with two acceptable identification documents, two proofs of Tennessee residency and proof of social security number (or sworn affidavit if no SSN has been issued) in addition to passing the required vision, knowledge and skills tests where applicable.

A list of acceptable documents for positive proof of identity, proof of Tennessee residency, and proof of U.S. Citizenship or Lawful Permanent Resident (LPR) status can be found in Chapter 2 of this Tennessee Driver Handbook.

The Certificate for Driving (CFD) is not available for commercial class vehicles (A, B, C). A CFD may be obtained for other non-commercial class vehicles including motorcycles and as a learner permit for non-commercial class vehicles.

The types used for CFD are the same as out-lined earlier in this chapter for licenses with the exception of the letter "T" that will precede each type designation to indicate it is a "certificate" and not a "license". For example:

TD = Certificate for Driving a Class D vehicle (page 7)
TM = Certificate for Driving a Class M vehicle (page 8)
TPD = Certificate for Class D vehicle learner permit (page 8)
TH = Certificate for Hardship driving approval (page 8)

Combinations of the above may also be issued such as:
TDM = CFD for a Class D and Class M vehicle
TMPD = CFD for a Class M and learner permit for Class D
TPDM = CFD for learner permit for both Class D and M

PENALTY FOR DRIVING WITHOUT A LICENSE

Driving without being licensed is a class B misdemeanor. The penalty is a fine up to five hundred dollars ($500) and/or six months in jail.

While driving in Tennessee you must have your driver license in your possession to display upon demand to any law enforcement officer. If you do not have your license with you, you may be fined not less than two dollars ($2.00) and no more than fifty dollars ($50.00).

Other Driver Related Topics

Anatomical Gifts

More than 82,000 Americans, including over 1,600 Tennesseans, are waiting for a life-saving organ transplant. Seventeen people die each day while waiting because there is a shortage of donors. Hundreds of thousands more need a life-enhancing tissue or cornea transplant. (Source: www.unos.org)

More than 750,000 Americans benefit from a life-enhancing tissue transplant each year another 46,500 have better vision each year as a result of corneal transplants. Your decision to become an organ and tissue donor can save or enhance someone's life.

By signing the back of your driver's license, you could be giving someone the ultimate gift — the Gift of Life. When you apply for a driver's license, or renew your current one, there will be a box for you to check which indicates your wishes to be an organ and tissue donor. If you are getting a new photo license a Red heart shape will appear in upper right corner of your photo for a visual notation of your choice to "share your life". You may fill out the Tennessee Organ Donor Card on the back of your license at any time or on the top portion of your renewal sticker if you make your choice as a part of your renewal by mail or internet.

In July, 2001, the law changed to make a signed driver's license or donor card the ultimate way to indicate a person's decision to become a donor. The law clarifies that only the person signing the driver's license can revoke this decision — no one else. It is important, however, for your family members to know

TENNESSEE DONOR AGENCIES
East Tennessee
Mountain Region Donor Services 888 562-3774
....or (423) 915-0808
East Tennessee Eye Bank ....(865) 544-9625
Knoxville Area
Tenn. Donor Services 888-562-3774
....or (423) 588-1031
East Tenn. Eye Bank ....(865) 544-9625
Nashville Area
Tenn. Donor Services Tissue Bank 888-234-4440
....or (615) 327-2247
Chattanooga Area
Tennessee Donor Services.........................(423) 756-5267
Lions Eye Bank..(423) 778-4000
Jackson Area
Tennessee Donor Services.........................(731) 425-6393
Memphis Area
Midsouth Transplant Foundation ....(901) 328-4438
Midsouth Eye Bank...................................(901) 726-8264
Regional Medical Center Skin Bank ....(901) 545-8313

your decision about donation so they can ensure your wishes are carried out.

For more information regarding organ and tissue donation, please contact the agencies in your area. You may also contact The Coalition on Donation at www.shareyourlife.org or 1-800-355-SHARE

"Motor Voter"

To make it easy for citizens to apply to register to vote, the law requires us to offer you the opportunity to register to vote, or to update your voting records, when you apply for a driver license or ID. The Department does not actually process your voter registration application. Instead, we forward your information to your local election commission, if you request.

• **REMEMBER:** *Only the Election Registrar can process and issue a voter registration card*. The Driver License Office simply transmits your application to the appropriate County Election Commission in order to save you an additional trip. **IF you have not received your Voter Registration Card within 30 days of applying at the DL Office you should contact you local County Election Commission immediately.**

International Driving Permit (IDP)

Possession of an International Driving Permit does not mean that the holder is valid to operate an automobile in Tennessee or any other state. Do NOT be fooled by Internet sites that claim that you can drive on such a permit if you license is suspended or revoked in any state. The facts about International Driving Permits (IDP) are as follows:

• *An International Driving Permit is an official translation of a driver's home state or country driver license into the nine official languages of the United Nations, including English. This translated document is to be **used in conjunction with** the valid driver license issued by the driver's home state or country.*

• *U.S. Citizens traveling abroad and/or foreign visitors to the Untied States are **NOT required** to have an International Driving Permit. However it can be useful in emergencies such as traffic violations or auto accidents when a foreign language is involved.*

• *The International Driving Permit MUST be obtained in the home country of the driver.*

   ° **U.S. Citizens:** In order to obtain an IDP a United States citizen must:

· Be at least eighteen (18) years of age

· Hold a VALID U.S. State, Territorial or U.S. Department of State Driver License, which is NOT under revocation or suspension at the time the IDP is issued.

The IDP is valid for one (1) year only from the date of issuance and if the applicant's state license expires and is not renewed or is suspended during that year the IDP becomes in-valid. The IDP is NOT valid for driving in the United States or its territories and it is NOT valid by itself for driving. The IDP MUST be carried with the driver's regular valid U.S. Driver License.

° NON-U.S. Citizens: must obtain their International Driving Permit in their native country prior to arrival in the U.S. if desired. An IDP can NOT be issued to a foreign visitor by any agency in the United States. The Tennessee Driver License Offices do NOT issue International Driving Permits. Any Tennessee resident who is interested in obtaining an IDP before traveling abroad should contact a local American Automobile Association (AAA) office or visit their website at: www.aaasouth.com

APPLYING FOR YOUR LICENSE

What Do You Need To Bring?

To reduce the potential for fraud, and to protect *you*, it is necessary for us to be able to determine that you are "who you say you are." This is why it is necessary for you to bring us positive proof of your name and date of birth, and why we require original or certified documents, not photocopies.

If your current name is different than the one shown on these documents, you must be able to show all of the links between your name currently on file with the department and the name you currently desire to have shown, with each link supported by original, certified legal documents. We cannot accept name changes through the mail.

You can apply for your license anywhere, not just in the county where you live. For a complete list of driver license stations, see the list of stations on last two pages of this handbook.

This chapter describes what you need to do to apply for your license (or CFD). For a quick overview, see the checklist at the end of this chapter.

Proof of Identity

The Driver License Examiner will require positive proof of date of birth and identification of any person applying for any class of driver license (or CFD) or photo identification license. The Examiner will ask for two (2) items of proof as follows:

- ORIGINAL applicants must have at least one item from the Primary Identification list. The second item may be from the Secondary Identification list or another item from the primary list.
- Applicants for DUPLICATES or RENEWAL of an existing Tennessee DL/ID generally must provide 2 items from either list.
- NEW RESIDENTS must surrender their license from the former state -OR- provide the same two (2) items of proof as required of an ORIGINAL applicant.
- CHANGE OF NAME: Applicant's will need proof (such as original certified court order, marriage certificate, divorce decree, etc.) of name changes when any of the primary or secondary documents detailed below have a name different than the applicant's current name.

Primary Identification

Acceptable primary identification includes but is not limited to original or certified documents with full name and date of birth, such as the following items:

Table: 2.1

Document	Notes
• U.S. photo driver license or photo ID card or license from another country. Photo document must be issued by state or federal agency.	May also include photo learner permits - Licenses not issued in English, must be translated and accompanied by a Certificate of Accurate Translation —or— a valid International Driving Permit.
• Original or Certified Birth Certificate	- Must be original or certified copy, have a seal and be issued by an authorized government agency such as the Bureau of Vital Statistics or State Board of Health. - Hospital issued certificates and baptismal certificates are **NOT** acceptable. - Foreign birth certificates, not issued in English, must be translated and accompanied by a Certificate of Accurate Translation.
• Military Identification	Active Duty, Retiree or Reservist military ID card Discharge papers Military Dependent ID card
• Passport (Valid)	Passports, not issued in English, must be translated and accompanied by a Certificate of Accurate Translation. Passports are not acceptable if expired.
• Immigration Naturalization Service documentation	*Certificate of Naturalization* N-550, N-570, N-578 *Certificate of Citizenship* N-560, N-561, N-645 Northern Mariana Card, American Indian Card U.S. Citizen Identification Card (I-179, I-197) Temporary Resident Identification Card (I-688) *Travel Documents* - Record of Arrival and Departure (I-94) I-551 U.S. Re-entry Permit (I-327) Employment Authorization card (I-688A, I-688-B, I-766) *Refugee I-94* Record of Arrival and Departure stamped "Refugee", not likely to be in a foreign passport Refugee Travel Document (I-571) *Canadian documents* Immigration Record and Visa or Record of Landing (IMM 100) Canadian Department of Indian Affairs issued ID card
• Marriage Certificate	Must include the applicant's full name and date of birth. The certificate must be the copy that is registered AFTER the marriage; NOT just the "license" authorizing the union.
• Federal Census Record	Must include the applicant's full name and date of birth (age)
• Applicant's Own Child's Birth Certificate	Must include the applicant's full name and date of birth (age)
• Adoptive Decree	Must include the applicant's full name and date of birth
• Legal Change of Name (Divorce, etc.)	As recorded in court decree with judge's original signature and/or official court seal
• Any confirmation of date of birth in court of law	As recorded in court document(s) with judge's original signature and/or official court seal

Any other documentary evidence which confirms to the satisfaction of the Department the true identity and date of birth of the applicant.

Secondary Identification

Document	Notes
• Computerized Check Stubs	Must include the applicant's full name pre-printed on the stub.
• Union Membership Cards	Must include the applicant's full name
• Work IDs	Preferably with photo
• Financial Institution Documents	Computer printouts of bank statements, savings account statements, loan documents, etc.
• Social Security Documents	SS Card (original only not metal or plastic replicas), printout, benefits statements, etc.
• Health Insurance card	TennCare, Medicaid, Medicare, etc.
• IRS / state tax form	W2 Forms, Property tax receipts, etc.
• Military Records	Assignment orders, selective service cards, Leave & Earnings Statement, etc.

NOTE: 2003 legislation prevents the Department of Safety from accepting the Matricula Consular Card as proof of identification for a Driver License.

Proof of Tennessee Residency

The Driver License Examiner will also require positive proof of Tennessee residency for the following applicants:

- ORIGINAL applicants for a first time ID, CFD, permit or license of any class.

- NEW RESIDENT applicants for an ID, CFD, permit or license of any class.

- RETURNING RESIDENT applicants for an ID, CFD, permit or license of any class (even when the applicant may have previously held a Tennessee ID or license before moving out of state).

Items that will be considered as acceptable proof of residency shall consist of two (2) separate documents from the lists shown in Table 2.2 as long as the documents contain the following information:

1. The applicant's name - OR -

2. The name of the applicant's spouse, if the applicant has a spouse (proof of relationship required) - OR -

3. If the applicant is a minor, the name of a parent or legal guardian (proof of relationship required)

4. The Tennessee residence address used on the application for ID, permit or license of any class. (NOTE: Most items in List B will NOT have the address but are still acceptable)

5. Documents must be originals; no photocopies or facsimile copies can be accepted.

NOTE: Proof of relationship is generally the certified marriage or birth certificate. (long-form)

Table: 2.2

Two Documents From List A Showing residence address used on application and your name, or name of your parent, guardian or spouse	OR	One Document From List A and One Document From List B
LIST A • Current utility bill including telephone, electric, water, gas, cable, etc. (Must include postmarked envelope bill was mailed in) Initial Deposit Receipt is NOT acceptable. • Current bank statement (not checks) • Current rental/Mortgage contract fully signed and executed or receipt including deed of sale for property • Current employer verification including paycheck / check stub, work ID or badge, etc. • Current automobile, life or health insurance policy (not wallet cards) • Current driver license or ID issued by the State of Tennessee to a parent, legal guardian or spouse of applicant (proof of relationship required) • Current Tennessee motor vehicle registration • Current Tennessee voter registration • Current IRS tax reporting W-2 Form • Receipt for personal property or real estate taxes paid within the last year • In case of student enrolled in public or private school in this state, student may provide a photo student ID and acceptable documentation that student lives on campus.		**LIST B** • Individual Taxpayer Identification Number (ITIN) issued by the IRS • Form I-94 issued to the applicant by the Immigration and Naturalization Service (INS) • Employment authorization document (E.A.D.) issued to the applicant by the INS • I-551 issued to the applicant by the INS

REMEMBER — NO PHOTOCOPIES!

Social Security Numbers

Tennessee law requires the social security number for all applications where the U.S. Government has issued the applicant a social security number. The department is also required to maintain this information on each applicant's record. However, you can choose whether or not to have it printed on your license.

Tennessee has a computer link with the Social Security Administration, so most applicants will not have to present proof of the social security number. The computer will simply return a message indicating that the number matches (or not). If the social security number provided fails to match with the computer records; the Examiner will then be required to ask for proof of the number from the applicant. Some documents the Examiner can use as proof are listed below. These documents may also serve as a second piece of identification.

- Your original Social Security card
- The Internal Revenue Service W-2 Wage and Tax Statement form
- A computer generated payroll check (check stub) or bank statement
- Health insurance card with both name and Social Security number

If You Have Never Been Issued a Social Security Number

New legislation passed in May of 2001 allows applicants who have never been issued a social security number to sign a sworn affidavit to that effect. This affidavit is available at any Driver License Station and must be signed in the presence of an Examiner or Notary Public. By signing this affidavit the applicant attests, under the penalty of perjury, that no social security number has ever been issued to them by the U.S. Government. This affidavit allows the Department of Safety to process the application without the requirement of the social security number.

Proof of U.S. Citizenship or Lawful Permanent Residency

Tennessee has a law requiring proof of U.S. Citizenship or Lawful Permanent Residency in order to obtain a Tennessee driver license or Identification Only License. This policy requires first-time applicants, new and returning residents, applicants reinstating a driver license after being revoked, suspended or cancelled (regardless of when the license was issued) and anyone issued a Tennessee driver license or photo identification license since January 1, 2001 upon renewing for the first time, to provide documentation they are either a U.S. Citizen or a Lawful Permanent Resident (LPR).

If an applicant is unable to provide the required proof discussed above or they only have "temporary" immigration status they will NOT be eligible of a regular driver license or identification only license. However, they may be issued a Certificate for Driving (CFD) as long as they have all the

Acceptable documents proving an applicant is a U.S. citizen or a lawful permanent resident include, but are not limited to, the following:

- Official Birth Certificate issued by a U.S. state, jurisdiction or territory (Puerto Rico, U.S. Virgin Islands, Northern Mariana Islands, American Samoa, Swain's Island, Guam);
- U.S. Government-issued Certified Birth Certificate;
- U.S. Certificate of Birth Abroad (DS-1350 or FS-545);
- Report of Birth Abroad of a Citizen of the U.S. (FS-240);
- Valid or expired U.S. Passport;
- Certificate of Citizenship (N560 or N561);
- Certificate of Naturalization (N550, N570 or N578);
- Unexpired U.S. Active Duty/Retiree/Reservist Military ID Card (DOD DD-2);
- U.S. Citizen Identification Card (I-197, I-179);
- INS I-551 Permanent Resident Alien Card;
- Foreign passport stamped by the U.S. Government indicating that the holder has been "Processed for I-551",
- Permanent resident Re-entry Permit (I-327);
- Temporary I-551 stamp on Form I-94 Arrival/Departure Record, with photograph of the applicant;
- U.S. Department of Receptions and Placement Program Assurance Form (Refugee) and I-94 stamped refugee;
- Form I-94 Record of Arrival and Departure stamped Asylee; Parolee or Parole, refugee, asylum, HP (humanitarian parolee or PIP (public interest parolee).

other required proofs of identification, Tennessee residency, social security number or affidavit and can pass the required examinations for the class of CFD needed. For more details on the Certificate for Driving (CFD) see Chapter 1 of this handbook.

License Fees At A Glance

Tennessee licenses now expire every five years on the driver's birthday evenly divisible by five (age 30, 35, 40 . . . 55, 60, 65, etc.). This makes it easier for drivers to remember when it is time to renew, and means they have to renew less often than before.

To get you on the "Drive for Five" cycle, your first license may be for a shorter or longer period than five years. If so, fees will be pro-rated. Everyone pays the same fees PER YEAR for each license. The fees shown in Table 2.4 as "standard fees" are calculated for a 5-year license and include an application fee.

Your actual fees may vary slightly depending upon your age at the time of applying. The actual fee and number of years issued will be determined by the age you are within 6 months of (i.e. 21 + 3 months = 21st birthday issue for 4 years, or 21 + 8 months = 22nd birthday issue for 3 years)

Table: 2.4

License Class (standard 5-year cycle)	License Fees	Minimum Age	Certificate Fees	CFD Type (standard 1-year cycle*)
D - Operator	$19.50	16	$19.50	TD - Class D Vehicle
D w/For Hire	$22.00	18	N/a	N/a
Adding For Hire	$4.50	18	N/a	N/a
PD - Learner Permit (over age 18)	$5.50 (1 yr)	18	$19.50 (1 yr)	TPD - Class D Permit (over age 18)
PD - Learner Permit (under age 18)	$10.50 (1yr)	15	$24.50 (1 yr)	TPD - Class D Permit (under age 18)
H - Hardship	$9.00	14	$19.50	TH - Hardship
ID Only	$5.00	Under 18	N/a	N/a
ID Only	9.50	Over 18	N/a	N/a
M-Motorcycle	$20.50	14	$20.50	TN - Class M Vehicle
DM - Operator & Motorcycle	$38.00	16	$38.00	TDM - Class D & M Vehicles
Class A	$46.00	21	N/a	N/a
Class B or C	$41.00	21	N/a	N/a
1st Duplicate - D or M	$8.00	—	$19.50	1st Duplicate - D or M
2nd or subsequent Duplicate - D or M	$12.00	—	$19.50	2nd or subsequent Duplicate - D or M
1st Duplicate - CDL	$12.00	—	N/a	N/a
2nd or subsequent Duplicate - CDL	$16.00	—	N/a	N/a
Intermediate Restricted - D	$24.50	16	$24.50	Intermediate Restricted - TD
Intermediate Unrestricted - D	$2.00	17	$2.00	Intermediate Unrestricted - TD
"Graduating" to Class D	$8.00	18	$19.50	"Graduating" to Class TD

*Certificate cycle could extend up to maximum of 5 years based on validity of immigration documents presented.

Certificate (CFD) Fees At A Glance

The Certificate for Driving (CFD) is NOT issued on the same schedule as a driver license. A CFD will generally be issued for only one (1) year from the date of issuance, unless the applicant provides immigration documentation with a valid expiration date of more than one year. In those cases the expiration date will be set to coincide with the expiration date of the immigration documents up to a maximum term of five (5) years.

The fees for a Certificate for Driving (CFD) therefore are fixed rates that do not change with the length of time the CFD is issued. The cost for a Certificate for Driving will be $19.50 regardless of the type issued (TD, TPD, etc.) or whether issued for one year, two years or the maximum of five years.

Additional fees are applied to the CFD cost the same as with a license. For example a minor applying for a GDL Certificate for Driving will pay the additional $5.00 GDL fee at the applicable levels for a total of $24.50. If getting a CFD for a motorcycle the additional $1.00 motorcycle fee will apply for a total of $20.50 and also if the applicant is getting a CFD for two types they will be charged for each type plus any applicable additional fees (for example $38.00 for a Class-Type TDM).

Other Applicants

New Residents

People who move to Tennessee must obtain a Tennessee driver license (or CFD) no later than thirty days after establishing residency. After passing the required tests, they must surrender all out-of-state driver licenses. Tennessee law does not allow a resident of this state to hold more than one valid license or ID.

If the new resident presents an out-of-state driver license that has not expired, only the vision test is required, unless otherwise deemed necessary by the Examiner. However, if the license has expired over six months, all tests are required.

New residents must also provide items for proof of residency as listed at the beginning of this chapter (Table 2-2) and proof of citizenship (Table 2-3).

Military Personnel

If a person holds a valid Tennessee license and is in or enters into the United States armed forces, that license shall remain valid as long as the person remains on active duty, and is based outside this state. Members of the National Guard and family members of military personnel are not eligible for this provision.

While on active duty and stationed outside of Tennessee, the military person may have a "Code 30" placed on the license to indicate that the license does not expire. To add this code, bring a copy of your military orders to the driver license station and pay the appropriate fees.

Note, after you have been honorably discharged or separated from the military, or reassigned to a duty station back in Tennessee, you have sixty (60) days following the date of separation on the DD214 form to renew your license without any penalty or added tests.

Other Common Questions

Q: How Do I Replace a Lost License?

If your driver license or learner permit is ever lost, stolen or destroyed, you may obtain a duplicate by applying at any driver license station or you can visit our website (www.tennessee.gov) to see if your eligible to apply for your duplicate on-line. If you must apply in person, you will need to present proper identification, and pay the appropriate fee. This fee may vary depending upon the number of duplicates applied for during the current renewal cycle of your license.

Q: How Do I Renew My License?

The department mails every driver a <u>courtesy</u> renewal notice from four to six weeks before their licenses expire. READ YOUR RENEWAL NOTICE CAREFULLY. There are several ways to renew a driver license, which will be explained on your notice.

- If you have a current valid photo license, you may renew by mail, or by Internet.

- If you renewed by mail or internet on your last renewal, or have certain types of licenses, your renewal notice will direct you to go to your nearest driver license station to have a new photograph made.

- If you are 60 years old or older and choose to have a non-photo license, you may obtain this by mail or internet. You will be sent a new non-photo license to replace your old license.

Don't Let Your License Expire. No matter how you renew, the important thing is to do so <u>before</u> your license expires. If you let 30 days go by after your expiration date, there will be a five-dollar late fee. After six months, the late fee doubles to $10.00. If you let five years go by without renewing, not only will you have to pay the $10.00 late fee, you will also have to pass vision, knowledge, and skills test.

NOTE:These are not "grace periods." **When your license expires, you are no longer entitled to drive**, and will be subject to the same penalties as someone who has never been licensed. It is your responsibility to maintain the validity of your license.

If you do not receive your renewal notice, you may simply take your current license to any driver license station. The renewal notice itself is not necessary for you to be able to renew your license.

Q: How Do I Change My Address?

It is important to notify the department of safety! If your residence address changes (even though you may not have moved) you are required by state law to notify the Department of Safety within **ten (10) days** of this change. Sometimes addresses are changed without people actually moving. For example, if your area installs an emergency "911" system, your address may be changed with the Post Office. But simply notifying postal authorities will not provide the information to us. By failing to notify us, you could miss the renewal date of your license, or even have your driving privileges suspended or revoked unnecessarily.

The law does not require the address to be changed on your actual license, just on our files. If you want to have your record updated, write to us and give us your name (as it appears on your license), date-of-birth, Social Security number and, of course, your driver license number. You may do this by letter, by picking up a change-of-address form at any driver license station, or by internet.

If you want a new license issued that reflects this change, you may go to a driver license station, pay the appropriate fees, and have a new license issued or you may visit our website at www.tennessee.gov and apply for a duplicate with the new address on-line.

When giving us your new address, remember that by law, your license must show your legal resident address: a house, and/or apartment number and the street or a route and box number. The city along with the correct zip code is also required. A post office box <u>alone</u> will not be accepted as a mailing address. For on-line service visit our web site at: http://www.tn.gov/safety

Q: How May I Choose to Release Personal Information From My Record?

The Federal Driver Privacy Protection Act (DPPA) prohibits the dissemination or disclosure of personal information from a motor vehicle record without the "express consent" of the person to whom such information pertains.

Therefore, in order to comply with the act, as of June 1, 2000 the personal information contained in your driver license record is protected. Without your express consent, **we will not** release your personal information to people wanting a mailing list or individuals who ask for your record for an unspecified purpose.

If you want us to release your information you should visit the local Driver License Station to file your request or visit our website at http//www.tn.gov/safety/dl/privacy.html

GRADUATED DRIVER LICENSE PROCEDURES

If Under Age Eighteen

First License or Learner Permit

Tennessee began issuing a Graduated Driver License on July 1, 2001.

Purpose: To incrementally teach young drivers how to drive by guiding their progression toward full, unrestricted driving.

Focus: To increase the young driver's awareness of the responsibility entrusted to those granted the privilege of driving.

Goal: To increase this awareness through requiring minimum levels of driving experience and safe driving history (record) before allowing teenage drivers to receive a "full-fledged" Class D driver license.

Graduated Driver License

The rules for getting a driver license (or CFD) for those under age 18 are covered in this chapter. Motor vehicle crashes are the major cause of death for young people between the ages of 15 and 20. By requiring more supervised practice, the State of Tennessee hopes to save lives and prevent tragic injuries.

LEARNER PERMIT

- You must be 15 years old and pass the standard written and visual exams.
- You must hold a learner permit for 180 days.
- You may drive a car only when accompanied by a license driver 21 years or older who is riding in the front seat of the vehicle.
- You may not drive between the hours of 10 P.M. and 6 A.M.
- Passengers between 4-17 years of age must wear a seat belt.

Intermediate License

There are two (2) Intermediate License levels for those who are under 18 years of age. The first level is the Intermediate Restricted License and the second level is the Intermediate Unrestricted License.

FIRST LEVEL - INTERMEDIATE RESTRICTED LICENSE

- You must be sixteen (16) years old and pass the driving test.
- You must have held a learner permit for 180 days.
- You cannot have more than six (6) points on your record during the immediate 180 days preceding your application.
- You must have verification from a parent, legal guardian or driving instructor stating you have fifty (50) hours (ten (10) hours at night) of driving experience.
- Passengers between 4 and 17 years of age must wear a seat belt.

SECOND LEVEL - INTERMEDIATE UNRESTRICTED LICENSE

- To obtain this license you must be 17 years old.
- No additional tests are required.
- You must have held an Intermediate Restricted License for one (1) year.
- You cannot have accumulated more than six points on your driving record.
- You cannot have had a traffic accident that was your fault.
- You cannot have 2 seat belt violations.
- Passengers between 4 and 17 years of age must wear a seat belt.

FINAL LEVEL - REGULAR DRIVER LICENSE

- You may obtain a Class D regular driver license when you are 18 years of age, or
- Upon graduating from high school or receiving a GED.

The word Intermediate" will be removed, however, the license will still include the "Under 21" indicators.

Proof of Behind The Wheel Driving Experience

Applicants under 18 applying for the Intermediate Restricted Class D must provide certification that they have completed fifty (50) hours of supervised driving experience while holding a valid permit. This experience must include a minimum of ten (10) hours of night-time driving.

Certification of driving experience must be made on the official form (SF-1256) provided by the Department of Safety. This form is available at all DL Stations or may be downloaded from our web site. This form must be signed by either a parent, legal guardian or licensed driving instructor.

Hardship Driver Licenses

The Graduate Driver License (GDL) law **DID NOT** affect or change the Hardship procedures in any manner.

- Hardships can still be issued at age fourteen (14) and will always expire on the driver's sixteenth (16th) birthday.
- Hardships will still automatically serve as a PD once the holder turns fifteen (15) years of age.

If the Hardship (or PD) has not been held by the driver for the minimum of 180 days by the time the Hardship expires on the sixteenth birthday the driver will have to be re-issued the learner permit. This permit will need to be carried for the remainder of time to complete the required 180 days before the issuance of an Intermediate Restricted (IR) can be allowed. The Hardship license still CAN NOT be renewed.

New Residents Under 18

If the minor is age fifteen (15) and has a valid permit from the previous state then a Tennessee learner permit is the only thing that may be issued. The minor must hold a valid permit for a total of 180 days and have attained the age of 16 before being eligible for the Intermediate Restricted License Class D.

- The length of time the minor has held the permit in the previous state may be included in the required 180 day period as long as the minor can provide a certified driving record from the previous state:

  1. Issued within the 30 days immediately preceding the date of Tennessee application and,

  2. Showing a clear driving record with absolutely no violations or accidents on their record. If there are any violations on the previous state record the minor will be required to obtain the Tennessee Learner Permit until the driving record can be reviewed by the Driver Improvement Section to see if the record complies with the "less than 6 points" requirement of Tennessee law.

If the minor is age 16 and holds a valid license (regular, provisional, probationary, graduated, etc.) from the previous state that has been issued for 90 days or more they may apply for an Intermediated Restricted license only.

- If the minor has held the out-of-state license for LESS than 90 days an Intermediate Restricted License may NOT be issued unless a clear driving record form the previous state is provided confirming:

  1. A valid learner permit and/or license class has been held for a combined period of not less than 180 days. (i.e. GA permit held for 120 days + GA license held for 60 days = 180 days total).

  2. NO violations or accidents on the driving record, if any violations on the record then the applicant may only be issued a learner permit, until the previous state record can be reviewed and evaluated by the Driver Improvement Section to see if it complies with the "less than 6 points" requirement of Tennessee law.

Regardless of the length of time the minor has carried the license in the previous state they will be required to hold the **Tennessee** Intermediate Restricted license for a full year before qualifying for the second level GDL.

- If the minor has graduated from high school or received their GED prior to turning 18 they may apply for the regular Class D operator's license as described previously.

Features of The GDL Photo License

(See next page for examples) All GDL levels will have the photo on the right side of the license and a yellow header bar.

Some of the features of the licenses issued to minors under GDL include:

- **Learner Permits** will have a red color coded Tennessee state imprint indicating GDL in the lower left corner.

  ° A minor who is issued a learner permit will be given a **"restriction card"** to carry along with the permit that explains the restrictions and requirements to advance to the first level of the Class D license under the GDL Program. An example is shown on page 18.

- **Both levels of the Intermediate License issued** under the GDL program will show the license class as Class D as well

as having the words INTERMEDIATE DRIVER LICENSE displayed in the yellow header bar on the front of the license. New Tennessee shaped designations on the face of the license document will indicate at which level the license holder currently is under the GDL Program. Yellow indicates 1st level Intermediate Restricted and Green will indicate Level 2 the Intermediate Unrestricted.

  ° A minor who is issued the first level **Intermediate Restricted (IR)** Class D will also be given a **"restriction card"** to carry along with the license that explains the restrictions and requirements to advance to the second level of the Class D license under the GDL Program. An example is shown on next page.

- A minor who is issued the second level **Intermediate Unrestricted (IU)** Class D will not be issued any special cards as there are not any restrictions upon their driving at this level of the GDL Program.

Additional Requirements for Minors

In addition to the requirements described in Chapter 2 (Proof of ID, TN Residency, SSN and U.S Citizenship / Lawful Permanent Resident) all applicants under the age of eighteen (18) must also meet the requirements described in this section.

Minor/Teenage Affidavits

Applicants not yet eighteen years old must have an adult sign a Minor/Teenage Affidavit and Cancellation form, available at all driver license stations. This form confirms that the adult signing the form joins in the application for the license and will be responsible for the actions of the minor driver. It must be signed by a parent, a step-parent living at the same address as the applicant, legal guardian, or a grandparent authorized by the parent, step-parent or guardian.

If adults cannot accompany the minor to the driver license station to sign the form, it may be picked up ahead of time and signed before a notary public.

If the grandparent is assuming financial responsibility for the youth, the grandparent must bring a notarized statement authorizing this, signed by the parent, step-parent, custodian or guardian, as appropriate. The statement is not on a department form, but should be in the following general format:

"I do hereby authorize _____
(name of grandparent)
to sign for a driver license for_____."
(name of minor)
Signed: _____
(name and relationship of adult granting authorization)
(Notary certificate)

- If a minor applies for a different class of license (such as motorcycle) the parents or legal guardian will be required to sign a second teenage affidavit for that license type.

Proof of School Attendance/Progress

Applicants under the age of 18 must prove they are either enrolled in or have already graduated from high school. Acceptable proof of this status must be provided to the examiner in one of the following methods:

Examples of the license documents issued under the Graduated Driver License (GDL) Program are shown below.

Learner Permit

Intermediate Restricted

Front of PD Card

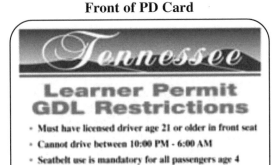

Front of IR Card

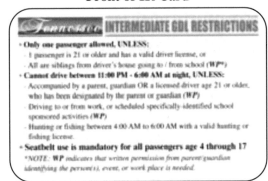

Back of PD Card

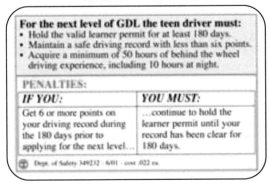

Back of IR Card

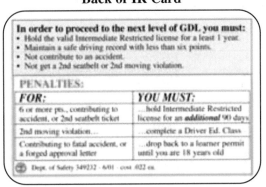

Intermediate Unrestricted

Note: No Restriction Card issued with this level. No driving restriction applied at this level.

1. If graduated the applicant must **bring their original high school diploma or G.E.D. certificate** with them when they apply (no photo copies).

2. If still enrolled in a Tennessee school the applicant needs to **ask their school to complete a Certificate of Compulsory School Attendance (Form SF1010) and take the original part of this form with them to a driver license station.** This form is valid for only one month (30 days) from the date of signing by the school official.

   - During the traditional summer vacation months a properly completed SF1010 form signed within the last 30 days of the school year will be accepted throughout the summer until 30 days after the start of the following school year (i.e. signed in May accepted through Aug/Sept approximately).

3. If the applicant is enrolled in school outside of Tennessee (or in an approved private or church school in Tennessee without access to the SF1010 forms) they must provide a statement from the school principal or headmaster **on official school letterhead specifically confirming that the applicant is not truant and is making satisfactory progress in their school classes**.

   - Grade cards or school transcripts are not acceptable as proof of compliance with this law. Due to the various grading scales, evaluation of excused / unexcused absences and other factors that differ from school system to school system the Driver License personnel are not authorized to interpret the information in these documents. It is the responsibility of the school system or Department of Education to confirm the applicants eligibility and of the applicant to provide satisfactory documentation of this eligibility as required by the Department of Safety.

4. If the applicant is being **Home Schooled the documentation required is as follows:**

   - **Letter from the Superintendent's Office** in the county of the applicant's legal residence confirming that the parent has registered their "intent to home school" with the County School System.

   - **Verification of Home School Enrollment (Form SF-1193)** signed and completed by the parent or legal guardian of the applicant affirming the attendance and satisfactory progress of the applicant in the home school courses. Generally home schooling is conducted by the parent/guardian and thus they have the responsibility to confirm this eligibility same as the regular school teacher or principal.

5. Tennessee Department of Education does **NOT** recognize completion of Internet or "correspondence school" courses and thus documentation from these sources would NOT be acceptable to the Department of Safety as meeting the requirements for licensing of minors.

Unsafe driving incidents or violations that could result in the suspension or automatic downgrade of license level under The GDL Program are outlined in the following table:

GDL Penalties (Table: 3.1)			
Incident	After PD Issued	After Intermediate Restricted Issued	After Intermediate Unrestricted Issued
(a) Six or more points on driving record	Requires the applicant to continue to hold the learner permit for an additional time period until they are able to maintain a record with less than 6 points for 180 consecutive days	Adds 90 days to the minimum 1 year teen required to hold Intermediate Restricted (Total = 1 year & 3 months)	If any of the violations listed in (a), (b), (c) or (d) occurred during the time the teen had an Intermediate Restricted license, but the DOS did not receive notice from the court until *after* we had already issued the teen an Intermediate Unrestricted license, **the penalties in the preceding column will still apply.** The teen will be "dropped back" to an Intermediate Restricted license for 90 days.
(b) Contributing to the occurrence of an accident	N/A	Adds 90 days to the minimum 1 year teen required to hold Intermediate Restricted (Total = 1 year & 3 months)	
(c) Conviction of a 2nd Seatbelt violation	N/A	N/A Adds 90 days to the minimum 1 year teen required to hold Intermediate Restricted (Total = 1 year & 3 months)	
(d) Conviction of a 2nd Moving violation	N/A	Requires completion of a certified driver education course	
(e) Forged letter of parental approval	N/A	Revocation of Intermediate Restricted and Re-issuance of a Learner Permit only until teen reaches the age of 18	If DOS notified *after* Intermediate Unrestricted issued, **teen's Intermediate privileges will still be revoked and a Learner Permit re-issued until the 18th birthday.**
(f) Contributing to the occurrence of a fatal accident	Must maintain a Learner Permit only until teen reaches the age of 18	Revocation of Intermediate Restricted and Re-issuance of a Learner Permit only until teen reaches the age of 18	Revocation of Intermediate Unrestricted and Re-issuance of a Learner Permit only until teen reaches the age of 18

If a student fifteen years old or older drops out of school, the school is required to notify the Department of Safety which suspends the student's driving privileges. The first time a student drops out, he or she may regain the privilege to drive by returning to school and making satisfactory academic progress. There is no second chance, however. the second time a student drops out he or she must wait to turn 18 years old before being eligible to apply.

If a person who dropped out does return to school, the appropriate school official can certify the student has returned by completing a different section of the Certificate of Compulsory School Attendance. They will give the student a pink copy of the form to take with them to a driver license station. The Student will be required to pay a $20 reinstatement fee on top of the appropriate application and license fees. Other fees may be added as well, depending on the individual's history.

Teen / GDL FAQs

1. What is the graduated license law?
The graduated licensing system places certain restrictions on teens under the age of 18 who have learner permits and driver licenses.

2. Are there any changes in how to apply for a learner permit or intermediate license under the GDL law?
The process to apply for a learner permit or intermediate license is the same with the exception of an additional $5 fee for each application. To apply for an intermediate license,a parent, legal guardian or license instructor must present certification that the intermediate license applicant has a minimum of 50 hours of behind-the-wheel driving experience, including a minimum of 10 hours of driving at night.

3. What are the restrictions for those with learner permits?
Anyone under the age of 18 who has a learner permit will be prohibited from driving between the hours of 10 p.m. and 6 a.m. When driving, permit holders must have a licensed driver age 21 or older in the vehicle with them on the front seat. Seatbelt use is mandatory for everyone in the vehicle under the age of 18 (passengers age 4 and under must be in an approved child restraint device).

4. How long must I have a learner permit before applying for an intermediate restricted license?
Under the new law, anyone under the age of 18 must have their learner permit for a minimum of six months before they can apply for an intermediate restricted license. The minimum age for applying for an intermediate restricted license is 16. If someone with a learner permit gets 6 or more points on their driving record during the 180 days before applying for the intermediate restricted license, they have to continue to hold the learner permit until their record has been clear for a full 180 consecutive days.

5. What are the restrictions for an intermediate restricted license?
A. Seatbelt use is mandatory for everyone in the vehicle age 17 and under (passengers age 4 and under must be in an approved child restraint device).

B. Those with an intermediate license can only have one other passenger in the vehicle

UNLESS:
• One or more of the passengers is age 21 or older and has a valid, unrestricted license;
  • The passengers are brothers and sisters, step-brothers or step-sisters, adopted or fostered children residing in the same house as the driver and going to and from school AND the intermediate license holder has in their possession written permission from their parent or guardian to transport their siblings.

C. *Those with an intermediate license are prohibited from driving between the hours of 11 p.m. and 6 a.m.*

UNLESS:
  • They are accompanied by a parent or guardian;
  • They are accompanied by a licensed driver 21 or older who has been designated by the parent or guardian. This designation must be in writing and be in the possession of the teen driver;
  • They are driving to or from a specifically identified school sponsored activity or event and have in their possession written permission from a parent or guardian to do this;
  • They are driving to or from work and have in their possession written permission from a parent or guardian identifying the place of employment and authorizing the driver to go to and from work;
  • They are driving to or from hunting or fishing between 4 a.m. and 6 a.m. and have in their possession a valid hunting or fishing license.

6. What would happen to an intermediate license holder who is caught with a forged or fake letter?
A driver with an intermediate license who is convicted of having a forged or fraudulent letter or statement will have their intermediate license revoked and will be reissued a learner permit until they reach the age of 18.

7. What will my intermediate license look like?
You may view examples of these licenses on page 17.

8. How long do I have to keep an intermediate restricted license?
Teens must hold their intermediate restricted license for a minimum of one year. After one year, they can apply for an unrestricted intermediate license. There is a $2 application fee. The word "Intermediate" will still be on the license, but the restrictions will be lifted.

HOWEVER:
If a teen driver has received six or more points (equivalent

of two minor traffic citations) on their intermediate restricted license; has contributed to a traffic crash; or has been convicted of a second seatbelt violation, they will have to wait an additional 90 days to apply for an unrestricted intermediate license, meaning they would be required to hold the intermediate restricted for a total of 15 months.

ALSO:

If the teen driver gets a second moving violation while holding the Intermediate Restricted Driver License, he or she will need to complete an approved Driver Education class before being allowed to get an Intermediate Unrestricted Driver License.

At age 18, a driver could apply for a regular unrestricted license without the word "Intermediate" printed on it. There will be an $8 duplicate fee unless the driver chooses to keep the license with the word "Intermediate" on it until that license is at the end of its five-year renewal cycle.

9. Are there any teens who will not be affected by the change in the law?

The GDL law will not apply to anyone age 18 and older OR anyone under the age of 18 who has graduated high school.

GDL At-a-Glance Review

Table: 3.2

PD → At least 6 months → **Level 1** → At least 12 months → **Level 2** → Until age 18 → **Level 3**

	LEARNER PERMIT CLASS PD	INTERMEDIATE RESTRICTED	INTERMEDIATE UNRESTRICTED	REGULAR CLASS D

Requirements:	• Must be 15 years old
	• Vision Exam
	• Knowledge Test
	• SF 1010 Form *(Proof of Compulsory School Attendance and Satisfactory Progress)*
	• Parent or Legal guardian must sign Teenage Affidavit of Financial Responsibility
	• Birth Certificate*
	• Social Security Number **
	• Proof of citizenship or lawful permanent Resident
		• Must be 16 years old
		• Held a valid PD for 6 months
		• Certification of 50 hours behind-the-wheel experience, including 10 hours at night
		• **Cannot have:**
		  ◦ six or more points on driving record during the 180 days immediately preceding application
		• Driving Test
			• At least 17 years old
			• Held a valid Restricted Intermediate for 1 year
			• **Cannot have:**
			  ◦ six or more points on driving record
			  ◦ have been at fault in a traffic crash
			  ◦ have been convicted of a 2nd seatbelt violation
			[*these would add a 90 day waiting period to the 1 yr Intermediate Restricted duration*]
				• Must be at least 18 years of age
				• Optional: can apply for a duplicate of license, without the word "Intermediate" on its face

Fees:	$10.50, any age under 18 years old.	Age 16 = $24.50 Age 17 = $21.00 Age 18 = Eligible for regular driver license	Age 17 = $2.00 Age 18 = Eligible for regular driver license ($8 duplicate fee if had Intermediate license)	$8.00 or $12.00, regular duplicate fee depending upon if 1st or subsequent duplicate
Issued for:	12 months	until age 21	Same expiration date @ age 21	Same expiration date @ age 21
Restrictions:	• Must have licensed driver age 21 or older in front seat • Cannot drive between 10:00 PM - 6:00 AM • Seatbelts mandatory for all passengers age 4 thru 17 (or child restraint device if under age 4)	• Only one passenger • Cannot drive between 11:00 PM - 6:00 AM • Seatbelts mandatory of all passengers age 4 thru 17 (or child restraint device if under age 4)	• Seatbelts mandatory for all passengers age 4 thru 17 (or child restraint device if under age 4) • No additional restrictions, however, license still states "Intermediate" prominently on the face of the license	• No restrictions and license looks like regular "Under 21 license"

* See Chapter 2, page 11 for information on acceptable forms of identification
** See Chapter 2, page 13 for more information in SSN requirements

THE EXAMINATIONS

General Information:

- Your driver license examination will consist of a vision test, a knowledge test, and a road test.
- Driver license tests are given at all driver license stations except for the express service stations. They are administered on a first-come, first-served basis.
- Due to the length of time to administer, road tests are cut off 30 minutes prior to the posted closing time.
- Road tests are not given in extreme weather (heavy rain/snow, dense fog, hail, high winds, icy roads, etc.)
- During winter months road tests are not given in the dark.
- No test may be repeated on the same day.
- Mandatory waiting periods are required when an applicant fails the written or road test for the original issuance of a Class D license or Learner Permit. For details on these waiting periods, see Table 4.2 and 4.3.
- When you return to take a test over, you must bring back all of the original documents you are required to provide.
- You will be required to pay the application fee each time you take a test and fail
  $2.00 for Class PD, D or For Hire tests
  $3.00 for Class PM or M tests
  $6.00 for Any CDL test including endorsements

Determining Which Tests Are Required:

Table: 4.1

Original License	**Class D or Class H** Full Tests: Vision, knowledge, road **Class PD** Vision and knowledge tests **Exchanging PD to D** Vision and road
Duplicate, Renewal	No Test
Adding For Hire Endorsement	Vision, knowledge
New residents, with out-of-state license	Vision only, if out-of-state license is valid and has not expired; otherwise, full tests.
New residents, from other countries (or no prior license)	Vision, knowledge and road test

Note: See Motorcycle Manual for Class M tests, and CDL Manual for Classes A, B, and C

Vision Screening Test

To determine if a driver can see well enough to drive, a screening test is required before any license or permit is issued. An applicant is required to have at least 20/40 vision in each eye individually and both eyes together. This may be with or without your glasses or contact lenses. If you cannot see this well, you must have an eye specialist of your choice fill out an eye statement for the department to evaluate.

Knowledge Test

You will be given an exam covering knowledge needed to drive safely. The test will consist of multiple choice questions based on information contained in this handbook. Roughly speaking, you can expect the test to cover the following areas:

Traffic signs and signals—25%
Safe driving principles—25%
Rules of the road—25%
Drugs and alcohol—25%

The knowledge tests are administered in either a written or computerized format dependent upon the station visited. As a rule stations that are equipped with the computerized testing machines routinely require the test be taken in that format on the first attempt.

Stations that have the computerized testing are also currently able to offer the test in 3 alternate language formats of Spanish, Korean or Japanese. Applicants for whom English is not their first language may also use a translation dictionary as long as there are no notes or other handwriting visible within the pages of the book. Electronic Dictionaries on "Palm Pilots" are NOT allowed to be used during testing. Interpreters are NOT allowed to assist with any of the driver license testing.

Oral tests are available by appointment at selected stations for applicants who have a learning disability or are illiterate. If the applicant requesting an oral test is under the age of eighteen (18) a written statement from a physician or educational specialist stating that the applicant has a medical condition or learning disability will be required before the test can be administered in the oral format. In the event the applicant requesting an oral test is deaf, the Department of Safety will furnish a certified sign language interpreter to assist with the administration of the exam.

Original Class PD or Class D License Testing:

In order to encourage the applicant to thoroughly study the Driver Handbook and cut down on repeat visits by applicants who are not yet prepared for the examination; **the following time restraints will be observed for all original applications for a Class PD or Class D license.** These guidelines are based on the number of questions answered correctly by the applicant on the initial test.

Table: 4.2

Number of questions answered correctly:	Allow retest after the following mandatory study time period:
24 to 30 Questions Correct	PASS no re-test needed
21 to 23 Questions Correct	Next (1) Day
18 to 20 Questions Correct	Seven (7) Days
15 to 17 Questions Correct	Fourteen (14) Days
14 and fewer Questions Correct	Thirty (30) days

*NOTE: The guidelines established above will also be applied to wait times between additional re-testing opportunities if applicant does not pass the examination on the second or subsequent attempts. **THESE GUIDELINES APPLY ONLY TO ORIGINAL ISSUANCE OF A CLASS PD OR CLASS D LICENSE.***

Any form of cheating by an applicant on a required examination will result in an automatic failure and the applicant will not be allowed to re-attempt the test for a minimum of thirty (30) days. Forms of cheating include, but are not limited to the following:

- Use of any form of written notes (including notes on paper, clothing, body, digital pagers, etc.)

- Talking during the examination (includes cell phone use)

- Attempting to allow another person to take the examination

- All cell phones, pagers or text messaging devices must be turned off during both written and road test administration

Road Test

Pre-Trip Vehicle Inspection

The motor vehicle you bring for the road test must meet all Tennessee motor vehicle registration (valid tags) and safety law requirements and have equipment in proper working order. In addition, applicants will be asked to demonstrate their ability to use each of the first eight items (indicated in bold with a '*').

*Seat Belts. Any passenger motor vehicle manufactured or assembled in 1969 or later must be equipped with safety belts and must be in good usable condition for both the applicant and the examiner.

*Brakes. (Emergency and regular). All automobiles must have two separate methods of applying brakes. They must have a regular foot brake and a parking brake.

*Headlights. (High and low beam). Motor vehicles must be equipped with at least two headlights but no more than four white headlights.

*Tail and Brake Lights. Passenger vehicles must be equipped with a rear license light, two red tail lights, and two red brake lights.

*Windshield Wipers. Every vehicle equipped with a windshield should have two (2) windshield wipers for cleaning rain or any other moisture in order to permit clear vision for the driver, unless one (1) wiper cleans to within one (1) inch of the inside of the windshield.

*Windshield Defroster and Fan Control. Applicants need to be able to demonstrate how to 'unfog' the windshield.

*Rear View Mirrors. At least one rear view mirror with nothing interfering with the driver's view of the rear. For applicants with certain vision or hearing impairments, two outside rear view mirrors are also required.

*Horns. A horn is required on all motor vehicles.

Also required:

Windows and windshields. Clear vision for the driver is required to the front, rear and both sides. It is unlawful to drive a motor vehicle with a windshield that is so cracked, or covered with steam or frost that clear vision is prevented. No tinting material may be affixed to the windshield of any motor vehicle. Standards for the other windows depend on the vehicle as follows: **Passenger Car**. No material which transmits less than 35% of visible light may be attached to any window. Multi-Purpose Vehicles: All windows behind the front seat are exempt. Windows immediately to the left and right of the driver must comply the same as for passenger vehicles.

Mufflers. Every vehicle must be equipped with a muffler to prevent excessive or unusual noises and annoying smoke.

Doors. Both the driver door and the passenger door must open from the inside and the outside.

Bumpers. Passenger cars must have bumpers which are within a range of 14 to 22 inches from the ground; 4x4 recreational vehicles must have bumpers with a range of 14 to 31 inches.

Speedometer. Every vehicle must have a working speedometer in order to gauge vehicle speed.

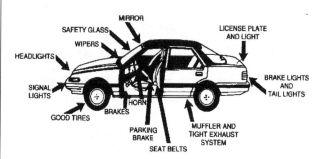

The Driving Test

The examiner will give you directions and evaluate whether or not you can drive safely. You will not be asked to do anything illegal. The only people allowed in the vehicle are you and the examiner (or other authorized personnel). No animal may be in the vehicle. During the test, the examiner will be observing the following:

1. How you prepare to drive. Have you checked your mirrors, fastened your seat belt, turned on any necessary lights or wipers?

2. How you start your vehicle. Do you look for other cars? Do you signal and wait until it is safe before entering traffic?

3. How you control your vehicle. Do you accelerate smoothly? Do you use your gas pedal, brake, steering wheel, and other controls correctly? Handle curves properly?

4. How you handle intersections and make left and right turns. Are you in the proper lane? Do you look both left and right for approaching vehicles? Do you make sure

your path is clear before proceeding? Do you simply rely on the traffic signals? Do you signal and change lanes carefully?

5. How you obey the traffic signals and posted signs.

6. How you drive in traffic. Do you pay full attention to driving? Do you scan carefully for signs, signals, pedestrians and other vehicles? Do you yield and take the right-of-way correctly?

7. How you stop. Do you stop smoothly and at the right spot? Can you stop quickly and safely in an emergency?

8. How you back up. Do you look over your shoulder? Can you back in a straight line? Can you turn safely while backing? Can you back into/out of a parking space?

9. How you judge distance. Do you maintain a safe distance from other cars?

10. How you communicate to other drivers. Do you make sudden changes, or signal too late or too early? Do you slow down as early as it is safe to do so, or do you catch other drivers by surprise?

11. How you share the road with others. Are you courteous and watchful?

12. How you change your speed to suit the situation. Do you take into account the speed limit, other cars, light, weather and road conditions?

Causes for Immediate Failure

The applicant will be failed immediately for any of the following:

- Violation of any traffic law
- Lack of cooperation or refusal to follow directions
- Any dangerous action
- Contributing to an accident

When You Don't Pass

Upon completion of the driving test, the examiner will advise you of your errors, how to correct them, and what maneuvers you should practice to improve your driving skill.

You should review the related material and/or practice the driving skills before returning.

Applicants who do not successfully pass the skills test on the first attempt are not permitted to take the examination again on the same day. Applicants may be allowed to re-test

after mandatory practice times as determined by their total score (number of errors) under the guidelines in Table 3.2.

In order to encourage the applicant to thoroughly practice their driving skills and cut down on repeat visits by applicants who are not yet prepared for the examination; the following time restraints will be observed based on the number of errors committed by the applicant on the initial test.

Table: 4.3

Number of errors committed during the skills test:	Allow retest after the following mandatory practice time period:
1 to 6 errors / points	PASS no re-test needed
7 to 9 errors / points	Next (1) Day
10 to 12 errors / points	Seven (7) Days
13 to 15 errors / points	Fourteen (14) Days
16 or more errors / points -OR- Automatic Failure	Thirty (30) Days

NOTE: *The guidelines established above will also be applied to wait times between additional re-testing opportunities if applicant does not pass the examination on the second or subsequent attempts.*

When You Pass

In most cases, after you have successfully completed the required tests, your photo will be taken and you will receive your photo driver license at this time.

Tips To Help Your Testing Go More Smoothly

✓ **Study and Practice Driving Ahead of Time**

Both the knowledge test and the road test will go more smoothly if you spend time reviewing this manual, and spend time on the road with an experienced driver before you come to apply.

✓ **Bring A Proper Vehicle**

All safety equipment must work (horns, lights, seat belts, brakes, signals and windshield wipers). The vehicle registration must also be current. Bring a vehicle that you are familiar with driving.

Problem Driver Pointer System

The Problem Driver Pointer System (PDPS) is a federally mandated program which requires Tennessee to do a national computer check **before** issuing a driver license. If you apply for a Tennessee license — whether it is your first license here, or some other transaction such as a renewal — and you have a problem in another state, we cannot issue you a license until the matter is resolved.

The national computer listing contains names and limited other identifying information about individuals whose licenses have been canceled, denied, revoked, or suspended, or who have been convicted of certain serious traffic violations. If you do have a problem in another state, the examiners will provide you the name of the state reporting the problem and a telephone number you can use to contact that state to clear your record there.

Please Note: To find out specific information about what the other state has reported to the PDPS system, you have to call the other state. Tennessee does not have this information. We are only provided with the fact that the other state has reported a problem.

Losing Your Privilege To Drive

In Tennessee, a driver license may be revoked or suspended for the following offenses:

1. Driving under the influence of alcohol or drugs, including implied consent
2. Allowing unlawful use of a driver license, including fraudulently altering a driver license or allowing another individual to use your license or identification
3. Mental or physical difficulties
4. Leaving the scene of a personal injury or fatal accident; failure to stop and render aid in an automobile accident
5. Perjury, or giving false information on the use or ownership of an automobile, or for the issuance of a driver license
6. A felony that involves the use of an automobile
7. Evading arrest while operating a motor vehicle
8. Manslaughter/vehicular homicide involving the operation of an automobile
9. Two (2) reckless driving violations within twelve (12) months
10. Drag racing
11. Habitual offenders of moving traffic violation
12. Unsatisfied judgment resulting from the negligent operation of a motor vehicle
13. Purchasing or possessing any alcoholic beverage if 18-20 years old
14. Failure to comply with child support requirements
15. Driving a motor vehicle away from a gas station without paying for dispensed gas or diesel fuel

16. Failure to show evidence of financial responsibility to officer when involved in an accident or charged with a moving violation.

In addition, persons under the age of 18 may lose their privileges for:

- Convictions of any drug or alcohol offense, whether or not the offense occurred while driving;
- Dropping out of school (which is defined as having ten consecutive or 15 total days in a semester of unexcused absences);
- Failure to make satisfactory progress in school (which in general means passing three subjects per grading period); or
- Weapons violations

Finally, commercial motor vehicle operators have separate rules and regulations governing their commercial driver licenses (CDL's) which can cause them to lose their driving privileges. These are discussed in the CDL Study Manual.

WHENEVER A DRIVER LICENSE IS SUSPENDED OR REVOKED, IT MUST BE TURNED IN TO THE DEPARTMENT OF SAFETY WITHIN 30 DAYS OF THE SUSPENSION OR REVOCATION.

The license may be mailed to the Tennessee Department of Safety, 1150 Foster Avenue, Nashville, TN 37249-4000. Any Tennessee Highway Patrol Office or Driver License Station can take your license and see that you are given credit for turning it in.

FAILURE TO SURRENDER YOUR LICENSE MEANS THAT YOU WILL BE FINED $75.00 IN ADDITION TO ANY OTHER FINES AND COSTS YOU MAY OWE.

Hearings

Before any license is suspended or canceled, the department will notify the licensee in writing of the proposed suspension or cancellation. If your license is about to be suspended or revoked, the department will give you an opportunity for a hearing prior to action, except in cases of final judgments and convictions.

Non-Resident Violator Compact

Tennessee is a member of the Non-Resident Violator Compact. The compact is an agreement between states to ensure that a person receiving a citation for a traffic violation appears in court or otherwise complies with the terms of the court for the citation.

In a nutshell, this compact means that regardless of where you receive a citation for a traffic violation, you must either appear in court to answer the citation or meet any other requirement the court may set out to satisfy the citation. If you ignore the citation — whether it was issued for a traffic violation here or in another member state, your driving privileges will be canceled or suspended.

The same consequences apply to non-residents who receive a citation in Tennessee and fails to answer the citation. The suspension remains in effect until the court notifies Tennessee that the citation has been properly disposed of and the proper fees are paid to this department.

Reinstatements

Steps you need to follow to have your driver license reinstated depend on several factors, including why you lost your license and what else is on your record. To clear your record, you must contact:

Tennessee Department of Safety
Financial Responsibility
1150 Foster Avenue
Nashville, Tennessee 37210

Phone: (615) 741-3954, or
TDD—Telecommunications Device for the Deaf:
(615) 532-2281
Email Address: FinResp.Safety@tn.gov

Driver Improvement Program

The Department of Safety keeps records of traffic violations and accidents for each driver. These records are based on reports forwarded to the department by the courts, and on reports of traffic accidents submitted by investigating officers. Drivers who accumulate twelve (12) or more points within a twelve (12) month period receive a notice of proposed suspension. In an effort to keep drivers aware of the possibility of losing their privilege to drive an advisory letter is mailed to a licensee having 6 to 11 points on their driving record within any 12 months.

A Defensive Driving Course may be attended as an alternative to suspension; however, the Defensive Driving Course may be taken only once in any five (5) year period. After a hearing, the department will take whatever action is necessary to correct and improve poor driving habits by education, re-examinations, placing necessary restrictions on the licensee and probation. Should these steps be unsuccessful, the department will have no other choice than to suspend the person's driving privileges.

The assignment of point values, for various offenses, is designed to impress upon drivers that unless they comply with traffic laws and regulations, they may establish a bad driving record leading to suspension of driving privileges.

Frequent Traffic Violations

Frequent traffic violations are a most dangerous and costly habit. If you are suspended for frequent violations, upon the completion of the suspension time, before you can receive your regular license, you must pay the appropriate reinstatement fees and establish future proof of financial responsibility (SR-22 Form) with the Department.

DRIVING WHILE YOUR LICENSE IS SUSPENDED WILL RESULT IN THE EXTENSION OF THE SUSPENSION PERIOD AND IN ALL LIKELIHOOD WILL RESULT IN CRIMINAL PROSECUTION.

Restricted Driver Licenses

When a driver license is suspended or revoked, but the driver depends on his or her driving to make a living or to continue schooling, there are certain conditions in which the driver may apply for a restricted driver license. The restricted license permits the driver to operate a motor vehicle for very specific purposes and only such purposes as are spelled out when the license is issued. The procedures for applying for a restricted license depend upon the reason the license was taken away in the first place, as summarized below:

1. **Financial Responsibility**: When a person's license is revoked for failure to provide proof of financial responsibility and they are employed to operate an employer's vehicle, they may apply for an approval letter from the Financial Responsibility Section and pass appropriate tests.

2. **DUI**: After the first conviction for DUI, provided the driver does not have a prior conviction of DUI, or adult driving while impaired within 10 years, or a prior conviction of vehicular homicide as the proximate result of intoxication aggravated vehicular homicide, or vehicular assault, the trial judge may issue an order for a restricted license to go to and from work, attend college full time, drive as part of employment or to attend certain court-ordered events. Persons serving a two year revocation, may after serving the first year, apply for a restricted driver license provided that an ignition interlock device is installed on the motor vehicle for the remaining period of revocation. When applying at the driver license station, these applicants must submit two (2) copies of the court order and proof of insurance (SR-22 from their insurance company), and pass all appropriate tests.

3. **Driver Improvement**: Any person whose driver license has been suspended for frequent traffic violations may obtain this type of license by applying to the Driver Improvement Section of the Tennessee Department of Safety. They will be required to submit their approval letter, present proof of SR-22 insurance and pass appropriate tests.

4. **Implied Consent**: A person whose license has been suspended by the court for Implied Consent may apply to the trial judge for a restricted license to operate a motor vehicle for going to and from work, full-time college and working at his or her regular place of employment. At the time of application, two (2) copies of a court order and proof of SR-22 insurance must be submitted.

5. **Juvenile**: Minors who lose their license because of the Drug Free Youth Act may apply to the trial judge for a restricted license. They must bring two copies of the court order to a driver license station and pass vision, knowledge, and skills tests. Proof of insurance is not required.

POINTS FOR MOVING TRAFFIC VIOLATIONS AND ACCIDENTS (Table: 5.1)

POINTS	SPEEDING	
3	Where speed not indicated	Construction Zone: 4 pts.
1	1 thru 5 m.p.h. in excess of speed zone	Construction Zone: 2 pts.
3	6 thru 15 m.p.h. in excess of speed zone	Construction Zone: 6 pts.
4	16 thru 25 m.p.h. in excess of speed zone	Construction Zone: 7 pts.
5	26 thru 35 m.p.h. in excess of speed zone	Construction Zone: 7 pts.
6	36 thru 45 m.p.h. in excess of speed zone	Construction Zone: 8 pts.
8	46 m.p.h. and above in excess of speed zone	Construction Zone: 8 pts.

POINTS	MOVING TRAFFIC VIOLATION
8	Operating without being licensed or without license required for type of vehicle being operated (under suspension)
8	Driving while license canceled
8	Reckless endangerment by vehicle — misdemeanor
8	Adult driving while impaired
6	Reckless driving
6	Passing school bus taking on or discharging passengers
6	1st Offense violation of driver license restrictions
6	Fleeing law enforcement officer
5	Leaving the scene of an accident (Property damage only)
4	Signs and control devices — Failure to obey traffic instructions
4	Improper passing — Passing where prohibited
4	Wrong way, side or direction
4	Failing to yield right of way
4	Careless or negligent driving
4	Violation of bumper law
3	Following improperly
3	Making improper turn
3	Speed less than posted minimum
3	Operating without being licensed or without license required for type of vehicle being operated (not under suspension)
3	Miscellaneous — Failure to maintain control, improper control, etc.
2	Failure to signal change of vehicle direction or to reduce speed suddenly
2	Following emergency vehicles unlawfully

POINTS	ACCIDENTS
8	Contributing to occurrence of an accident resulting in the death of another person
4	Failure to Report Accident
4	Contributing to occurrence of an accident resulting in bodily injury
3	Contributing to occurrence of an accident resulting in property damage

Physical Or Mental Disabilities

When evidence is received by the department that an individual's ability to drive may be affected by a physical or mental disorder, the licensee will be required to submit within twenty (20) days of notification, a medical certificate from a competent doctor stating the effects of the illness or disability on the individual's ability to safely operate a motor vehicle. If the report is unfavorable, the driving privilege will be suspended until the condition improves.

Re-Examination Of Drivers

If there is evidence a licensee's ability to safely operate a motor vehicle is questionable, he or she may be directed to report to the nearest Driver License Station and submit to a complete driver examination. Appropriate corrective action may be directed and certain restrictions (should they be required) may be placed on the license.

NOTE: Failure to respond to departmental requests for a medical certificate or submission to a driver license examination within the prescribed time will result in the suspension of the driving privilege.

Financial Responsibility

The purpose of this law is to protect you and the public from financially irresponsible drivers who become involved in an accident, as well as from drivers who have repeated violations and disregard of the law.

The best way to protect yourself and your driver license would be to have adequate insurance to cover death, bodily injury, and property damage.

First, a few definitions:

• *Liability insurance* provides coverage for damages you cause to other persons.

• *Collision insurance* provides coverage for damages sustained by your vehicle.

• *Uninsured motorist insurance* provides for coverage for the damages uninsured persons cause you.

Collision insurance is not required by law. However, the Financial Responsibility Law requires drivers to produce evidence of financial responsibility to the officer when charged with a moving violation or involved in a motor vehicle accident, without regard to apparent or actual fault. Evidence of financial responsibility presented to the officer can be in the form of a declaration page of your insurance policy, an insurance binder, an insurance card from an insurance company authorized to do business in Tennessee, a certificate issued by the Commissioner of the Department of Safety stating that a cash deposit or bond in the amount required by statute has been paid or filed with the Commissioner, or proof of qualification as a self-insurer as provided by statute. If unable to present evidence and convicted on the charge of failure to show evidence of financial responsibility, your driving privileges will be suspended. Before reinstatement of your driving privileges, you would be required to submit evidence of financial responsibility along with any other requirements.

Reporting Accidents

Drivers must notify local law enforcement officials of any accident involving death, injury, or property damage over fifty dollars ($50).

In addition, certain accidents — called "reportable accidents" — must be reported to the Tennessee Department of Safety. These include any accident within this State in which any person is killed or injured, or in which damage to the property of any one person, including oneself, is in excess of four hundred dollars ($400.00).

Regardless of who is to blame, the operator and/or owner of a vehicle involved in a reportable accident in this state must file a report of the accident within 20 days to the Tennessee Department of Safety. The accident report forms can be obtained at any Highway Patrol office or from your local police. Failure to report an accident may result in suspension of your driving and registration privileges.

If you contribute to a reportable accident and a claim is filed with the Department of Safety by the other party, you must also do one of these three things: (1) Show proof you had liability insurance at the time of the accident; (2) obtain notarized releases from all parties that file claims with the department; or (3) post cash or corporate surety bond with the department for the amount of damages sustained by other parties. IF YOU DO NOT COMPLY WITH THESE REQUIREMENTS YOU WILL HAVE YOUR DRIVING AND REGISTRATION PRIVILEGES REVOKED.

If your driving privileges are revoked due to a conviction or failure to file security after an accident, in addition to all other requirements you must have a liability insurance carrier file an SR-22 Form with this department before your privileges can be reinstated.

Traffic Accidents

If You Are Involved In An Accident — STOP! The law requires drivers of vehicles involved in an accident to stop immediately at the scene, or as close to the scene as possible without obstructing traffic. Notify the police immediately.

After stopping your vehicle, give your name, address, driver license number, and vehicle registration number to the other driver, and ask him for the same information.

Remain calm and stay at the accident scene. Don't blame other people or accept blame, and don't discuss the accident. Wait for the law enforcement officer and answer all questions truthfully and calmly.

As discussed above, you must report the accident to the Department of Safety if it involved death, personal injury, or property damage in excess of $400 to any one person. They must be completely filled out and filed within 20 days of the accident. If the driver sustained an injury and cannot complete the report, it can be filed by a passenger, or by the owner. If the accident involved an unattended vehicle or a domestic animal, and you cannot locate the owner, report the accident to the police.

If You Arrive First At An Accident Scene — If you can help, park your car off the road and turn on your emergency flashers.

If you have them, warn oncoming traffic with flares so that cars approaching the accident scene will not strike the wrecked vehicle.

Have someone notify the police.

Turn off the ignition in the damaged vehicle to prevent a fire. If the car is on fire, help the people out and take them away from the vehicle to prevent further injury in the event of an explosion.

If someone is pinned under a wrecked car, don't try to lift it unless you have enough strong people available to help, and not until after you have checked to make sure that no one will be pinned under the other side. Generally, unless you know what you are doing it is best to wait for the police and emergency squad to free crushed or pinned victims.

If you are not the first at an accident scene and your assistance is not needed, drive on. Do not slow down or stop just to satisfy your curiosity. Move on so that you do not interfere with the arrival of the police and emergency equipment.

Emergency First Aid — Generally, medical assistance should be given only by properly trained persons. However, you may find yourself in a situation where immediate assistance is unavailable and you may have to help the injured victims. In these cases, remember these basic first aid rules:

Unless absolutely necessary because of the danger of fire or some other hazard, avoid moving the injured person. If he must be moved, get help and try not to change the position in which he was found. If possible, cover him with coats or blankets to keep him warm. Never lift a victim by holding him under the shoulder (armpits) and knees.

If a victim appears to have a broken back or a broken neck, and you bend him forward or sit him up, you may cut his spinal cord and paralyze him permanently.

Control excessive bleeding with thick cloth pads, as clean as possible, applied with pressure by hand or by bandaging.

Cover burns with clean cloths to reduce the pain. Apply no ointments. Do not offer the injured anything to drink.

If the injured person does not seem to be breathing, attempt to revive breathing through emergency artificial respiration.

ALCOHOL, OTHER DRUGS AND DRIVING

Drinking and Driving

Alcohol and You

Researchers estimate that between the hours of 10 p.m. and 2 a.m. one out of every ten drivers is intoxicated. More than one-third of these drivers have been drinking at someone else's home. Nearly 50 percent of the drivers arrested for driving under the influence (DUI) are social to moderate drinkers. Don't think that it won't happen to you. In your lifetime, there's a 50-50 chance that you'll be involved in an alcohol-related crash.

An Overview Of The Effects Of Alcohol

Before the motoring public can fully understand why drinking and driving result in fatalities on our highways, we first need a better understanding of the effects of alcohol on the body.

How Does Alcohol Affect the Body?

Alcohol begins to be absorbed into the bloodstream within one to two minutes after an alcoholic beverage is consumed. As you consume alcohol it accumulates in your blood. Intoxication occurs when you drink alcohol faster than the liver can oxidize it. As the percentage of alcohol in your blood increases, you become more intoxicated.

Once in the bloodstream, the alcohol is distributed to all parts of the body, including the brain and liver. Upon reaching the liver, the alcohol immediately begins to be oxidized. The liver can only oxidize about one drink per hour. Contrary to popular belief, this rate cannot be increased by drinking coffee, exercising, taking a cold shower, or anything else. **Only time can sober a person who's been drinking. And remember, it is a slow process.**

What Is Blood Alcohol Concentration (BAC)?

BAC stands for Blood Alcohol Concentration. BAC is expressed in percentage of alcohol to blood. The higher the BAC number, the more impaired a person is. In most states, including Tennessee, .08 is the level of intoxication which is always illegal. This means that for every 800 drops of blood in a person's body, there is at least one drop of alcohol. BAC changes with body weight, time spent drinking, and the amount of alcohol that is consumed.

Amount of Alcohol Consumption. Each drink consumed within an hour increases the BAC level. Therefore, the more you drink in a fixed amount of time, the higher your BAC will register. This happens no matter what you weigh — or what kind of alcoholic beverage you drink.

Rate of Alcoholic Consumption. Drinking three drinks in one hour will affect you more than drinking three drinks in three hours. Spacing your drinks over a longer period of time will slow the rate at which you become intoxicated and indicates responsible drinking habits.

Body Weight and Fat. The heavier the person, the more alcohol it takes to raise the BAC. Be aware of your size when drinking with others. If you are smaller than your friends and try to drink as much as they do, your judgment and inhibitions will probably be affected before your friends are.

Body fat also affects how quickly you are affected by alcohol. Alcohol is able to be absorbed in water, not fat. This simply means that those with less body fat have more water in which to dilute the alcohol. So, drink for drink, if people weigh the same, the one with more body fat will show signs of intoxication first.

Amount of Food in the Stomach. All the alcohol consumed eventually gets into the blood whether you have eaten or not. Food in the stomach causes alcohol to be absorbed more slowly, thus slowing down the rate, and the amount of intoxication.

Overall Condition of the Body. Heavy and chronic drinking can harm virtually every organ and system in the body. The liver is particularly vulnerable to alcohol's harmful effects since it oxidizes approximately 90 percent of the alcohol in the body. If the liver is damaged or diseased, the rate of oxidation is reduced, causing the alcohol to stay in the body longer and the BAC to be higher for a longer time. Further, the effects of alcohol on the liver can lead to such diseases as hepatitis and cirrhosis.

Relationship of Alcohol To Traffic Crashes and Accident Risks

Driving after drinking is a widespread problem. It is estimated that two in every five Americans (or 40%) will be involved in an alcohol-related crash at some time in their lives.

Each drink drastically increases your risk of having an accident. Look at the table below. With a BAC of .10%, you are **seven** times more likely to cause an accident than if you were sober. As your BAC increases to .15%, your chances increase to **twenty-five** times and at .17% BAC, you are **fifty** times more likely to cause an accident.

Alcohol's Effects At A Glance   Table: 6.1

BAC	Rough Number of Drinks	Risk of Automobile Crash	Comment
.01-.03%	◊ 1 drink within 15 min.	Rises for young adults, others with low tolerance for alcohol	Stiff penalties for BAC as low as .02 if driver under age 21
.04-.07%	◊ 2 drinks within 1/2 hour	Definite risk for anyone with low tolerance levels	Most people feel high and have some loss of judgment. You may get louder and have some loss of small muscle control, like focusing your eyes.
.08%-above		**LEGAL INTOXICATION*** — Judgment and reasoning powers are severely hampered; cannot do common simple acts. **Definitely unsafe to drive**.	
.10-.12%	◊ 4 drinks within 2 hours	Risk of automobile crash increases 7 times normal rate	Many people claim they're not affected anymore, as if they could drink themselves sober — definitely not thinking straight.
.13-.15%	◊ 5-7 drinks within 3 hours	Crash risk 25 times normal rate	You have far less muscle control than normal and feel happy even though stumbling and acting foolishly.
.16-.25%	◊ 8-12 drinks within 4 hours	Crash risk 50 times normal rate	You are confused and need help doing things, even standing up. Alcohol-related highway fatalities sharply increase.

*Lower levels are set for younger drivers, commercial drivers, and subsequent offenses, as discussed later in this chapter.

Behavior at each BAC level may differ somewhat with the individual. ALL people at the .10% level are definitely too impaired to drive safely. **Research has proven driving skills, good judgment and vision are greatly impaired at BAC levels as low as .03 and .04%, especially for young drinkers.** The table, **Alcohol's Effects at a Glance,** describes different levels of intoxication and degree of behavior impairment at each level.

Alcohol's Effects On Driving Ability

Driving involves multiple tasks, the demands of which can change continually. To drive safely one must maintain alertness, make decisions based on ever-changing information present in the environment, and execute maneuvers based on these decisions. Drinking alcohol impairs a wide range of skills necessary for carrying out these tasks. Fatal injuries resulting from alcohol-related traffic crashes represent a tremendous loss of human life.

The plain and simple fact is that you cannot drive safely when you are impaired by alcohol. The two abilities most important to the driving task are *judgment* and *vision* — both of which are affected by small amounts of alcohol. Your ability to judge speed, time, and distance are altered even after having only one drink. Each drink thereafter markedly affects your driving ability. In addition, your *reaction time* and *coordination* begin to deteriorate, while your *alertness* and *concentration* fade. All of this adds up to a deadly combination.

Judgment — *Ability to think clearly and make quick decisions*

Good judgment decreases with the use of alcohol. The concern for physical well being is lessened. This causes unnecessary and dangerous risks to be taken when drinking and driving. Examples are driving too fast, passing cars without enough clear distance and speeding around curves. "Showing off" is another example of impaired judgment.

Vision — *Ability to see clearly straight ahead, to the side, and at night*

Alcohol decreases clearness of vision. Seeing clearly at night is reduced by more than half. Glare vision is poor because of relaxed eye muscles. Glare recovery is also slowed by alcohol. Side vision is reduced by about 30% at .05% BAC. Judging depth or distance is affected because alcohol causes each eye to get a slightly different picture. These vision impairments greatly increase chances of a head-on or rear-end collision. **Eye muscles are relaxed by alcohol and cannot focus properly. Because the eyes provide almost 90 percent of the information used in driving, any restriction in vision can cause disastrous results.**

Reaction Time and Coordination — *Ability to react quickly and safely to an emergency or hazardous situation — being able to keep eyes, hands and feet working together*

Reaction and coordination are impaired by alcohol as low as .02% BAC. It takes longer to react. The skills necessary to drive safely, coordination to control the car with hands, feet and eyes in response to other vehicles and the road are drastically reduced as alcohol intake increases.

Alertness and Concentration — *Being ready to react to changing driving conditions or situations — keeping your mind on driving and paying attention to the task at hand.*

Alcohol, in any concentration, is a depressant, not a stimulant. Alcohol slows all nerve impulses and body functions. The false feeling of stimulation, with small doses, comes from lessening of inhibitions due to the particular portion of the brain controlling this part of behavior being relaxed. In reality, alcohol has the effect of "fuzzing" a driver's ability to be alert and to concentrate.

"Every Day" Drugs

One of the most common and most dangerous instances of drug abuse occurs when people mix alcohol with prescription and over-the-counter drugs. For example, when alcohol is combined with another depressant, like tranquilizers or sedatives, etc. the results are not just added together, they are multiplied. Even some over-the-counter medicines can affect driving. The effects are much stronger, much more dangerous and can affect your driving skills.

If your doctor prescribes a tranquilizer or sedative, make a point to discuss how the drug will affect your ability to drive safely. Just because a drug is prescribed is — by law — no defense for driving under the influence of it.

Non-prescription drugs, such as cold tablets, cough syrups, allergy remedies, etc., purchased over-the-counter may contain antihistamines, alcohol, codeine, and other compounds that can be especially dangerous for drivers. You should read labels and pay attention to warnings (e.g. "may cause drowsiness," "do not operate machinery," "caution against engaging in operations requiring alertness").

Again, if you have questions about a particular drug or combination of drugs, check with your doctor or pharmacist.

Driving Under The Influence Of Drugs Or Alcohol (The "DUI" Law)

Studies indicate that marijuana and other drugs also affect judgment and motor functions, making driving under the influence of drugs other than alcohol **dangerous**. In Tennessee it is unlawful for any person to drive or be in physical control of an automobile or other motor-driven vehicle on any public street, highway, road, or alley, or while on the premises of any shopping center, trailer park or any apartment house complex, or any place frequented by the public while

1. under the influence of any intoxicant, marijuana, narcotic drug, or drugs producing stimulating effects on the central nervous system; or

2. while the alcohol concentration of the operator's blood or breath is .08% or higher.

It is not only unlawful if the alcohol concentration of a person's blood or breath is **.08%**, there is a presumption that the defendant's ability to drive is sufficiently impaired to constitute a DUI violation.

Strictly speaking, a driver can register a BAC of **.00%** and still be convicted of a DUI. The level of BAC does not clear a driver when it is below the "presumed level of intoxication." If a law enforcement officer observes such

things as erratic driving behavior, or maintaining an inappropriate speed (too fast or too slow), this would be cause for stopping the vehicle to investigate. Further sobriety checks could lead to the conclusion that the driver was indeed "Driving Under the Influence" of an intoxicant, narcotic drug, or other drug-producing stimulating effects on the central nervous system including prescription drugs. If you have any doubt about your ability to drive, don't get behind the wheel.

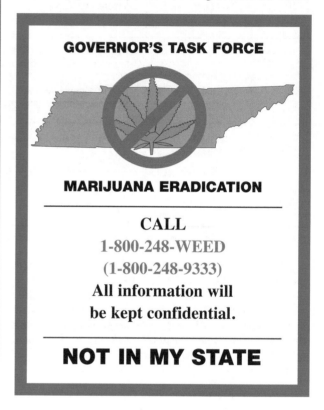

Implied Consent Law

By law, when you drive in Tennessee you have given your consent to be tested to determine the alcohol or drug content of your blood. This test must be administered at the request of a law enforcement officer having reasonable grounds to believe you have been driving under the influence of an intoxicant or drug.

If you are placed under arrest and a law enforcement officer asks you to take the test and you refuse, the test will not be given. The court will send notification of action to the Department of Safety and your driver license will be suspended for twelve (12) months.

Consequences Of DUI Arrest

Drinking and driving poses several problems. One is the probability of an accident and another is being arrested for DUI. The penalties for a DUI arrest are the same whether the driver was drinking alcohol or taking drugs (even prescription or over-the-counter drugs). If you are arrested for DUI, the consequences can be severe.

Minimum DUI Penalties   Table: 6.2

	Minimum Jail Time	Minimum Fines/ Revocation Period	Vehicle Seizure
FIRST CONVICTION	48 hours	$350.00/ One (1) year	Does not apply
SECOND CONVICTION	45 days	$600.00/ Two (2) years	If your second violation occurs within five years of your first DUI conviction, and both events happened after January, 1997, your vehicle is subject to seizure and forfeiture.
THIRD OR SUBSEQUENT CONVICTION	120 days	$1,100.00/ Three (3) years – Ten (10) max.	Vehicle is also subject to seizure and forfeiture.

Penalties Applying To Any DUI Conviction

Regardless of whether the conviction for driving under the influence is a driver's first or not, several other laws apply:

- **ID'S With "DUI Offender."** If a person with a license revoked for DUI applies for a photo identification license to carry during the period before his or her license can be restored, the department is required to indicate on the ID that the person is a DUI offender.

- **Seizure of Vehicle.** Beginning January 1997, if a person's driving privileges are revoked for DUI, and he or she is charged with driving on a revoked license, the driver's vehicle can be seized and forfeited. This holds true for any DUI conviction, whether it is the driver's first or not.

There are two basic instances where your vehicle can be subject to seizure:

1. If a driver is charged with driving on a revoked license when their driving privileges are already revoked as a result of any DUI conviction (first or subsequent).

2. If a driver has two DUI convictions within five (5) years and both events happened after January, 1997.

- **Vehicular Homicide.** If you are operating a motor vehicle under the influence of a drug or alcohol and you are involved in an accident that results in the death of another person(s), you may be charged with vehicular homicide and if convicted, **you may be fined and sentenced to prison**. These laws have recently been strengthened so that it is possible to be imprisoned for **up to 60 years**.

- **Aggravated Assault** — If you are operating a vehicle under the influence of a drug or alcohol and you are involved in a motor vehicle accident that results in the injury of another person you may be charged with aggravated assault and if convicted, **you may be fined and sentenced to prison**.

- **Child Endangerment** — Known as the Drunk Driving Child Protection Act, this law adds penalties for those who violate DUI laws when accompanied by a child under thirteen (13) years of age. There is a mandatory minimum incarceration of thirty days and a mandatory minimum fine of $1,000, both of which are added onto any other incarceration and fine required by law.

If the child suffers serious bodily injury, the violation is a Class D felony, and if the child actually dies, it is a Class C felony of especially aggravated child endangerment.

Additional DUI Penalties

In addition to the minimum penalties, the judge shall impose the following conditions:

- Participation in an alcohol safety DUI school program, if available; or

- Upon the second or subsequent conviction, participation in a program of rehabilitation at a treatment facility, if available; and

- The payment of restitution to any person suffering physical injury or personal losses as the result of such offense if such person is economically capable of making such restitution.

Courts may also, at their discretion, order the person to operate only a motor vehicle which is equipped with a functioning **ignition interlock device**, and may order this restriction to continue for a period of time up to one year after the person's license is no longer suspended or restricted under normal provisions. Effective October 1, 2002, a person with 2 DUI's in a five year period MUST operate a motor vehicle with the ignition interlock device for six months after reinstatement of driving privileges.

DUI's Are Expensive!

Besides being extremely dangerous and against the law, DUI's are costly. In addition to the fine and court costs, a person charged with DUI can be faced with posting bond to get released from jail, attorney fees, loss of time from work to attend court hearing(s), fees for an alcohol safety course, increased insurance premiums, and other expenses. This can add up to several thousand dollars.

Can you afford a nearly $10,000 night on the town? Approximately $9,115.50 is probably more than you plan on spending for a night out with a friend. Or is it? A first offense DUI (Driving Under the Influence) charge could easily add up to such a staggering cost! The cost could be even higher if you don't qualify for the restricted driver license for driving to work during your suspension. This could add expense for alternate transportation (taxi, bus fare, etc.) or even worse the complete loss of your employment.

Young Driver Risks And Laws

Not Just Driving — Riding With Others!

Young people remain especially vulnerable to the threat of alcohol and other drugs, not only from impairment of their own driving, but from getting in the car with other drivers who are not sober. TRAFFIC CRASHES ARE THE LEADING KILLER OF YOUNG PEOPLE, AND NEARLY HALF ARE ALCOHOL RELATED. In a national survey, nearly half of 10th graders and a third of 8th graders reported having ridden during the past month with a driver who had used alcohol or other drugs before taking the wheel.

Accident records indicate that young drivers under the influence of small amounts of alcohol appear to have more driving problems than older drivers. Most teenagers are intoxicated at low BAC levels. The young driver's chance of an accident is much greater with BAC between .01-.09% than older drivers. This is due to low tolerance of alcohol and driving experience.

The decision is yours. Be responsible and smart — help yourself and your friends!

Under Twenty-One Laws

In addition to the standard penalties for driving under the influence of drugs or alcohol discussed in the next section, there are three special laws that apply to people under the age of twenty-one:

- **"18-20 Alcohol Violations"** — If you are 18, 19, or 20 years old and are convicted of purchasing, attempting to purchase, or possessing any alcoholic beverage, you will lose your privilege to drive for one year. If it

REMEMBER, DRIVING WHILE UNDER THE INFLUENCE OF DRUGS — EVEN PRESCRIPTION DRUGS — CARRIES THE SAME PENALTIES AS FOR ALCOHOL.

happens again, you will lose your license for two years. The law applies to *any* alcohol-related conviction, whether or not you were driving or even in a vehicle. Just having a can of beer at a party could cost you your driver license.

- **"Juvenile Offenders"** — If you are between the ages of 13 and 17 and found to have possessed, consumed, or sold either alcohol or drugs, your driving privilege will be suspended for one year or until age 17, whichever is longer. Even if you have never been licensed, you could lose your privilege to drive until you reach age 17. If you have a second conviction, the suspension is for two years or until age 18, whichever is longer.

- **"Under 21 BAC"** — A person age 16 or over but under the age of 21 who is found driving with a BAC of .02%, or under the influence of alcohol or any other drugs, commits the act of driving while impaired. Penalties include losing your license for one year, a fine of $250, and public service work.

Prevention Of Drinking And Driving

The best advice, of course, is simply to not drink when you know you are going to drive. One of the most successful programs in recent years has been the "designated driver" concept, where friends agree ahead of time which person will remain strictly sober. Many night clubs will offer the designated driver free non-alcoholic beverages for the evening. Young people who do not want to drink in the first place are finding it more socially acceptable to offer to be the designated driver.

Avoiding The Risks

Alcohol-related crashes are not accidents. They can be prevented. If you are planning a night on the town, decide before you start drinking that you are not going to drive. Remember, alcohol affects your judgement. It's a lot more difficult to make the decision not to drive after one or two drinks. Use the following tips to keep from drinking and driving and still have a good time.

Drive to social events in groups of two or more and have the driver agree not to drink.

Arrange to ride with a friend who is not drinking.

Before you start drinking, give your vehicle keys to someone who isn't drinking and who won't let you drive after drinking.

If someone offers you a drink and you plan to drive, simply say, "No thinks, I'm driving."

If You Choose To Drink

If you choose to drink alcoholic beverages you should control your drinking to stay within your limit. Drinking in a responsible and mature manner means that you are aware of your physical and mental condition. You also:

- Set a limit in advance and stick to it
- Drink at a slow pace
- Watch for signs of impairment
- Use time to get rid of alcohol

If despite your best intentions you realize you have had too much to drink, consider using public transportation to get home. Taking a cab could be a lot cheaper than paying a fine or losing your driver license! Beyond taking a cab, you could:

- Offer the keys to a non-drinking friend
- Stay over night at the party giver's home or a hotel within walking distance
- Call a parent or friend to pick you up and take you home

If You Are the Host

You assume a great amount of responsibility when you entertain your friends at home and serve alcoholic beverages. To help prevent the consequences of drinking and driving, you should do the following during the party:

- Encourage some of the guests to be designated drivers
- Serve food, such as cheese and crackers
- Always offer non-alcoholic drinks
- Do not mix strong drinks or be in a hurry to refill glasses

- Close the bar at least two hours before guests depart
- Do not serve additional drinks to a guest who has had too many!
- Do not serve additional drinks to a guest who has had too many.

Did You Know?

1. Alcohol, in any concentration, is a depressant not a stimulant. Alcohol slows all nerve impulses and body functions. The false feeling of stimulation, with small doses, comes from lessening of inhibitions due to the particular portion of the brain controlling this part of behavior being relaxed.

2. The amount of alcohol in one (12 oz.) bottle of beer is about equal to that in a (1 oz.) shot of whiskey.

3. When alcohol is consumed, it quickly reaches the brain where it, in effect, short-circuits the parts that control judgment, emotions and confidence.

4. The first thing affected after drinking alcohol is a person's **judgment**.

5. Reliable research studies show that 2 or 3 drinks of alcohol impair the driving ability of most individuals.

6. A driver with a BAC of .08% or more is intoxicated (in the presumptive level).

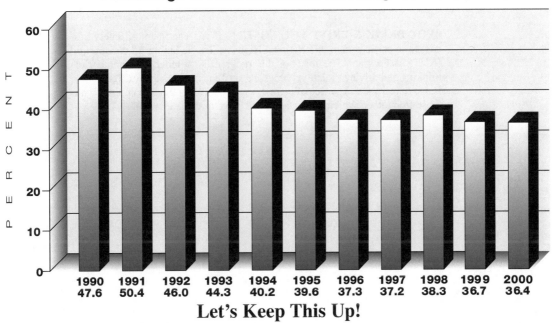

Percentage of Fatal Accidents Involving Alcohol (Table 6.3)

	1990	1991	1992	1993	1994	1995	1996	1997	1998	1999	2000
PERCENT	47.6	50.4	46.0	44.3	40.2	39.6	37.3	37.2	38.3	36.7	36.4

Let's Keep This Up!

NOTE: This chapter was written in consultation with the Tennessee Statewide Clearinghouse for Alcohol, Tobacco & Other Drug Information and Referral.

For further information on the general subject of drug and alcohol use and abuse, or for referrals for help with such problems, they may be reached at their toll-free "Redline" at 1-800-889-9789. Or, check their Website: www.tnclearinghouse.com.

7. It takes about one hour to cancel the effects of one drink. It takes about 3 hours to cancel the intoxicating effects of 3 drinks.

8. Alcohol-related vehicle accidents are the number-one killer of people under the age of 40.

9. Many drugs, including the "miracle" drugs, can impair your ability to drive. They can make an ill person feel well enough to drive, but can also affect alertness, judgment, coordination and vision.

10. The combined use of alcohol and other depressant drugs, such as antihistamines, may be more dangerous to health and highway safety than the effects of either the alcohol or drugs alone.

We Are Doing Better

Over the past few years, Tennessee has seen a progressive decrease in the percentage of fatal accidents involving alcohol. Prior to 1990 it was common for half of all fatal accidents to involve alcohol. Since then there has been a steady decline, so that in 2000 (the most recent year for which data is available), the percentage has dropped to 36%.

"YOU DRINK & DRIVE YOU LOSE" — The Department of Safety has chosen to participate in this National Highway Traffic Safety Administration (NHTSA) Program. The focus of this program is to reduce the number of drinking and driving violations occurring on Tennessee roadways. Tennessee is one of many states participating in this program. Our efforts, combined with those from other participating states, will serve to make all roadways safer.

PROTECTING PASSENGERS/DRIVERS

Tennessee Safety Belt Laws
"It's the Law"
(T.C.A. 55-9-602, 55-9-603)

Effective July 1, 2004 a law enforcement officer no longer has to stop a violator for a separate violation in order to issue a citation for failure to observe the seatbelt or child restraint laws in Tennessee. Seatbelt and Child Restraint Device (CDR) violations are now known as primary enforcement statute and just as any other rule of the road a driver can be stopped and ticketed solely for disobeying these laws.

A. No person shall operate a passenger motor vehicle in the State of Tennessee unless such person and all passengers four (4) years of age or older are restrained by a safety belt at all times the vehicle is in forward motion.

B. Children are further protected by the law, which makes the **driver responsible** for their protection up to the age of sixteen (16). If children under age 16 are not properly restrained the driver may be charged and fined $50.00 for violation of the law.

- If the child's parent or legal guardian is present in the car but not driving, then the parent or legal guardian is responsible for making sure that the child is properly transported and may be fined for non-compliance.

C. Further revisions to the Tennessee Child restrain Law that took effect on July 1, 2004 include:

- Any child under one (1) year old (even if he or she weighs over 20 pounds) or any child weighing 20 pounds or less must be in a rear facing child restraint, in the rear seat, if available.

- Any child aged one to three (1 – 3) years old weighing more than 20 pounds must be transported in a forward facing child restraint system in the rear seat, if available.

- Any child aged four to eight (4 – 8) years of age, measuring less than 5 feet in height must be in a belt positioning booster seat, in the rear seat if available. (**NOTE:** If the child is not between age 4 and age 8, but is LESS than five feet (5') in height, he/she must still use a seat belt system.)

- Any child aged nine to twelve (9 – 12) years of age measuring 5 feet or more in height must use a seat belt system and be placed in the rear seat, if available. (Note: If the child is not between age 9 and age 12, but is five feet (5') or MORE in height, he/she must still use a seat belt system.)

- Any child aged thirteen to fifteen (13 – 15) years old must use a passenger restraint system (seat belt system).

- Provision is made for the transportation of children in medically prescribed modified child restraints. A copy of a Doctor's prescription is to be carried in the vehicle utilizing the modified child restraint device (CRD) at all times.

All child passenger restraint systems (car seats or booster seats) referenced above must meet federal motor vehicle safety standards.

D. Tennessee law further requires every occupant sixteen (16) years through seventeen (17) years of age to wear a safety belt throughout the vehicle. Failure to comply could result in a $20.00 fine for the occupant.

SEAT BELTS SAVE LIVES

Safety Belts Facts

Seat belts and child safety seats help prevent injury five different ways. By:

1. Preventing ejection

Ejection greatly increases the chance of death or serious injury, in fact the chance of being killed in a crash by being ejected from a vehicle is 1 in 8. Safety belts virtually eliminate ejection. The belted driver stays inside the car often protected from injury.

2. Shifting crash forces to the strongest parts of the body's structure.

- To get the most benefit out of your seat belt, you should be aware of the following points:

- The lap belt should be worn low over the pelvis with the bottom edge touching the tops of the thighs snugly.

- The shoulder belt should be worn over the shoulder and across the chest, *NOT* under the arm and over the abdomen. Make certain that the shoulder belt is not worn so loosely that it slides off your shoulder.

- Pregnant women should wear the lap belt below the abdomen and the shoulder belt above the belly.

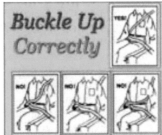

3. **Spreading forces over a wide area of the body.** Safety belts reduce the possibility of injury from "hostile" surfaces inside the car (steering wheel, dashboard, windshield, controls, etc.). Even if the belted driver does collide with some of these surfaces, they do so with much less force and are often spared more serious injury.

4. **Allowing the body to slow down gradually.** The belt keeps the driver "in the driver's seat." The belted driver is better able to deal with emergencies and often avoid more serious trouble.

5. **Protecting the head and spinal cord.** The belted driver is less likely to be stunned or rendered unconscious by the accident and is better able to cope with the situation. Research has found that proper use of lap/shoulder belts reduces the risk of fatal injury to front seat passenger car occupants by 45% and the risk of moderate-to-critical injury by 50% (for occupants of light trucks, 60% and 65% respectively).

- Every 14 seconds someone in the U.S. is injured in a traffic crash, and every 13 minutes someone is killed.

- Seat belts are the most effective safety devices in vehicles today, reducing the chance of injury or death in a crash by 45% and saving nearly 10,000 lives annually.

- Failure to use a seat belt contributes to more fatalities than any other single traffic safety-related behavior.

- In 2001, traffic crashes on Tennessee's roadways killed 1,251 people and caused 74,856 injuries. Sadly, many of those deaths and injuries could have been prevented if only the victims had taken the time to buckle up.

Road Test Reminder

Any passenger motor vehicle manufactured or assembled in 1969 or later must be equipped with seat belts and they must be in good usable condition for both applicant and examiner use.

The Belted Driver Has Better Control of the Car
The seat belt holds the driver in the driving position designed to give maximum comfort and maximum control of the car. Belts also tend to reduce fatigue. The belted driver stays more alert. *Also the facts are clear:* **In an accident, the belted driver is much more likely to survive uninjured.**

Common Fears and Misconceptions about Seat Belts:
Many people still have *"bad information"* about using safety belts. For example:
- *"Safety belts can trap you inside a car."* It takes less than a second to undo a safety belt. Crashes where a vehicle catches fire or sinks in deep water and you are "trapped", seldom happen. Only one-half of one percent of all crashes ends in fire or submersion. Even if they do, a safety belt may keep you from being "knocked out".

Your chance to escape will be better if you are conscious.

- *"Some people are thrown clear in a crash and walk away with hardly a scratch."* Most crash fatalities result from the force of impact or from being thrown from the vehicle. Your chances of not being killed in an accident are much better if you stay inside the vehicle. Safety belts can keep you from being thrown out of your vehicle, into the path of another one. Ejected occupants are four times as likely to be killed as those who remain inside the vehicle.

BUCKLE UP

IT'S WORTH THE EFFORT

- *"If I get hit from the side, I am better off being thrown across the car; away form the crash point."* When a vehicle is struck from the side, it will move sideways. Everything in the vehicle that is not fastened down, including the passengers, will slide toward the point of the crash, not away from it.

- *"Safety belts are good on long trips, but I do not need them if I am driving around town."* Over half of all traffic deaths happen within 25 miles of home. Many of them occur on roads posted at less than 45 m.p.h.

Tennessee's Child Passenger Protection Laws

Tennessee cared enough about children to become the <u>first State</u> in the country to pass a Child Passenger Protection Law. This law requires:

That any person transporting a child under the age of four (4) years old in a motor vehicle upon a road, street, or highway in Tennessee shall be responsible for protecting the child and properly using a child passenger restraint system meeting federal motor vehicle safety standards.

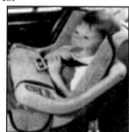

- A 2001 amendment allows a mother to remove a child under four (4) years of age from a child passenger restraint system only when the mother is nursing the child.

Remember, holding a child in your lap, even if you have on your seat belt, does not protect the child. In fact, your own body weight in an impact could add serious damage to the child. While the above makes it legal for a mother to nurse while the vehicle is in motion; the <u>safest recommendation</u> is still to pull over and stop briefly for this need.

By promoting child passenger safety, Tennessee attempts to protect its most precious resource from needless death and injury. Why needless? Consider the following:

• Motor vehicle crashes are the leading cause of death for children 5 to 14. An average of eight children are killed and more than 900 are injured in crashes every <u>DAY</u>.

• Children who are properly secured in safety seats survive three quarters (3/4) of the crashes that would otherwise be fatal.

• The proper use of child-restraint devices could prevent **nine out of ten deaths** and **eight out of ten serious injuries** to child passengers under the age of four.

Unfortunately, many of these needless injuries result in permanent disabilities such as paralysis, brain damage, epilepsy, etc.

Set a Good Example - Always Buckle Up

Think about what your child sees you do in the car. Do you wear your safety belt? Children follow their parents' example. Set a good example and remember you want to stay alive to share the beautiful years of your child's growth.

There have been studies conducted that show children's behavior in the car improves when they learn how to ride in their child-restraint device and it becomes habit. Make it a habit for your child. A habit you can both live with.

Put children in their place—in child-restraint devices or seat belts!

Tips For Using Seat Belts With Children

When your child "graduates" from the child-restraint system to seat belts, it is very important for the belts to lie across the correct area of the child's body.

Basically a child is big enough to use the vehicle lap and shoulder belt when they can sit with their back against the vehicle seat back with their knees bent over the edge of the vehicle seat without slouching. The lap belt should lie securely on the child's upper thigh, low and snug around the hips. The shoulder belt should fit snugly across the chest and rest between their neck and shoulder. Never put the shoulder belt behind the child's back or under their arm.

Always remember **"Belts to Bones"**. The pelvic bone and the collar bone should bear the pressure of the seat belts. If the safety belt system seems to ride up too high on the child's stomach or the shoulder harness lays across the face or neck area of the child, you should continue to use a booster seat or one of the many models of high back booster seats that incorporate the vehicle's existing safety belt system.

Air Bag Safety

Air bags can HELP save your life. There have been over 800,000 air bag deployments, and air bags have been

Children ages 12 and under are safer in the back seat of a vehicle.

credited with saving more than 4,011 lives since 1987 according to information provided by the National Highway Traffic Safety Administration. Even if your car has airbags, always wear your seat belt. *Airbags are supplemental restraint systems that work* **WITH** *seat belts, not in place of them.* They help protect adults in a frontal crash, but they don't provide protection in side or rear impact crashes or in rollovers. Most tragedies involving air bags could be prevented if air bags are used in combination with a safety belt and if children under 12 are properly restrained in the rear seat of the vehicle.

"The Back Is Where It's At" for children 12 and under. While air bags have a good overall record of providing supplemental protection for adults in the event of a crash, they pose a severe risk for children ages 12 and under. Research shows that children and air  bags simply do not mix. Children are safer properly restrained in a child restraint-device or seat belt in the **back seat** of a vehicle, regardless of whether the vehicle is equipped with a passenger side airbag. **NEVER PLACE A CHILD SAFETY SEAT IN THE FRONT SEAT WHERE A FRONT MOUNTED PASSENGER AIR BAG IS PRESENT.**

An important item to remember is that an air bag is not a soft, billowy pillow. Air bags were developed to prevent vehicle occupants from striking the steering wheel or dashboard. The air bag deploys and immediately deflates — faster than the blink of an eye. Air bags **combined with** safety belts are the most effective protection currently available in a car or truck.

If you drive, own or ride in a vehicle equipped with either a driver-side and/or passenger side air bag you should follow the following safety points:

Adults

• Always wear the lap AND shoulder safety belts

• If you have an adjustable steering wheel always try to keep it tilted down in a level or parallel position.

• Sit as far as possible from the steering wheel (or  dashboard on passenger side) to give the air bag room to deploy and dissipate its energy; ten (10) to twelve (12) inches between the chest and the air bag module is recommended by the National Highway Traffic Safety Administration (NHTSA).

Children

• Children 12 and younger should always ride in the back seat, properly buckled up or restrained in a child restraint device.

• Infants in rear-facing seats should NEVER be placed in the front seat of a vehicle with a passenger-side air bag.

- Infants should be properly restrained in the back seat.

- If a child must ride in the front seat of a vehicle with a passenger-side airbag, the seat should be moved back as far as possible and the child should be properly buckled up.

Air Bag Deactivation?

Should air bags be deactivated? No, not unless you meet one of the four following criteria:

1. The driver cannot sit 10 to 12 inches from the steering wheel and air bag module, and drive the car safely.

2. The driver and/or passenger(s) has one of several unusual medical or physical conditions.

3. The driver must transport children under 12 in the front seat because the car has no rear seat or because of a car pool situation.

4. An infant in a rear-facing infant seats must be transported in the front seat because the car has no rear seat.

Vehicle owners and lessees can obtain an on-off switch for one or both of their air bags only if they can certify that they are, or a user of their vehicle is in one of the four risk groups above. To be considered eligible for an on-off switch a NHTSA request from must be filled out and returned to the National Highway Traffic Safety Administration (NHTSA). Forms are available from state driver license and registration offices and may be available from automobile dealerships and repair facilities. Forms may also be requested by contacting NHTSA's Auto Safety Hotline at 1-888-DASH-2-DOT (1-888-327-4236) or visiting the NHTSA Web site at http://www.nhtsa.dot.gov.

As of May 19, 2003 Tennessee law makes it a Class A misdemeanor for any person to knowingly install or re-install any object in lieu of an air bag that was designed in accordance with federal safety regulations for the make, model and year of the vehicle, as part of the vehicle's standard inflatable Restraint System.

Other Child Passenger Protection Laws

It is now not only common sense, but against the law to allow children under the age of twelve to ride in the bed of a pickup truck. The only exceptions are:

1. When the vehicle is being used in an organized parade, procession, or other ceremonial event.

2. When the vehicle is being used for agricultural purposes.

3. In certain local areas where children over age six who are not yet 12 year old are in vehicles traveling on local streets and roads.

Even with these exceptions, if a child under the age of six is in the pickup truck bed, the vehicle must travel 20 miles per hour or less.

Each year more than 200 people die as a result of riding in the cargo area of pickup trucks. More than half of these deaths are children and teenagers.

TRAFFIC SIGNS AND SIGNALS

Traffic signs give you information about the road, the highway system, traffic flow, and the local regulations and laws. They warn you about hazards, identify your route, and direct the speed and movement of traffic. These signs also provide directions and let you know about places of interest, from the huge overhead green interstate signs to the little blue rectangles that direct you to a library or hospital.

Every traffic sign has a definite shape and colors that announce their purpose and specific meanings. You should be able to recognize them immediately. Even if a stop sign is damaged or blocked by dirt, limbs or snow, you should know by the octagonal shape and red color that you must stop.

Sign Shapes and Colors

Learn the standard colors and shapes (shown below) so you know what a sign means, even at a distance. For example, a rectangle is always a regulatory sign, telling you about laws and regulations or giving you instructions such as speed limits or lane uses.

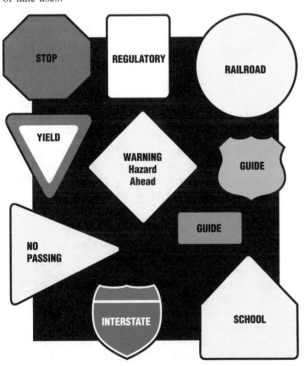

Color Codes On Highway Traffic Signs

Colors of Signs Series

The colors to be used on standard signs shall be as follows:

RED is used only as a background color for STOP signs, multiple supplemental plates, DO-NOT-ENTER messages, WRONG WAY signs and on Interstate route markers; as a legend color for YIELD signs, parking prohibition signs, the circular outline and diagonal bar prohibitory symbol.

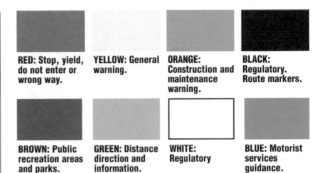

The meanings of the eight basic background colors of signs should be memorized.

BLACK is used as a background on ONE-WAY signs. Black is used as a message on white, yellow and orange signs.

WHITE is used as the background for route makers, guide signs, the Fallout Shelter Directional sign, and regulatory signs, except STOP signs, and for the legend on brown, green, blue, black and red signs.

ORANGE is used as a background color for construction and maintenance signs and shall not be used for any other purpose.

YELLOW is used as a background color for warning signs, except where orange is specified herein, and for school signs.

BROWN is used as a background color for guide information signs related to points of recreational cultural interest.

GREEN is used as a background color for guide signs (other than those using brown or white), mileposts, and as a legend color with a white background for permissive parking regulations.

BLUE is used as a background color for information signs related to motorist services (including police services and rest areas) and the Evacuation Route Marker.

Four Other Colors — Purple, light blue, coral, and strong yellow-green have been identified as suitable for highway use and are being reserved for future needs.

Whenever white is specified herein as a sign color, it is understood to include silver-colored reflecting coating or elements that reflect white light.

Traffic signs are placed to help you and to instruct you in the best and safest use of the highway. All signs must be obeyed at all times unless a policeman or other traffic officer directs you to do otherwise. Study and learn the signs on the following pages and notice that the shape of each sign has a general or specific meaning.

Octagon Shape — Stop

This sign is the only eight-sided sign you will see on the highway. It always means that there is danger. It will always be red with white lettering. It tells you that you are approaching an important street or highway and that you must bring your car to a complete stop, not going beyond the crosswalk. IF you cannot see, then proceed cautiously to a point where you can see, and then go only if you can do so safely.

4-Way or All Way: Red Rectangle — Added below a stop sign, means all traffic approaching this intersection must stop.

Triangular Shape — Yield

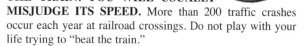

This three-sided sign means that you are approaching an intersection and must stop and wait if any other vehicles are approaching from the right or left on the other highway. If you are sure no other cars are coming you need not come to a complete stop but you must slow down and enter the intersection with caution. You must stop when traffic warrants.

Round Shape — Railroad Ahead

This circular sign always means that you are approaching a railroad grade crossing. You must slow down and be ready to stop. This sign tells you that it is up to you to stop if you see a train coming. **NEVER TRY TO "BEAT" THE TRAIN. YOU WILL USUALLY MISJUDGE ITS SPEED.** More than 200 traffic crashes occur each year at railroad crossings. Do not play with your life trying to "beat the train."

Broad "X" Shape — Railroad Here

This is known as a crossbuck sign. It is placed at all railroad grade crossings, and tells you exactly where the tracks are located. Notice the smaller signs placed on the post directly below the crossbuck. They will tell you the number of tracks at a particular crossing. This is very important because, when there are two or more tracks, one train passing might hide the approach of a train from the other direction.

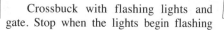

Flashing lights on a crossbuck mean that a train is coming. Always stop when the lights are flashing. Remain stopped until the train has passed. If there is more than one track, be sure all tracks are clear before crossing.

Crossbuck with flashing lights and gate. Stop when the lights begin flashing

and before the gate comes down. Remain stopped until the gates are raised and the lights stop flashing.

Diamond Shape — Hazardous Or Unusual Condition Ahead

These signs call for caution and usually for a slower speed. Some carry written information. Others are miniature symbolic road maps that warn of highway conditions ahead. This sign tells you that you are approaching an intersection. The black lines show you just what kind of intersection this is. This sign tells you it is a crossroad. *(See more examples of warning signs on pages 43-44)*

Rectangular Shape—Special Laws, Regulations Or Important Information Applies Here

• **Lane Control**

The signs below indicate that traffic in the respective lanes must either move straight through or turn left. They may also direct certain vehicles (such as trucks) as to which lane

they must travel. Variations of these signs will limit turns by showing an arrow with the word "Only," and others will indicate that traffic must turn right. These signs are sometimes mounted overhead.

The sign shown at right (High Occupancy Vehicle) indicates lanes reserved for buses and vehicles with the minimum number of occupants specified on the sign.

• **Speed Control**

Speed Limit Signs. These signs tell you the maximum speed allowed, the minimum speed required, or of a change in speed limit.

The sign on the far right is used whenever children are within walking distance of school. It tells you that children may be crossing the street on their way to and from school.

This type of sign is controlled by a time clock and flashes yellow lights while illuminating the speed limit. Failure to obey the posted school zone limit could result in serious injury or loss of life to **Tennessee's most valuable asset, its children**.

Regulatory Signs

These signs which have a white background and a red circle and line diagonally through them mean "NO" according to what is shown behind the red symbol. For example:

STOP FOR SCHOOL BUS LOADING OR UNLOADING	PEDESTRIANS BICYCLES MOTOR-DRIVEN CYCLES PROHIBITED	COMMERCIAL VEHICLES EXCLUDED

NO TRUCKS

NO BICYCLES

WEIGHT LIMIT *T *T

PEDESTRIANS AND BICYCLES PROHIBITED

END 15 MILE SPEED

NO PARKING 8:00 AM TO 4:00 PM

ONE WAY

NO LEFT TURN

NO U TURN

SLOWER TRAFFIC KEEP RIGHT

This sign is used on a highway which has four lanes or more. It means that you must drive in the extreme right-lane unless you want to pass a slower-moving car or make a left turn. Never straddle lanes or drive in the center lane when you are moving more slowly than other traffic around you.

This sign tells you that, in the area where this sign is placed parking is forbidden.

• *No Passing Signs* - These signs tell you where passing is not permitted. Passing areas are based on how far you can see ahead. They consider unseen hazards such as hills and curves, intersections, driveways and other places a vehicle may enter the roadway.

DO NOT PASS

This sign tells you that you are approaching a one-way street and that you must not enter from the direction you are traveling.

DO NOT ENTER

NO PASSING ZONE

A triangular No Passing Zone sign can also be used. These signs are yellow or orange and placed on the left side of the roadway.

Tennessee law (T.C.A. 55-8-139) makes it illegal to stand in a roadway to solicit a ride. Hitchhiking is not only dangerous to the pedestrian, but also to the driver of the vehicle who stops to pick up a stranger. It is recommended that you neither hitchhike nor pick up hitchhikers.

Warning Signs

This sign tells you to be prepared for a rather sharp turn to the left. The turn sign is used to mark turns with a recommended speed of 30 m.p.h. or less.

Curve Sign

This sign tells you that you must be prepared for a curve to the right. The curve sign is used to mark curves with recommended speed in the range between 30 and 55 m.p.h.

Reverse Turn Sign

This sign tells you that you must turn right, then left. The reverse turn sign is used to mark two turns in opposite directions that are less than 600 feet apart.

Advisory Speed Plate

The smaller sign on the post beneath this sign is used to supplement warning signs. It gives you the recommended maximum safe speed.

You will see this sign — or one saying, "SLIDES" in some hilly areas. Both of these signs warn of rocks which may be in the road; not of rocks which may strike you from overhead. Watch the roadway, not the hill.

This sign indicates that there is a STOP sign you can't yet see just ahead — so you should start to slow down at this point. A similar sign using a symbol shaped like a traffic light and the black arrow indicates there is a "traffic signal ahead."

This sign indicates that there is a YIELD sign you can't yet see just ahead — so you should start to slow down at this point.

This sign warns you that the road ahead narrows and that you must plan to move into the left lane. Don't forget to check behind you before you begin this maneuver and signal your intentions.

This sign alerts you to the possibility of traffic blending into the main stream of travel. After checking to your rear you should move into the other lane, if possible, to allow the merging motorist a clear path.

This sign tells you that the bridge is too narrow to be safe at average passing speeds; you must slow down and drive cautiously when you are crossing a bridge which displays this sign.

You will see the following sign near school grounds or buildings. This sign warns you to slow down, drive with caution, and watch for children. It is placed as you approach a school.

Warning Signs

SLIPPERY WHEN WET

CATTLE CROSSING

TWO-WAY TRAFFIC

LEFT LANE ENDS

BIKE CROSSING

WINDING ROAD

LOW CLEARANCE

CHEVRON
A sharp change in
direction ahead

T-INTERSECTION AHEAD

T-INTERSECTION
You must turn right or left. Be
prepared to yield.

Work Area Signs - These construction, maintenance or emergency operations signs are generally **diamond or rectangular** shaped, **orange with black letters or symbols** and warn you that people are working on or near the roadway. These warnings include reduced speed, detours, slow moving construction equipment and lane closures. In work areas, a person with a sign or flag may control traffic. You must obey the directions of these persons.

Construction Signs

MEN WORKING

ROAD CONSTRUCTION 500 FT.

DETOUR 500 FT.

STOP AHEAD

FRESH OIL

Channeling Devices

Barricades, vertical panels, concrete barriers, drums and

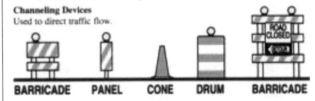

Channeling Devices
Used to direct traffic flow.

BARRICADE PANEL CONE DRUM BARRICADE

cones are the most common devices used to guide drivers safely through work zones. When driving near these devices, keep your vehicle in the middle of the lane and obey the posted speed limit. As you leave the work zone, stay in your lane and maintain your speed. Don't change lanes until you are completely clear of the work zone.

Electronic Message or Arrow Signs - These are mobile devices that are often used on some roadways to give you advance warning of construction zones, special traffic directions, road closures or in some cases weather hazards.

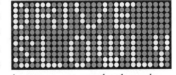

Flashing arrow panels advise approaching drivers of lane closures. You must begin to merge into the remaining open lane(s) well in advance of this sign.

Highway Flaggers

You will see flaggers such as these pictured below at numerous construction sites along our highways. Please learn these three simple signals since they are the most commonly used by construction flaggers.

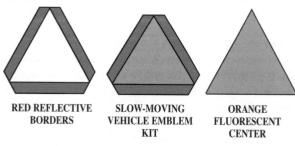

TO STOP TRAFFIC

TRAFFIC PROCEED

TO ALERT AND SLOW TRAFFIC

Flaggers at some worksites may use paddles with the word stop on one side and slow on the other instead of red flags. The basic hand movements for stop and proceed remain the same whether a flag or paddle is used.

Slow-Moving Vehicle (SMV) Emblem

| RED REFLECTIVE BORDERS | SLOW-MOVING VEHICLE EMBLEM KIT | ORANGE FLUORESCENT CENTER |

Recognize this sign. Some day (or night) it may save your life. Look at it!

During daylight the bright fluorescent orange solid triangle in the center of the SMV emblem is highly visible. At night, the SMV emblem glows brilliantly in the path of approaching headlights.

You may see this emblem on slow-moving vehicles such as farm tractors, machinery, construction equipment, or horse-drawn vehicles.

Object Marker

These markers warn you of objects not actually in the roadway but so close to the edge of the road that they need marking.

Typical applications include bridge ends, underpass abutments and other obstructions closely adjacent to the edges of the roadway.

Hazard to left

Hazard to right

Guide Signs For Highways

PRIMARY ROUTE
(Primarily Connects Cities)

A sign such as the one below will show two highways are coming together or separating. The sign to the left denotes a State secondary highway while the one to the right indicates a U.S. highway that will reach into another state. Drivers should become thoroughly familiar with route numbers and signs they must follow when beginning a trip from one area to another. They should approach signs such as the one below with caution and should be alert for drivers nearby who are not familiar with the area highways.

Interstate Route Marker

Indicates that the route is one of the routes comprising the national system of interstate and defense highways. These highways join centers of population and defense establishments and join with the major international highways at the Mexican and Canadian borders, they constitute a nationwide network of the most important highways.

Guide Signs On Interstates

These are signs to help you while driving on Tennessee's  Interstate and Defense Highways. The signs are above or to the right of the highway with the arrows pointing to the lane you should be in if you intend to enter or leave the road.

This sign is seen on Interstates and Expressways. The background is green with white lettering and/or numbers visible at some distance. Such signs give information vital to selection of lane, proper exits, etc.

If an Interstate guide sign is marked with the above sign, all traffic in the lane(s) directly below the arrows MUST exit.

Service Signs

The blue color of these signs indicates that they provide direction to motorist service facilities. Word message signs will also be used to direct motorists to areas where service stations, restaurants and motels are available.

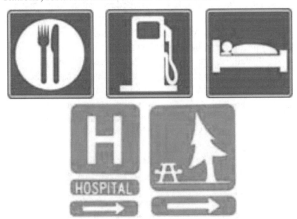

Handicap Symbol

Parking spaces displaying this blue sign are reserved for vehicles bearing disabled veteran or handicapped license plates, or a special handicapped decal. The use of reserved handicapped spaces by others is prohibited by law. Please be courteous!

Directional Signs

The green background signs indicate that the message is providing directional information. New directional signs will point to bike and hiking trails.

Reference Markers

RAMP SIGN

In order to help motorists better identify their location on urban interstates, the state has installed interstate reference markers every 1,000 feet along heavily traveled sections. These have been installed in Nashville and Knoxville, and are planned for Memphis and Chattanooga in the near future.

The signs display information about the route number, direction of travel, and the "log mile" in tenths of a mile. Most are mounted on the median dividers. Thus, motorists with mobile phones who notify emergency operators about incidents will be able to give an accurate description of the exact location where assistance is needed. This will help emergency personnel respond more rapidly, and possibly make the difference between life and death. It will also help clear the highways more quickly. *In the sample (at right) this sign* **MAIN LINE** *indicates the location as: West Bound on* **SIGN** *Interstate 40 at mile marker 223 and 6 tenths. So the driver would be between mile markers 223 and 224.*

Uniform Highway Markings

The information in Chapter Seven is taken from the United States Department of Transportation's Federal Highway Administration's (FHWA) Manual on Uniform Traffic Control Devices, which all highway agencies must use in marking and signing roadways under their jurisdiction. Until all states have completed marking, drivers may encounter both the old and new markings. BE ALERT and follow directions.

Word and symbol markings on the pavement are used for the purpose of guiding, warning, or regulating traffic.

Symbol arrows indicating more than one movement is permitted; arrows indicating only one movement is mandatory.

Traffic Signals

Traffic signals are used to control drivers of vehicles and pedestrians at some intersections and crosswalks. Signals promote better movement of traffic on busy roads by assigning right of way. Tennessee state law requires that if a signal is not working, the intersection is to be treated as if it were a four-way stop intersection. Stop as you would if there were stop signs in all directions and do not proceed until it is safe. Common courtesy and the right-of-way law instructs that if there are two or more vehicles at the intersection that stopped at the same time, the driver on the left would yield to the driver on the right. The driver on the right who arrives first gets to go first. However, stay cautious and be sure it is safe to proceed even when you are the first vehicle to reach the intersection.

Traffic control devices include traffic signals, signs and pavement markings. Traffic control can also be provided by law enforcement, highway construction personnel or school crossing guards. You must obey directions from these individuals, even if their directions are different than what the traffic lights and signs indicate. Also remember that regardless of the color of a traffic signal ALL vehicles must yield the right-of-way to any approaching emergency vehicles.

1. *Traffic Signals* are usually placed at heavily traveled intersections. These lights tell you when or where to stop and go. A green light means you can go if it is safe. A yellow light means caution, prepare to stop for the red light and the red always means stop. Standard traffic lights are red, yellow and green, from top to bottom respectively.

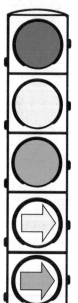

RED — Stop behind crosswalk or stop line. Unless otherwise posted, you may turn right on red after coming to a complete stop and when no pedestrians or cross traffic are present.

YELLOW — Caution, prepare to stop. Red stop signal will be exhibited immediately thereafter. Adjust your speed immediately so you may come to a smooth stop. You must stop if it is safe to do so. ***DO NOT SPEED UP TO BEAT THE LIGHT.*** If you are already IN the intersection when the yellow light comes on, do not stop but continue cautiously through the intersection. Tennessee law only requires the yellow light to be exhibited for a minimum of **3 SECONDS before the red light.**

Collisions often happen at intersections on yellow lights. Not only is it dangerous for you to ignore the yellow light because you may hold up oncoming traffic that receives the green light, you also must be aware that some drivers often "jump the green" and start through an intersection because they have seen the yellow light come on from the crossing directions. **If you try to "beat the yellow" and another driver decides to "jump the green" the results could be deadly!**

GREEN — Go IF the intersection is clear. <u>You must yield to pedestrians and vehicles still in the intersection at light change</u>. The green signal gives you the permission to proceed, however you must still observe the laws of the right-of-way. Yield to oncoming vehicles if you are turning left. Never attempt to "jump the gree" by starting through the intersection early or by making a quick left turn in front of oncoming traffic. This is extremely dangerous!

Protected Arrows - At many intersections you may see what is called a "protected turn arrow". when the arrow is green, you have the right-of-way and may drive the vehicle only in the direction of the arrow after yielding to vehicles and pedestrians already in the intersection. When the arrow changes to yellow, prepare to yield to oncoming traffic. When the arrow is red or your lane has the red light, all turns are prohibited, even if other lanes of traffic have a green signal and your path through the intersection appears to be clear.

When traffic lights have added lights with directional arrows, drivers may cautiously enter the intersection only to make the movement indicated by the arrow. The light for your lane controls the direction in which you may lawfully proceed.

If traffic circumstances have left you in an intersection waiting to make a left turn, and the light turns red, you should complete the turn when the traffic clears. Do not try to back up, or stay in the intersection blocking traffic. Better yet, don't find yourself in this situation! You should not

FLASHING YELLOW	FLASHING RED
Slow down and proceed with caution at the intersection.	*Complete stop. Same as stop sign. Look both ways, yield to traffic and pedestrians and proceed when it is safe to do so.*

pull into an intersection to make a turn until your path is clear.

2. *Pedestrian Signals* - allow pedestrians to know when it is legally permitted and safe to cross a street or intersection. Pedestrians can promote traffic safety and protect themselves by observing the following rules:

A. "Walk" Sign: Many streets with significant pedestrian traffic will have a pedestrian signal that displays the word "WALK" or a symbol of a person walking when it is legally permitted and safe to cross the street or intersection.

Pedestrians who have started to cross the street or intersection when the "WALK" sign or walking person symbol appears should continue as quickly as possible to the other side of the street if the signal shifts to "DON"T WALK".

Please note: At some intersections there is a button near the base of the pedestrian signal or stop light that must be pushed by the pedestrian to activate the pedestrian signal to show the "WALK" sign.

B. "Don't Walk" Sign: Pedestrian signals indicate when it is not legally permissible nor safe to cross a street or intersection. When the pedestrian signal shows the words "DON'T WALK" or a symbol of a raised hand appears it is not legally permitted nor safe to begin crossing a street or intersection.

3. *Lane Control Signals*

| Driving in this lane is permitted | If flashing lane is for turning only, if solid direction of lane is changing | Driving is NOT Permitted in this lane |

The above signals may appear as single or multiple units over each lane of the roadway, and are most often used when the direction of the flow of traffic changes during different hours of the day. Also indicates toll plaza lane open or closed. (See Chapter 8, page 66 for details on reversible lanes)

General Principles of Pavement Lane Markings

Lines and symbols on the roadway divide it into lanes, tell you when you may pass other vehicles or change lanes, which lanes to use for turns, define pedestrian walkways and show where you must stop for signs or traffic signals. Line colors tell you if you are on a one-way or two-way roadway.

1. **Edge and Lane Lines** - Lines along the side of the road show you where the edge of the road is located. A solid white line indicates the right edge of the traffic lane on a road. A solid or broken yellow line indicates the left edge of traffic lanes going in your direction.
   ° If you ever find yourself with yellow to your right and white to your left, you are going the wrong way. Remember, on a divided highway **the side of the roadway to the left of the driver** and nearest the median, **always has a yellow line. The right side of the roadway will always have a white line.** It is a good way to confirm you are traveling the right direction when entering an unfamiliar interstate.

A. **Yellow Lane Markings** - Lines separating traffic moving in opposite directions are yellow. Yellow lines are also used to mark a boundary or barrier of the travel path at the location of a particular hazard such as bridge supports, etc.

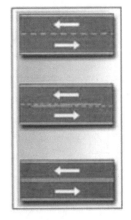

   ° **Broken yellow lines** mean that you **MAY cross the line to pass** if there is no oncoming traffic and it is safe to do so.
   ° **Two solid yellow lines** between lanes of traffic means you **MAY NOT cross the lines from either**

direction to pass even if no oncoming traffic is in view. You may cross a solid yellow line to turn into a driveway or side road if it is safe to do so.
   ° **One solid yellow line and one broken yellow line:** Where there is both a solid and a broken yellow line between opposing lanes of traffic, you **may not pass if the solid yellow line is on your side**. If the **broken yellow line is on your side, you are in the "*passing zone*" and may pass** if it is safe to do so. You must safely return to your side of the roadway **before** the passing zone ends.

B. **White Lane Markings** - Multiple lanes of traffic that flow in the same direction are separated by white lane markings.

You will find white lane markings on freeways, limited access highways, by-passes and one-way streets.
   ° **Broken white lines** between lanes of traffic mean you **MAY cross the lines to pass** or change lanes if it is safe to do so.
   ° **One solid white line** between lanes of traffic means that you should stay in your lane and **MAY NOT cross the line to pass** (unless an emergency situation requires you to change lanes).

2. **Crosswalks** - White crosswalk lines are painted across a road to indicate pedestrian crossing areas. Crosswalks define the area where pedestrians may cross the roadway and can be at intersections or in the middle of a block. However, not all crosswalks are marked. You must yield the right-of-way to pedestrians who are in or are about to enter crosswalk or street.

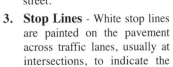

3. **Stop Lines** - White stop lines are painted on the pavement across traffic lanes, usually at intersections, to indicate the vehicle stopping position before traffic signs or signals. If the motorist is required to stop at the intersection the vehicle must be stopped behind this stop line (**A**). If no

Stop Line (A)	Crosswalk (B)	Neither (C)

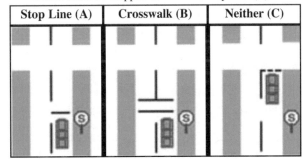

stop line is painted on the pavement all vehicles required to stop must: (**B**) Stop the vehicle before crossing the first line of the crosswalk (if crosswalk marked) and: (**C**) Stop the vehicle before the front bumper crosses the white edge line of the cross street in order to keep the vehicle from protruding out into the cross street traffic.

4. **High Occupancy Vehicle (HOV) lanes** are designated on highways by a diamond-shaped marking in the center of the lane. HOV lanes may also be special lanes separated by a barrier. During heavy traffic periods, HOV lanes are reserved for buses, vanpools, carpools and other high occupancy vehicles. Road signs indicate the

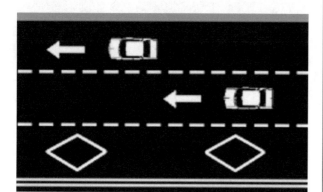

In the accompanying three-lane diagram, the far left travel lane is reserved for buses or high-occupancy vehicles (HOVs), like those used in carpools.

minimum number of passengers a vehicle must carry to use the HOV lanes and the times that HOV restrictions are in effect.

5. **Turn Lane Arrow**
If you are traveling in a lane marked with a curved arrow and the word ONLY, you must turn in the direction of the arrow. If your lane is marked with both a curved and a straight arrow, you may turn in the direction of the arrow or you may go straight.

A white cross-buck and the letters RR are painted on the pavement as a warning marker for many railroad/highway grade crossings.

RULES OF THE ROAD

This chapter highlights key traffic laws. To a certain extent, safe driving principles related to the laws are also discussed here, however a more complete discussion of driving techniques will be found in Chapter 11.

Even on a short trip, you may be faced with many dangerous driving conditions. Statistics show that half of all vehicle crashes occur within 25 miles of home.

The rules of the road are those laws, regulations and practices that provide safe and efficient vehicle movement on the roadways. This includes such things as signaling, turning, passing and stopping.

Learn the traffic rules and follow them; be willing to yield to other drivers to avoid a crash; always watch carefully for advance warning and information signs; and be a courteous driver. This will help you avoid snap decisions.

Obeying Officers

You must obey traffic officers at all times. There will be times when one will instruct you to do something that ordinarily would be a violation of traffic regulations. The officer will do this only in case of an emergency when it is the only way to keep traffic flowing smoothly and safely. A common example: A police officer holding up traffic at a green light and permitting a funeral procession to continue through a red light.

In the United States, Canada, and most other countries, right hand traffic is the rule. This means we drive on the right side of the road, and bear right when going around traffic circles, roundabouts or town squares.

Coasting Prohibited

The driver of any motor vehicle traveling on a downgrade shall not coast with the transmission of the vehicle in neutral. Vehicles shall not coast with the clutch disengaged.

Use Of Headlights

- **Required Night Use:** Your car headlights must be turned on between 30 minutes after sunset and 30 minutes before sunrise.
- **Dimming of Headlights Required:** When your vehicle's high beam headlights are on, you must dim or lower the beam when an oncoming vehicle is within 500 feet (approximately the distance of one city black) or when you are following another vehicle within 500 feet. Dimming headlights when following other vehicles is a practical

safety step. The glare from your headlights in a rearview mirror can blind another driver.

- **Special Daylight / Inclement Weather Uses:** Tennessee law requires that headlights must be turned on.

  1. at any other time when daylight is not good enough for you to see persons or vehicles clearly at a distance of 200 feet ahead, and

  2. when rain, mist, snow, or other precipitation requires constant use of windshield wipers.

Headlights turned on during daylight hours will make your vehicle more visible to oncoming vehicles and pedestrians. Use headlights when driving at dusk. Even if you can see clearly, headlights help other drivers see you as much as they help you see them.

Get into the habit of turning your headlights on when you use your windshield wipers. And don't forget using headlights when wipers are needed is not just a good safety precaution — **it's Tennessee law!**

- **Limited Use of Parking Lights or Auxiliary-Fog Lights:** The following procedures should be followed when using these type of lights -

  1. The law requires a vehicle stopped or parked on a road or shoulder to have parking lights on when limited visibility conditions exist.

  2. Do not drive a vehicle with only the parking lights on when driving at night or in inclement weather. The small size of parking lights may cause other drivers to think your vehicle is farther away than it actually is. Use of parking lights alone when there is limited visibility is not only unsafe it is against the law.

  3. It is also illegal to have auxiliary lights or fog lights on by themselves or on at times when you are required to dim your headlights. These very bright lights make if difficult for oncoming drivers to see and the glare may reflect blindingly in the rearview mirror of vehicles you are following.

Daytime Running Lights - Some newer vehicles have headlights that are on anytime the vehicle is running. These lights make it easier for others to see the vehicle, even in daylight, thereby reducing the likelihood of collisions. However, they are not meant to replace the use of headlights as required by law (night driving, inclement weather, etc.).

Littering

Throwing papers, bottles, cans, or disposing of other material from vehicles are all forms of littering. Littering is not only an offense against state law, with maximum fine of up to $500 and ten (10) days in jail. Littering is also an offense against common decency — something no respectable person would do.

Tennessee Driver Handbook   51   Rules of the Road

Slow-Moving Vehicles

It is against the law for you to drive slower than the posted minimum speed under normal driving conditions. You may drive more slowly than the minimum speed if you are driving in bad weather, heavy traffic or on a bad road. If there is no posted minimum speed, it is still against the law for you to drive so slowly that you block traffic.

You are considered to be driving a SLOW-MOVING VEHICLE if you are traveling at a rate of speed that is ten (10) miles per hour or more below the lawful maximum speed. Whether you are operating a passenger vehicle or a commercial vehicle, if five (5) or more vehicles are lined up behind you, the law requires you to turn or pull off the roadway as soon as you can do so safely. Slow drivers who block other traffic cause many accidents. Remember, slower is not always safer.

Funeral Procession

In Tennessee it is a common and accepted practice for oncoming traffic to pull to the side of the roadway as a sign of respect when meeting a funeral precession.

Tennessee law instructs the following:

• Vehicles following a funeral procession on a two-lane highway may not attempt to pass such procession; and

• No operator of a vehicle shall drive between vehicles in a properly identified funeral procession except when directed to do so by a traffic officer.

The Basic Speed Rule

The speed at which you drive determines how much time you have to act or react and how long it takes to stop. The higher the speed you are traveling, the less time you have to spot hazards, judge the speed of other traffic and react to avoid the mistakes of other drivers.

The Basic Speed Rule (B.S.R.) is not a Tennessee law but it is a general safety principle. The B.S.R. does not set an exact speed limit; instead it teaches that the speed you may drive is limited by the current conditions. For example, the posted speed limit is 65 M.P.H., but if you are driving at night on a two-lane state highway, it's raining, or it's foggy, 65 M.P.H. is **TOO** fast for those conditions.

To obey the B.S.R., you need to think about your speed in relation to other traffic (including pedestrians and bicycles), the surface and width of the road, hazards at intersections, weather, visibility and any other conditions that could affect safety.

Principles of the Basic Speed rule

1. Your speed must be **careful and prudent** (using skill and good judgment).
2. Your speed must be **reasonable and proper,** not too fast and not too slow, for any conditions including:
   • Amount of Traffic - how many cars on the road
   • Speed of Traffic - how fast or slow it's moving
   • Whether pedestrians are present - *especially children in school zones or neighborhoods*

• Surface of the road - rough or smooth, paved, gravel, etc.
• Width of the road - 1-lane, 2-lane, 4-lane
• Structure of the road - straight, curving, bridges, narrow shoulders, etc.
• Visibility - how far ahead you can see clearly
• Weather conditions - rain, snow, ice, fog, etc.
• Your own driving ability

3. You must not drive so slowly that you block, hinder, or interfere with other vehicles moving at normal speeds.
4. Your speed must be adjusted to conditions so you can stop within a clear distance ahead.

If you drive at a speed that is unsafe for existing conditions in any area, even if you are driving slower than a designated or posted speed or a maximum limit, you are violating the basic rule.

Suppose you are driving in a line of downtown traffic and the car ahead of you stops suddenly. If you can't stop in time to avoid hitting that car from behind, you are either breaking the "B.S.R." - even if you were driving within the posted speed limit - or you are following too closely.

TRAVELER'S NOTE: *Even though the B.S.R. is not a part of Tennessee law, you should be aware that many states have incorporated the principles of the B.S.R. into their actual state laws. Be extra careful when traveling in other states as you might find yourself receiving a "speeding" ticket if you violate the principles of the B.S.R. (i.e. driving too fast for conditions) even when you weren't over the posted limit.*

TENNESSEE SPEED LAWS

Speed is a major contributing factor causing fatal accidents in Tennessee. It is closely followed by failure to yield right-of-way and driving left of the centerline.

Unless otherwise posted the speed limit on primary and secondary state and federal highway is 55 M.P.H.

When driving, you should adjust you speed to flow along with the speed at which other traffic is moving - provided the other traffic is traveling within the posted speed limit provided under Tennessee law! Studies have shown there is more chance of an accident when the difference increases above or below the average. Slow drivers are as likely to become involved in accidents as speeders. If most of the cars are traveling between 50 and 55 miles per hour, you are least likely to have an accident if you stay with that speed range.

INTERSTATE SPEED LIMITS: The maximum speed set by Tennessee law for interstate highways is 70 M.P.H. However this speed does not apply to ALL sections of the interstate highway and may be set as low as 55 M.P.H. in some larger urban areas where there is more traffic congestion. The maximum limit should be driven only in ideal driving conditions and you must reduce your speed when conditions require it. For example, you should reduce your speed for curves and when the roadway is slippery (during rain, snow, icy conditions), or when it is foggy and difficult to see clearly down the road.

Rural - 70 M.P.H. is the speed that is posted on most of the rural sections of Tennessee interstate highways.

Urban - In the more congested urban or metropolitan areas of Tennessee interstates the limit is typically 55 M.P.H.

NOTE: It is unlawful for any person to drive a vehicle less than **55 m.p.h. in the left most lane** of any Interstate highway; unless traffic congestion and flow prevent safe driving at such speed. Also on the Interstates the minimum speed limit **in the right lane(s) is 45 M.P.H.** and under normal driving conditions all vehicles must travel at least this fast so they are not a hazard to other drivers. If the minimum posted speed limit is too fast for you, you should use another road.

<u>**Watch for speed limit changes**</u>! The state, counties and municipalities each have the authority to set speed limits for the roadways/highways under their control. Therefore you could see some sections of Interstate within some city limits set at 60 or 65 m.p.h.

Also on the secondary streets and highways these limits will change according to certain zones. Some residential roads or city streets may have limits as low as 25 or 35 M.P.H. at all times. Watch carefully and obey speed limit signs in business, residential, and school zones.

Speeding in School Zones: Speed limits in all school zones are regulated when children are going to or from the school or during a school recess hour. **Exceeding the school zone speed limit is by law considered to be reckless driving**. Penalty includes an **<u>automatic 6 points</u>** added to your driving record, which in turn automatically results in an advisory letter sent to you.

Speeding in Highway Work Zones: Highway work zones are those portions of a street or highway where construction, maintenance or utility work is being done to the road, its shoulders, or any other items related to the roadway. This includes work such as underground and overhead utility work, tree trimming, and survey activities. Highway work zones are easily recognized by

the presence of orange signing and other orange traffic control devices, flashing lights on equipment, and workers dressed in highly visible clothing.

Highway workers are trained on how to set up safe zones with directional traffic signs and devices. Motorists and pedestrians are responsible for knowing how to read and react to these directions. Paying attention, and driving cautiously and courteously are the most important steps to preventing crashes while driving through highway work zones.

TENNESSEE LAW MANDATES A MINIMUM FINE OF $250 DOLLARS AND UP TO A MAXIMUM FINE OF $500 DOLLARS FOR VIOLATIONS OF THE SPEED LIMIT POSTED IN ACTIVE WORK ZONES.

Each year nearly a thousand people are killed and thousands are injured as a result of crashes in highway work zones across the nation. Some of these are highway workers, flaggers, or law enforcement officials. However, drivers, passengers, and pedestrians suffer over 80% of these fatalities and injuries. Many of these work zone crashes are preventable.

State figures for 2000 indicate that, 22 people died 1,379 were injured and there were another 2,576 cases of property damage in work zone accidents in Tennessee. Nationwide in 2001 nearly one thousand (962) people lost their lives in work zone accidents.

BRAKING, FOLLOWING AND STOPPING DISTANCES

Just as important as being aware of speed limits and the effects of speeding, drivers must know and understand the safe and proper braking procedures for vehicles. Along with this come the principles of allowing adequate following distances or "safety cushion" around your vehicle and the laws of required stops (signs, signals, railroad crossings, school bus, etc.).

1. BRAKING: You will encounter numerous driving situations, such as speed zone changes and merging traffic, that will require you to know proper braking techniques.

You should apply your brakes slowly and evenly by applying gradual pressure. Start braking early as a signal to the cars behind you. If you brake too strong or quickly, you could skid and lose control of your vehicle. You also

make it harder for drivers behind you to stop without hitting your vehicle. As a general rule, if the car starts to skid, take your foot off the brake and turn the steering wheel in the direction of the skid; if you can do so without running off the road, hitting something, or steering into oncoming traffic.

- With a standard transmission, you can use your gearshift to slow down when you're approaching a stop sign or signal. First, flash your brake lights to signal any cars behind you, then shift down to a lower gear.
- Many of today's cars are equipped with anti-lock braking systems (ABS), however few drivers know how to use them properly. *Read the instructions in your car's owner's manual to learn the safe and proper operation of ABS. Look for additional tips on ABS in Chapter 11 of this manual.*

A general overview of ABS braking procedures includes:

- When slowing or stopping apply **firm, steady pressure to the brake pedal.** *(Never pump the pedal with ABS)*
- If you are braking to avoid an emergency or accident **gradually steer the car** around any obstacles. *(ABS was designed to prevent vehicles from locking wheels and to allow drivers to steer when skidding.)*
- **Release pressure on the brake pedal.** *(Do not release the steady pressure off the brake pedal until you have slowed to the speed you desire or stopped, otherwise you will disengage the ABS.)*
- **Resume driving normally.**

Regardless of the type of brake system your vehicle is equipped with you need to always be prepared to brake unexpectedly. there are some areas where drivers should be especially aware of this need including:

- When driving next to parked cars
- When approaching any type of intersection
- When approaching traffic signals and crosswalks
- When driving in a school zone or residential area
- When seeing brake lights of other cars
- When driving in heavy, slow moving traffic

Drivers should be able to distinguish situations, like those above, when the brake needs to be covered in preparation for use. "Covering the brake" means the driver's foot needs to be hovering over the brake or between the brake and gas pedals for quicker response time. You should not confuse this practice with "riding the brake." (Keeping your foot resting or slightly pressed down on the brake) Riding the brake not only adds much wear and tear on your vehicle brake system, but it also gives other drivers the false impression that a stop is imminent. *However, covering the brake is often prudent and a safe driving practice, **riding the brake is not a safe practice.***

2. **FOLLOWING DISTANCES:** Obeying the speed limit laws and knowing proper braking procedures must be accompanied by allowing for a reasonable and safe following distance between your car and other vehicles. This section will discuss principles that you can use to assist in determining safe following distances.

Tennessee law states: *"The driver of a motor vehicle shall not follow another vehicle more closely than is reasonable and prudent, having due regard for the speed of such vehicles and the traffic upon and the condition of the highway."*

When another driver makes a mistake, you need time to react. Give yourself this time by keeping a "space cushion" around your vehicle. This space cushion will give you room to brake or maneuver to avoid hazards when needed. Good drivers keep this safe following distance or space cushion to have a better view of the road. The more space you allow between your car and the car ahead, the more time you will have to see and anticipate traffic hazards, or accidents down the road.

Many drivers don't see as well as they should because they follow too closely (tailgating), and the vehicle ahead of them blocks their view of traffic and road conditions. Rear-end crashes are very common and most of these crashes are caused by drivers who are "tailgating".

Two Second Rule: Nationally, safety agencies and driver education programs have tried to define a safe following distance for drivers to maintain. This has ranged from a 2 to a 4 second following distance. To share the road safely, make sure you are a safe distance from the vehicle in front of you. Use the following tips to determine if you following too closely:

A. As the car ahead of you passes a stationary point on the road (a sign post, driveway, utility pole, etc.) count the seconds it takes you to reach the same spot. *(In the illustration at right and below "you" are driving the red vehicle.)*

B. Count to yourself "one-thousand-one, one-thousand-two," etc. You should NOT reach that same point on the road before you finish counting at least "one-thousand-two". If you do you are definitely following too close.

- You should slow down slightly to increase the space between you and the other vehicle. Find another spot to check your new following distance. Repeat this exercise until you are following no closer than two seconds.

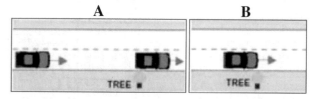

This principle will hold true at any speed on State and U.S. Highways with moderate speed limits. However, during inclement weather, Interstate Highway driving at higher speeds and night driving the 2-second rule should be increased to allow for limited visibility. A minimum of 4 seconds should allow for better reaction time and a safer space cushion under these conditions.

3. STOPPING DISTANCES: Be alert so that you know when you will have to stop well ahead of time. Stopping suddenly is dangerous and usual points to a driver who was not paying attention, speeding or not allowing a safe following distance. Try to avoid panic stops by seeing events well in advance. By slowing down or changing lanes, you may not have to stop at all, and if you do, it can be a more gradual and safer stop. As a rule it is best to never stop on the road, unless necessary for safety or to obey a low (stop sign, etc.).

There are three steps in stopping your vehicle:

- Driver perception time (length of time it takes to see and recognize a dangerous situation).

- Driver reaction time (time from perception of danger to start of braking - average is 3/4 second noted in blue section of charts below).

- Braking ability includes the type and condition of vehicle brakes as well as vehicle speed.

PERCEPTION, REACTION AND BRAKING TIME		
Step	**Time**	**Explanation**
Perception	About .50 second	See/hear danger
Reaction	About .66 second	Brain tells foot to brake
Braking/ Stopping	Varies by speed	Foot presses brake pedal until car stops

Stopping distance can vary widely due to many factors:
- ° Type and condition of the road/pavement.
- ° Type and condition of vehicle tires.
- ° Vehicle design and condition of the shock absorbers.
- ° Vehicle weight when loaded or towing.

You need to know how long it takes to stop any vehicle you drive. Vehicles cannot stop all at once. It takes long distances to come to a controlled, safe and complete stop.

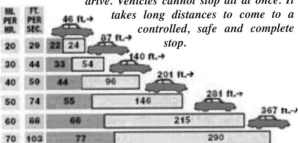

It takes longer to stop than most people realize. Suppose you're driving on the interstate at night at the maximum limit of 70 M.P.H. A deer suddenly appears in your headlights. Will you be able to stop in time? It will take 1.16 seconds for you to see the deer and move your foot to the brake. Before you even start to brake, you will have traveled 128 feet. If you're

on a good road in good weather, the braking distance at 70 M.P.H. will be 290 feet. Your total stopping distance has now reached 418 feet nearly the length of one-and-a-half football fields!

The chart in the previous column shows "average" stopping distances (stopping distances are based on tests made by the Federal Highway Administration) for vehicles under ideal conditions. *Note this chart does not include the distance you will travel in the 1/2 second of time required for perception of the hazard.* According to the National Safety Council, a lightweight passenger car traveling at 50 M.P.H. can stop in about 200 feet. The distance required to stop your vehicle is important in helping you choose a safe driving speed. These charts can be used as a rough guide, but your actual stopping distance will depend upon many factors specific to the situation you encounter.

STOPS REQUIRED BY LAW

Tennessee law states: *Every driver of a vehicle approaching a stop sign shall stop before entering the nearest side of a crosswalk, or stop at a clearly marked stop line, but if neither are present, then at a point nearest the intersecting roadway where the driver has a view of approaching traffic on the intersecting roadway before entering the actual intersection.* Tennessee Code defines **"stop"** as **"complete cessation of movement"**.

You are responsible for knowing the proper stopping procedures required by this law. At stop signs and right-turn-on-red intersections, come to a COMPLETE stop (not a rolling stop) and go only when the traffic is clear. The approaching traffic should not have to slow down or change lanes for your vehicle. You should:

- Come to a full and complete stop at the stop sign (or traffic signal). Often a wide white stop line will be painted on the pavement in line with the sign. You must stop your vehicle behind this line.

- If such pavement marking is not present you should stop with the front of your vehicle even with the stop sign's placement on the roadside.

- If you can't see whether the crossing traffic is clear, edge up slowly until you can clearly see the traffic crossing from both directions.

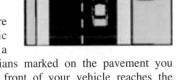

- If the intersection where the stop sign/traffic signal is placed has a crosswalk for pedestrians marked on the pavement you must stop before the front of your vehicle reaches the nearest white line marking the border of the crosswalk.

- If there are pedestrians in the crosswalk or about to enter the crosswalk you must wait for them to cross before you proceed.

- Once the crosswalk is clear you may slowly edge forward to check traffic before crossing the intersection or entering the roadway.

- When stopping behind another vehicle already stopped at the intersection, make sure you allow adequate "gap" space between the vehicles so you are not "tailgating".

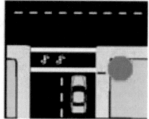

- A basic rule of thumb is that you should be able to see the license plate and/or the other vehicle's back tire where it meets the pavement.

- This "gap" provides a safety zone in the event the other vehicle rolls back slightly or stalls. If the vehicle stalls you would still be able to maneuver around it when safe. It also provides you with an evasive "out" in the event of an emergency such as another vehicle approaching from behind so fast that you may need to move to avoid a rear-end collision.

- Once the vehicle in front of you has moved on through the intersection you may move forward to the stop line. Remember you still must bring **your** vehicle to a FULL STOP at the stop line.

- A complete stop is required at a flashing red traffic light, just as with a stop sign.

- After you have stopped, if there is no traffic from the right or left you may proceed. When there is traffic on the crossroad (right to left) and/or oncoming traffic (heading toward you) from the other side of the intersection you must following the right-of-way procedures. (Right-of-Way rules are discussed in depth later in this Chapter.)

- You must stop completely when directed to stop by a flag person at a road construction site or by a police officer directing you to stop in any situation.

Rolling Stops: Rolling stops or "California rolls" are dangerous and illegal. A rolling stop occurs when the driver only slows down for a stop sign or traffic signal and proceeds through the intersection or turn without ever bringing the vehicle to a full and complete stop as required by law. Most law enforcement officers and driver education instructors agree that a vehicle has not come to a complete stop until the driver feels the car lurch after all forward motion has ceased. *You should remember that rolling stops are grounds for receiving a traffic ticket AND for failing the driver examination road test.* The following are also excellent reasons you should not get in the habit of rolling stop signs:

- A driver may not see a child or other pedestrian who assumes the car will follow the law and come to a complete stop.

- There is a better chance of seeing possible hazards because the driver who comes to a full stop has a longer observation period of the intersection.

- If two drivers are traveling at right angles to one-another, and both fail to stop, a collision is almost a certainty.

- Police and insurance companies will hold the driver

who fails to stop completely liable in the event of an accident, possibly resulting in fines, loss of license, increased insurance rates or loss of insurance coverage.

Stopping for Railroad Crossings

Railroad crossings have pavement markings that include a large cross buck ("X"), the letters "RR", a no-passing zone stripe and a stop line. Railroad crossing collisions should not happen. When they do, it usually means drivers are not paying attention to signs, pavement markings, and other warnings that tell when a train is coming.

Tennessee law states: *"Whenever any person driving a vehicle approaches a railroad grade crossing,...the driver of such vehicle shall stop within fifty feet (50') but not less than fifteen feet (15') from the*

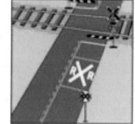

nearest rail of such railroad, and shall not proceed until that driver can do so safely. The foregoing requirements shall apply when:
1) *A clearly visible electric or mechanical signal device gives warning of the immediate approach of a railroad train;*

2) *A crossing gate is lowered or when a human flagger gives a signal of the approach or passage of a train;*

3) *A railroad train approaching within approximately 1,500 feet of the highway crossing emits a signal audible from such distance and such railroad train, by reason of its speed or nearness to such highway crossing, is an immediate hazard; and*

4) *An approaching railroad train is plainly visible and is in hazardous proximity to such highway crossing. No person shall drive any vehicle through, around or under any crossing gate or barrier at the railroad crossing while such gate or barrier is closed or is being opened or closed."*

STOP—LOOK—LISTEN—LOOK AGAIN!

Every motor vehicle should be driven at a rate of speed that will permit the vehicle to be stopped before reaching the nearest rail of a railroad crossing. The vehicle should not be

driven over the crossing until all railroad tracks are completely clear of train traffic. Violations of railroad signals or signs carry the same penalties as violations of other traffic control devices.

CERTAIN VEHICLES REQUIRED TO STOP AT ALL RAILROAD CROSSINGS: Tennessee law also states that certain vehicles must stop at all railroad grade/highway crossings whether or not any signs or signals are activated at the time the vehicle approaches the crossing. As a driver you must be aware of this requirement so you will be prepared for meeting or following these vehicles when they have stopped at the crossing.

The vehicles listed below are required by law to stop before crossing ANY railroad grade crossing:

- Church or School buses regardless of whether such school bus is carrying any school child at the time of crossing.

- Common carriers such as taxis or other vehicles transporting passengers for hire.

- Vehicles transporting flammables, explosives or other dangerous articles as cargo or part of a cargo.

When it is safe to do so, the driver may proceed across the tracks in a gear that permits the vehicle to complete the crossing of the track(s) without a change of gears.

Buses at a railroad crossing should pull to the right. This side movement of the vehicle along with its stoplights is a very clear signal, day or night, that the vehicle is preparing to stop. You must be alert to this type of movement by buses. Also tanker trucks or other vehicles required to stop at all railroad tracks will generally signal such stop by displaying the emergency flashers of the vehicle to alert other drivers to the impending stop.

The School Bus Stop Law

Meeting A School Bus — The driver of any vehicle approaching from the front, a school bus or church bus on
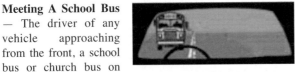
which the red stop warning signal lights are flashing, should reduce the speed of the vehicle and bring the vehicle to a complete stop while the bus stop signal arm is extended. The vehicle must remain stopped until the stop arm is retracted and the bus resumes motion.

Overtaking A School Bus — The driver of any vehicle approaching a school bus or church bus from the rear shall

not pass the bus when red stop warning signal lights are flashing and must bring the vehicle to a complete stop when the bus is stopped. The vehicle must remain stopped until the stop arm is retracted and the bus resumes motion.

School Bus Warning Lights

YELLOW FLASHING:

When the yellow lights on the front and back of the bus are flashing the bus is preparing to stop to load or unload children. Motorists should slow down and prepare to stop their vehicles.

RED FLASHING:

When the red lights are flashing and the stop arm is extended this indicates that the bus HAS stopped and that children are now getting on or off the bus. Motorists must stop their cars and wait until the red flashing lights are turned off, the stop arm is withdrawn, and the bus begins moving before they start driving again.

IT IS ILLEGAL IN ALL 50 STATES TO PASS A SCHOOL BUS THAT HAS STOPPED TO LOAD OR UNLOAD STUDENTS.

Never pass on the right side of the bus, as this is where the children enter or exit. This is illegal and can have tragic results. You must stop and remain stopped until:
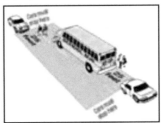

- The bus has started moving, OR
- The driver motions for you to proceed, OR
- the red flashing lights go off and/or the stop arm is pulled back.

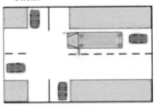
When a school bus is stopped at an intersection to load and unload children, drivers from ALL directions are required to stop until the bus resumes motion. (As shown by the red vehicles in the diagram at left.)

When driving on a highway with separate roadways for traffic in opposite directions, divided by median space or barrier not suitable for vehicular traffic, the driver need not stop but should proceed with caution.

Note: A turn lane in the middle of a four-lane highway is NOT considered a barrier, but a fifth lane that is suitable for vehicular traffic, drivers meeting a stopped school bus on this type of road would be required to stop in both directions.

T.C.A. 55-8-151(A)(5)(B)
IT IS A CLASS A MISDEMEANOR PUNISHABLE ONLY BY A FINE OF NOT LESS THAN TWO HUNDRED FIFTY DOLLARS ($250) NOR MORE THAN ONE THOUSAND DOLLARS ($1,000) FOR ANY PERSON TO FAIL TO COMPLY WITH PROVISION OF THIS SUBSECTION REQUIRING A MOTOR VEHICLE TO STOP UPON APPROACHING A SCHOOL BUS.

Stopping for Police Vehicles

Police vehicles which are attempting to stop drivers will do so by means of a visual, flashing blue or flashing blue and red lights, or audible signal. Remember, a police officer never knows what to expect when stopping a driver. Don't let your emotions or sudden unexplained movements (or those of your passengers) introduce an element of tension and anxiety into the occurrence. A police officer may be more likely to listen to what you have to say and less likely to feel threatened by you (or your passengers) if you follow these guidelines.

- Drive as close as is safely practical to the right-hand edge or curb of the road, clear of any intersection, stop and park.
- Limit the movements of the driver and/or passengers while stopping your vehicle
- <u>Drivers should keep their hands on the steering wheel</u> and passengers should keep their hands in plain view. **Drivers should advise officers if they have a handgun permit and if they are armed.**
- Provide your driver license and/or vehicle registration when requested.
- Keep all vehicle doors closed and remain in the vehicle unless requested to get out.
- If stop is made after dark, turn on the vehicle's interior light <u>before</u> the officer approaches
- If enforcement action is taken against you that you disagree with, do not argue with the officer at the scene. Traffic violations and traffic crimes charged against you are decided in court.
- If you find yourself being directed to pull over and stop by someone in an UNMARKED police car it is acceptable for you to drive a *short distance to the nearest* area where there are other people, such as the next business parking lot or the next exit if on the Interstate. This is especially prudent if traveling at night and/or alone.

INTERSECTIONS

Now that you have studied the effects of speed, following distances, stopping distances and legally required stops, it is time to look at the complex issue of Intersections. This includes rules for the right-or-way, pedestrians, right turns, left turns and turn signals.

Intersections are places where traffic merges or crosses. They Include:
- cross streets,
- side streets,
- driveways, and
- shopping center or parking lot entrances

More crashes happen at intersections than any other place. Intersections constitute a very small part of rural and urban street/highway systems, yet they are implicated in 40% of all motor vehicle crashes and more than 9,000 deaths per year (1998 NHTSA data). Be very careful when approaching any intersection or driveway. Never assume another driver will yield the right-of-way to you. Always be prepared to stop.

APPROACHING INTERSECTIONS SAFELY

Traffic checks are the process of looking frequently and carefully for vehicle traffic approaching your car from each direction. Traffic checks are especially important when merging or changing lanes and particularly when approaching and crossing intersections.

- **Look:** Look both ways as you near an intersection. Before you enter an intersection continue checking traffic from both the left and right for approaching vehicles and/or crossing pedestrians.

1. Look first to the left to make sure cross traffic is yielding the right-of-way, then look for traffic from the right. If stopped, look both left and right <u>just before you start moving</u>. Look across the intersection before you start to move to make sure the path is clear through the intersection when driving straight through.

2. As you enter the intersection, check again for unusual or unexpected actions to the left and right.

3. It is also important to watch for vehicle traffic from the front (oncoming traffic) and rear (approaching/overtaking traffic) of your vehicle at intersections. Be especially aware of vehicles behind you. If the light changes and/or you encounter a vehicle violating the right-of-way, causing you to need to stop suddenly will the vehicle behind be able to stop? It is unfortunately not uncommon for drivers to run red lights or stop signs which could result in you being involved in a head-on or rear-end collision.

- **Control Speed:** Be prepared to brake or stop unexpectedly at intersections if the above traffic checks alert you to a possible hazard. You should slow down **before** reaching the intersection, drive at your slowest speed just before entering the intersection and gradually increase you speed safely as you cross the intersection.

- **Use Proper Lane:** You should be in the proper lane for the direction you intend to travel **before** you reach the intersection. Do not make last minute lane changes as you start through an intersection. Do NOT pass a vehicle in an intersection.

- **Safety:** Most importantly you must know and obey
1. the proper right-of-way procedures for vehicles and pedestrians at intersections,
2. the purpose and meaning of pavement markings.
3. the purpose and meaning of traffic signals, stop or yield signs posted at intersections,
4. proper lane usage and speed at intersections,
5. proper use of you own vehicle turn signals

THE RIGHT-OF-WAY PROCEDURES

Vehicles or pedestrians are likely to meet one another where there are no signs or lights to control traffic. There are rules on who must yield the right-of-way. These rules tell who goes first and who must wait in different traffic situations. However if another driver doesn't follow these rules, give him the right-of-way. In all driving situations think of the right-of-way as something to be given, not taken. All drivers should know and understand the following rules which determine the right-of-way.

You Must Not Insist On The Right-Of-Way

The law does not really give anyone the right-of-way. It only says who must yield it. A driver must do everything possible to avoid a traffic accident. Rules for the most common situations drivers encounter include:

1. **Yielding to Pedestrians** crossing the road or your path of travel:

   - When pedestrians are in a crosswalk (marked or unmarked) and there are no traffic lights or police at the intersection.

   - When your car is turning a corner and pedestrians are crossing with the light.

   - When your vehicle crosses a sidewalk when entering or exiting a driveway, alley or parking lot. It is illegal to drive on a sidewalk except to cross it.

   - When a blind pedestrian using a guide dog or carrying a white cane with red tip is crossing any portion of the road way, even if not at an intersection or crosswalk. Do not use your horn as it could startle the blind pedestrian. If you see anyone in the roadway with a dog guide or a white cane, stop at least ten feet away until the person is off the roadway.

   - Persons operating motorized wheelchairs on a sidewalk or roadway are also granted the same right-of-way as pedestrians.

   - You must yield to children playing in the streets. In crowded downtown areas and in suburban residential neighborhoods, children play in the streets because there may not be parks or playgrounds nearby. Even though they have been told not to run into the street, children won't always put safety ahead of a runaway puppy or a bouncing ball. Children on bicycles can easily forget to slow down before entering an intersection or to signal and look behind before they turn. You are responsible for driving with extreme caution when children are present. Slow down near schools, playgrounds and residential areas.

2. **Yielding to Oncoming Traffic:** When meeting other traffic at intersections or when entering the roadway make sure the other drive sees you. Make eye contact whenever possible. Drive cautiously and defensively. Drive friendly. Remember the right-of-way is something to be given, not taken.

   - When you are starting from a parked position you should wait for all moving traffic to pass.

   - When turning left you must wait for oncoming traffic going straight ahead or turning right.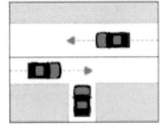

   - When you are entering a main road from a driveway, alley, parking lot or roadside you must yield to all vehicles already on the main road. (The blue car in the diagram at right must yield the right-of-way.)

   - When you are entering a roundabout, traffic circle or rotary (also known as "town squares") you must yield to traffic already in the roundabout.

   - When approaching a MERGE onto a busy highway or Interstate you must increase or decrease speed as needed to avoid an accident and yield the right-of-way if necessary to the oncoming traffic.

   - When approaching a fire station you should yield to any emergency vehicle that is about to back into, or is already in the process of backing into, the driveway entrance to the station.

3. **Yielding at Intersections:** The right-of-way should be determined by each driver before entering an intersection. If you have the right-of-way and another driver yields it to you, proceed immediately. However YOU must yield:

   - When oncoming vehicles (including bicycles) are proceeding straight or making a right turn you must yield the right-of-way to those vehicles.

   - At intersections where YIELD signs are posted the driver must slow down or stop to avoid an accident with oncoming traffic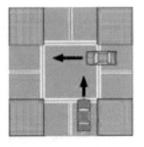

   - To any vehicles that are already in the intersection even if you have the green traffic light. (The red vehicle in the diagram at right must yield to the green vehicle.)

   - At "T" intersections where one road "dead-ends" into another main crossing roadway, the vehicles on the road ending must yield to oncoming traffic from both directions on the main road.

   - When turning left at intersections you must yield to any oncoming vehicle proceeding straight or turning right, unless you have a traffic light where your left turn is on a protected green arrow. (The red vehicle shown at right must yield.)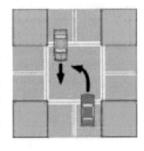

- At intersections marked as 4-way or All way stops, the vehicle reaching the intersection first gets to go first (of course, ALL vehicles must stop). If more than one vehicle arrives at the same time, yield the right of way to the vehicle on your right.

- Where roads cross and there are no stop signs or signals, wait for any vehicle coming at the same time on your right.

- You should not enter an intersection unless you can get through it without having to stop. You should wait until traffic in front of you clears so that you are not blocking the intersection. If your vehicle is left blocking an intersection (with or without a traffic signal) it prevents other traffic from proceeding and you could be ticketed for this type of action.

4. Yielding to Emergency Vehicles and Transit Buses

- You must yield the right-of-way to a police vehicle, fire engine, ambulance or other emergency vehicle using a siren, air horn or a red or blue flashing light.

- **It is against the law for an unauthorized private vehicle to have a blue flashing emergency light or combination of blue and red flashing emergency lights installed, maintained or visibly exhibited on the vehicle in any manner.**

- **Following Fire Apparatus:** The driver of any vehicle, other than one on official business, shall not follow any fire apparatus traveling in response to a fire alarm or drive into or park any vehicle within the block where the fire apparatus has stopped in response to a fire alarm. No vehicle shall be driven over any unprotected hose of a fire department without the consent of the department official in command.

- Tennessee law requires that upon the *immediate approach of an emergency vehicle all traffic meeting or being overtaken must YIELD the right-of-way and shall immediately drive to a position parallel to, and as close as possible to the right hand edge or curb of the roadway clear of any intersection and stop. Remain in that stopped position until the emergency vehicle has passed or you have been directed to move by a police officer. Proceed with caution. There may be other emergency vehicles coming.*

A. If you are in an intersection, drive on through the intersection before you pull over otherwise you may inadvertently block the emergency vehicle's path through the intersection.

B. Do not pull over to the right where you will be blocking a side road or driveway. The emergency vehicle may need to turn into that road or driveway to get to the incident scene.

C. If the traffic light is red, stay where you are. If the light turns green before the emergency vehicle has passed do NOT proceed on green - wait until the emergency vehicle has passed or turned onto a different street.

D. When yielding to emergency vehicles you should get in the habit of turning down the volume on the radio (if on) so that you may hear any instructions or directions given out over the emergency vehicle's loudspeaker. Your immediate reaction to such directions may be critically needed.

- You must yield the right-of-way to any transit vehicle (metro bus) that has signaled and is pulling back onto the roadway from a bus stop. Generally this occurs on urban roadways in areas usually marked by "bus stop" signs or benches. However occasionally you may encounter cross-country commercial buses signaling to re-enter traffic after allowing passengers to disembark on rural roadways in smaller communities and towns.

A. You are not required to stop for, nor forbidden to pass, these transit buses when they are stopped for passenger pick-up or drop-off as you would be for a school bus in the same situation. (See"The School Bus Stop Law" section of this manual for complete details.)

B. However you should be extremely cautious near such stopped buses and be watchful for passengers (including elderly and children) who may be attempting to cross the road in these areas.

5. Slowing and Yielding to stationary vehicles on the roadside: New legislation enacted on July 1, 2003 requires that drivers upon approaching any stationary vehicles must proceed with due caution and, if possible, make a lane change into a lane not adjacent to that of the vehicle, or proceed with due caution by reducing the speed of the vehicle and maintaining a safe speed for the current road conditions. Examples are:

- "authorized emergency vehicle", (police, fire, ambulance or rescue)
- "highway maintenance vehicle", (state, county, city or vendor vehicles used for road repair, maintenance or construction)

— or —

- "recovery vehicle" (tow truck or wrecker)

This is required only on multi-lane roadways where there are two or more lanes of traffic moving in the same direction and the stationary vehicles are along the roadside in the direction of the driver's travel.

TURNING

The most common faults when making turns are failing to signal, not signaling long enough, failing to search for hazards, turning from the wrong lane, and failing to turn properly. Rules for turning apply at all locations, even driveways and alleys, not just at intersections. *The first rule of turning is to turn from the closest lane in the direction you are traveling to the closest legal lane in the direction you want to go.* The law designates which lanes and

positions you must use when turning, and the required signaling distances for such turns. This section will expand on those rules and help you to learn the proper procedures for signaling and making safe turns.

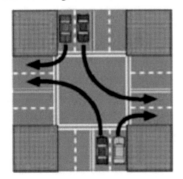

1. SIGNALING
A TURN: Before making any turn, whether the turn is into another roadway, a parking lot, another traffic lane, or leaving a parked position, it is extremely important that you signal. Other drivers expect you to keep traveling the path of the roadway and using the lane in which you vehicle is positioned. Your signal lets other drivers, cyclists, and pedestrians know your intentions to make a change in your vehicle's path of travel and give them time to react to your intended movements. However signaling does NOT give you the right-of-way.

You should always use your turn signals before you:

| LEFT TURN | RIGHT TURN | STOP OR SLOW |

- Change lanes or make any movement of your vehicle to the right or left
- Turn at an intersection or into a driveway, alley or

parking lot

- Enter or exit the interstate or other controlled access roadway
- Pull away from a parked position along the curb
- Pull over to the curb or roadside
- Slow down or stop your vehicle suddenly

You may use either your vehicle turn signal lights or hand and arm signals. Make sure your signals can be easily seen by others. The illustration below shows the standard positions for hand and arm signals. Extend your hand and arm well out of the car window and signal in plenty of time.

A. Hand Signal Tips:

- When you use hand signals, bring your arm in during the actual turn to keep control of the steering wheel.
- During non-daylight hours, hand and arm signals are usually not visible except in well lighted areas.
- Hand signals should also be used when the sun is shining brightly and may make your turn signal light harder for other drivers to see easily.
- In heavy traffic a hand signal may be seen by drivers who are several cars back and the line of cars following you could obscure their view of your turn signal light.

B. Electrical Turn Signal Tips:

- Check your vehicle's turn signals often to be sure your signal lights are working properly.
- Be sure that your turn signal lights (front and rear) are clean and free from dust, dirt, ice or snow.
- When signaling a stop, pump your brakes a few times to attract attention.
- Be sure to turn off your turn signal light after you use it.

YOUR UNINTENDED SIGNAL STILL MEANS "TURN" TO THE OTHER DRIVERS. You might tempt other drivers to pull out in front of you.

You should not assume that all drivers will respond to your signaled intentions. Also be aware that some drivers will not signal their intentions. Therefore, maintain control of your vehicle at all times and "drive defensively". Your signal helps other drivers plan ahead. A surprise move often results in accidents. As a good driver you should be alert and emphasize your intentions to turn by giving the proper signal or signals.

- At least 50 feet before the turn, you must turn on your flashing directional signals.
- You should use your turn signals **ONLY** to indicate when **YOU** plan to turn or change lanes.
- If you are parked at a curb or roadside and about to re-enter traffic, use a signal long enough to alert oncoming traffic that you are moving from the parked position back into the traffic lane.
- You should look back, using your rear-view mirrors.
- You must get into the correct lane. This is most important, for now, your car becomes a big signal to help indicate your intention to turn.

- If you plan to turn beyond an intersection, *do not signal until you are in the intersection*. If you signal earlier, another driver may think you intend to turn at the intersection and might pull into your path.

- You should get in the habit of signaling ever time you change direction. Signal even if you do not see anyone else around. *It is the car you do not see, that is the most dangerous.*

- When you slow down and your brake lights flash as a signal. Slowing down, itself, acts as a signal.

C. You should NOT use your turn signals:

- To signal a driver behind you to come around to pass your vehicle.

> **Proper signaling is a key to safe driving. Failing to signal is dangerous and inconsiderate. Communicating while driving is a must. Safe drivers are good communicators. They are always aware of surrounding conditions and readily communicate their intentions to other drivers by using their signals at ALL times.**

- To relay the turn intentions of vehicles ahead of you to those drivers behind your vehicle. This is misleading to other drivers and your brake lights will be sufficient to warn those behind you to slow down. If you see someone ahead signaling they are about to turn, do NOT turn on your turn signals unless you also plan to turn.

2. MAKING TURNS: Before making a turn, be sure you can do so safely. Check traffic ahead, behind and to the side. Become familiar with the following Do's and Don'ts:

DO:

- Use your turn signal at least 50 feet before the turn or lane change.

- Make thorough traffic checks, looking behind and on both sides to see where other vehicles are, so you can change lanes and make the turn safely.

- Move into the correct lane as soon as possible. The faster the traffic is moving, the sooner you should move into the proper lane. Go from one lane to the other as directly as possible without crossing lane lines of interfering with the traffic.

- Slow down before you reach the stop line or crosswalk, select the proper gear before entering the intersection and accelerate slightly through the turn.

- As you turn, make sure to check for pedestrians, cyclist and other traffic as you turn. Make the turn correctly staying in the proper lane and maintaining a safe speed.

- Finish the turn in the proper lane. Once you have completed your turn, you can change to another lane if you need to.

DON'T:

- Don't turn unless the turn is permitted and can be made safely; be aware of signs prohibiting right or left turns at certain locations.

- Don't try to turn from the wrong lane. If you aren't in the proper lane, drive to the next intersection and make the turn from the proper lane there. Circle back if you have to, this may take you some extra time and miles however it will be much better than causing an accident, injury or worse.

- Don't "swing wide" or "cut the corner" when making your turns. Don't turn too short so as to cut corners on left turns or run over the curb on right turns. Turning too wide or too late, straddling lanes, or turning into the wrong side of the street will result in not being able to turn into the correct lane. Always follow the white lines in intersections using multiple turn lanes.

- Don't turn your wheels in the direction of the turn while waiting for oncoming traffic to pass. If you are hit from the rear while your wheels are turned, the impact can push you right into oncoming traffic. Keep your vehicles wheels straight until you begin the turn. Wait until you are sure you can complete the turn before turning the wheels.

- Don't enter the intersection if traffic ahead may keep you from completing the turn before the traffic light changes. Stay behind the stop line or crosswalk until you can fully complete the turn without the risk of blocking the traffic flow.

- Don't brake or depress the clutch while actually turning.

- Don't shift gears in the intersection (if you stall you could cause and accident and/or block the intersection to other traffic).

3. LEFT TURNS: You should study the diagram showing the five basic steps in making left turns from routine 2-way streets to 2-way streets.

When you are meeting another driver at an intersection and both of you want to turn left, each will turn to the left of the other. Leave from the left lane or as close to the yellow center line as possible and enter in the left lane or as close to the yellow center line as shown in the diagrams below.

A. From A Two-Way Street Onto A Two-Way Street

Remember these tips:

- Reduce speed and get into the lane just to the right of the center line well ahead of time.

- Signal your intentions for at least 50 feet and approach the turn with your left wheels as close to the center line as possible. *Failure to signal is dangerous, inconsiderate and illegal. Your signal makes it possible for other cars to complete a turn.*

- Look out of your left window for pedestrians and other traffic in your turn path. Yield to any oncoming cars or pedestrians.

- Begin your turn when you enter the intersection. Keep your wheels straight until you can turn; turn just before the imaginary center point in the intersection. Drive just to the right of the center line of the street you're entering and be sure to turn into the first lane past the center line. This avoids conflict with other traffic making either right

HOW TO MAKE A LEFT TURN
There are five steps in making a left turn. Take care to keep close to the centerline, but don't cross it.

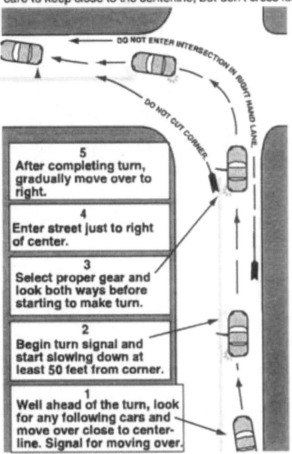

5 After completing turn, gradually move over to right.

4 Enter street just to right of center.

3 Select proper gear and look both ways before starting to make turn.

2 Begin turn signal and start slowing down at least 50 feet from corner.

1 Well ahead of the turn, look for any following cars and move over close to center-line. Signal for moving over.

or left turns. Never turn "wide" into the right lane. *The right lane will be used by any oncoming vehicles turning right.*

- If the intersection has a lane signed or marked for making left turns, do not make this turn from any other lane. At some areas you may make turns from more than one lane. Signs and pavement markings will tell you if this is allowed. If there are multiple lanes you must keep your vehicle in the lane you start from throughout the turn. Be alert for signs that may also PROHIBIT left turns at some intersections.
- Pay close attention to the traffic light cycle. If the light turns yellow while you are waiting for oncoming vehicles to clear the intersection, **do NOT proceed into the intersection**.

B. From A Two-Way Street Onto A One-Way Street

Keep in mind the following differences when turning on one-way streets:

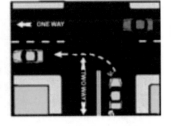

- When making left-hand turns, be alert for "one-way" street signs on traffic lights, posts and stop signs.
- Center lines on two-way streets are yellow.
- Center lines on one-way streets are white.
- Make the proper "two-way" approach next to the center line.
- Turn sharply into the FIRST lane. Remember you are turning onto a one-way street so both lanes will be traveling in the same direction and you should turn into the first lane closest to the left curb.

C. From A One-Way Street Onto A One-Way Street

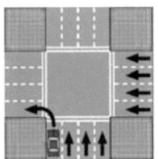

- Make your approach in the traffic lane furthermost to the left curb of the street.
- Turn sharply into the first lane on the left side of the one-way street. DO NOT TURN WIDE.
- At intersections that are not marked for "No Turns on Red" you may make a left turn on red when turning from a one-way street onto a one-way street. You must come to a complete stop at the light prior to making the turn, same as right turns on red.

D. From A One-Way Street Onto A Two-Way Street

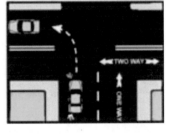

- Make your approach in the traffic lane furthermost to the left curb of the street.
- Don't start your turn at the crosswalk. Drive into the intersection and then turn sharply into the first lane to the right of the yellow lane on the two-way street.
- If the two-way streets has multiple lanes you may move into the right lane ONLY AFTER giving the proper turn signal and checking traffic to your right.
- You can NOT make this left turn on a red light.

E. Notes on Multiple Turn Lanes

- A vehicle in the second lane can make the same turn as a vehicle in the first lane only when a lane use control sign or marking permits it.
- You'll often see white channel lines & arrows on the pavement. These lines help to direct you into the correct lane while turning.

4. RIGHT TURNS: Making right turns can be just as dangerous as left turns. Study the diagram showing the 4

HOW TO MAKE A RIGHT TURN

There are four steps in making a right turn. Be careful not to swing to the left before or during the turn.

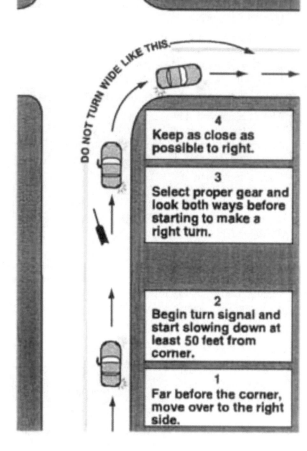

DO NOT TURN WIDE LIKE THIS.

4 Keep as close as possible to right.

3 Select proper gear and look both ways before starting to make a right turn.

2 Begin turn signal and start slowing down at least 50 feet from corner.

1 Far before the corner, move over to the right side.

basic steps making right turns. You should also remember these tips:

- On right turns, avoid moving wide to the left before going into the turn or as you make the turn. If you swing wide, the driver behind you may think you are changing lanes or turning left and may try to pass you on the right. If you swing wide as you complete the turn, drivers who are in the far lane will not expect to see your vehicle in that lane of traffic.

- Well ahead of the turning point check for traffic behind and beside your vehicle. Get as close as is practical to the right curb or road edge without interfering with pedestrians, bicyclists or parked vehicles.

- Give a signal for a right turn for at least 50 feet .

- Before starting to turn look to the left and right for cross traffic on the intersecting street and oncoming traffic that may also be turning. Always check for pedestrians or bicyclists to your right before turning. Remember to yield the right-of-way, if necessary.

- Move your vehicle around the corner and into the travel lane closest to the right curb.

A. Turn Warning: Trucks and Buses Turning Right

When driving in city traffic, pay special attention to the turn signals of large trucks and buses.

- Large trucks and buses MUST make wide turns.

- Sometimes they must leave an open space to the right just before the turn. To avoid and accident, don't pass a truck on the right if there is a possibility that it might make a right turn.

B. Turns Permitted on Red

Tennessee law allows a right turn on red and left turns on red at certain one-way to one-way intersections, unless otherwise posted.

- When making a right turn at a red light, you must first come to a complete stop before reaching the marked or unmarked crosswalk or stop line. Always yield the right-of-way to pedestrians, bicyclists and of course, oncoming traffic. Be sure to check for signs that prohibit turns on red and/or requires you to use specific lanes for turns.

- A left turn on a red or stop signal shall be permitted at all intersections where a one-way street intersects with another one-way street where traffic is moving in the same direction into which the left turn would be made. You must follow the same rules for complete stop, yielding and observing signs prohibiting turns as you would for a right turn on red.

5. SPECIAL TURNS: Roundabouts and U-Turns

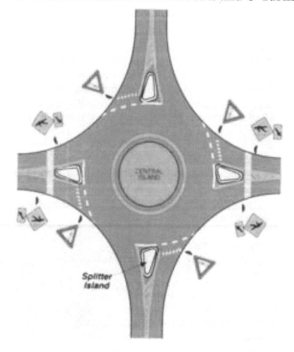

Splitter Island

A. Roundabouts: A roundabout is an intersection control device with traffic circulating around a central island. Such traffic circles are usually used to discourage drivers from using neighborhood street for commuting thoroughfares, to slow speeds, and to reduce accidents. You may think that a roundabout is a type of intersection that you would only encounter in a European country. However roundabouts are gaining more favor in American urban and residential areas. Also many of your home towns may have a form of roundabout that has been in use for years known as the "town square".

• You always travel around a traffic circle or roundabout to the right in a counter clockwise direction.

• On approaching the roundabout, stay in your lane and to the right of the splinter island or yellow pavement markings/curbs directing traffic to the right. These islands or medians are used to prevent vehicles from attempting to travel left around the circle.

• Upon reaching the roundabout, you must yield to vehicles already within the circulating traffic. You should observe the standard right-of-way procedures as with regular intersections controlled by yield signs. Enter the roundabout when there is a gap in traffic and once inside do not stop unless directed to do so by signs, signals or a traffic officer.

• Within the roundabout, proceed at a slower speed (usually posted at 15 to 25 M.P.H.). You may exit the roundabout at any street or continue around again if you miss the street you wanted to turn on .

• In a multi-lane roundabout, do not overtake or pass any vehicles. Remember the roundabout is a low speed traffic control device. Be prepared to yield to vehicle turning in front of you from the inside lane to exit the roundabout.

• Exit the roundabout carefully; always indicate your exit using your right turn signal. Watch for pedestrians in or approaching the crosswalk on the street you are exiting onto and yield the right-of-way if necessary.

B. U-Turns: A U-turn is a turn within the road, made in one smooth u-shaped motion, so as to end up with your vehicle traveling in the opposite/reverse direction as before the turn. *Some towns and cities do not allow U-Turns on the streets and roadways under their control. Check with local police to be sure.*

You may NOT make a U-Turn:

• At any intersection where a traffic light or police officer is controlling the traffic flow.

• At any rural or urban location where you cannot see traffic coming from both directions for at least 500 feet in each direction.

• At any location where U-Turns are prohibited by official signs or markings.

• Between intersections in a city. The safest thing to do is drive around the block.

• At or near a curve or the crest of a hill when the driver cannot see 500 feet or more in each direction. Improper turns are a major contributor to traffic crashes.

• It is illegal in Tennessee for any driver to make a U-Turn on an interstate highway. Emergency crossovers are for the use of emergency vehicles and highway maintenance crews only. It is extremely dangerous and illegal to use them to "turn around" in the event you missed an exit or are in a traffic jam. Drive on to the next exit ramp. Don't cut across the median strip as this maneuver is also illegal.

TRAFFIC LANES AND LANE USAGE

A traffic lane is a part of a roadway wide enough for a car or a single line of vehicles to travel safely. Most lanes on hard-surfaced roads are marked with white or yellow pavement line markings. On dirt or gravel roads, some rural roads, private drives and other roadways (such as parking lot rows and shopping center perimeter roads) the lanes may not be marked, but they are there anyway. When driving on a road without any centerline markings and where vehicles are coming from each direction, drivers must give others going in the opposite direction at least half the road.

1. **Overview of Lane Usage**

"White on Your Right, Yellow on Your Left" this simple statement sums up the principle of "right hand traffic" on which all traffic must move upon American roadways. If you ever find yourself driving with the yellow line on to your right pull over immediately. You are driving on the wrong side of the road!

Always drive on the right side of a two-lane highway except when passing. If the road has four or more lanes with two-way traffic, drive in the right lanes except when overtaking and passing other vehicles safely and legally.

Left lanes on some interstate highways are reserved for car pool vehicles with two or more occupants in the car - watch for diamond signs in the median or painted on the pavement. The center lane of a three-lane or five-lane highway is used only for turning left.

Keeping Right - Drive on the right of the road except when:

• Passing another vehicle going in the same direction as your vehicle.

Drive in the Proper Lane

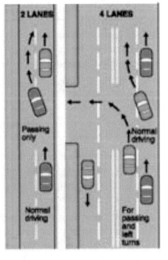

- Driving to the left of center to pass an obstruction. (Whenever possible always drive around obstructions or accidents to the right side to avoid the possibility of becoming involved in a head-on collision.)
- A road is marked for one way traffic.
- You are turning left.

2 LANES - Two-lane highways have a single broken yellow centerline. You should always drive to the right of the centerline, except to pass, when you can pass safely.

4 LANES - A four-lane (or more) highway is divided in half by two solid yellow lines in the center. The two lanes on each side are divided by a dashed white line. Drive in the extreme right lane except when passing another vehicle or to make a left turn.

ONE WAY - A one-way highway is generally composed of two or more lanes restricted to moving in one direction.

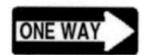

There should not be any vehicles traveling in the opposite direction on these roads.

2. Divided Highways

Always use the road on the right when driving on a divided highway, such as an interstate, unless directed to do otherwise. Do not drive within, across or over any median strip or barrier separating these roadways. It is only allowed at an authorized crossover or intersection, or when you are officially directed to do so.

On a divided 4-lane highway when using a designated crossover for a left turn (or a U-Turn where permitted) you should treat the crossover/opening the same as a cross street by keeping to the right side of the crossover paved area.

A. If a vehicle is already in the crossover waiting for traffic to clear you should remain stopped in the left most lane of the 4-lane highway with your turn signal on until the waiting vehicle has cleared the crossover.

B. DO NOT "swing" into the left side of the crossover or "bunch-up" behind the waiting car. This creates a dangerous situation for any vehicle attempting to use the crossover for a left turn coming from the opposite direction. additionally:

- It leaves your vehicle with its rear-end partially sticking out in the left traffic lane. In this position approaching vehicles coming upon your car are less likely to notice your turn signal than if your vehicle was fully stopped in the left lane.

- It places your car on the "wrong side of the road" in the crossover and could cause a head-on collision with a vehicle attempting to turn left in the crossover from the opposite direction.

C. Remember such a crossover is PERMITTED ONLY at paved openings provided on 4-lane highways. There are NO crossovers provided for traffic on interstates. It is

ILLEGAL to crossover or cross the median on the interstate unless directed to do so.

Driving the wrong way on a one-way road or street is very dangerous and illegal. If you see red reflectors facing you on the lane lines, or red "Wrong Way" and "Do Not Enter" signs, you are on the wrong side of the road. Get

into the proper lane immediately! If you see red reflectors on the lines on the edge of the road, you are on the wrong freeway ramp. Pull over immediately! Red reflectors always mean you are facing traffic the wrong way and could have a head-on collision.

3. Dual Use Lanes

Dual use lanes have both a turn arrow and a straight arrow. You can proceed straight or make the indicated turn from these lanes as shown by the pavement markings and/or signs erected at the intersection. Unless the intersection has a protected arrow for

your turn you must follow the standard right-of-way rules.

4. Shared Center Turn/2-Way Left Turn Lane

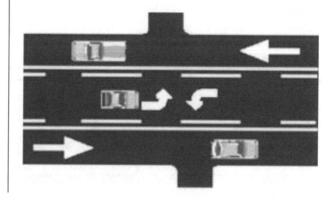

These center lanes are reserved for vehicles making left turns in either direction from or into the roadway. These lanes cannot be used for passing and cannot be used for travel further than 300 feet. On the pavement, left turn arrows for traffic in one direction alternate with left turn arrows for traffic coming from the other direction. These lanes are marked on each side by solid yellow and broken yellow lines. Enter the shared lane only when safe to do so.

If this special lane has been provided for making left turns, do not make a left turn from any other lane. Enter the shared center turn lane just before you want to make the turn. If you enter too soon, you may interfere with another driver's use of the lane. Wait in the special lane until traffic clears enough to allow you to complete the desired left turn movement. Do NOT travel in the center turn lane to access a left turn lane at an intersection.

You may turn from a side street or driveway into a shared center turn lane, stop, and wait for traffic to clear before merging into traffic in the lane immediately to your right. Make sure the lane is clear in both directions and then turn into the lane only when it is safe.

Be sure to give the proper signal while waiting to move into the right lane and also when moving out of the turn lane back into the right lane of traffic

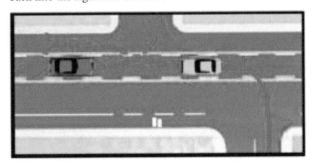

If another vehicle is already in the turn lane from the other direction you may NOT enter if it will interfere with the other vehicle's intended turn. When vehicles enter the turn lane from opposite directions the first vehicle to enter the lane shall have the right-of-way.

5. Reversible Lanes

Some travel lanes are designed to carry traffic in one direction at certain times and in the opposite direction at other times. These lanes are called "reversible lanes" and are usually marked by double-broken yellow lines. Before you start driving in them, check to see which lanes you can use for the direction of travel at that time. There may be signs posted by the side of the road or overhead. Special lights are also often used.

- A green arrow means you can drive in the lane beneath it.

- A red "X" means you can NOT drive in the lane below.

- A flashing yellow "X" means the lane is only for turning.

- A steady yellow "X" means that the use/direction of the lane is changing and you should move out of it as soon as it is safe to do so.

These type of lanes and control devices are usually found in heavily traveled industrial areas where there is a high volume of rush hour traffic coming in during the morning and going out during the afternoon.

6. Reserved Lanes

On various roadways, one or more lanes may be reserved for special vehicles. Reserved lanes are marked by signs stating that the lane is reserved for special use, and often have a white diamond posted at the side of the road and/or painted on the pavement surface. Do NOT travel in one of these lanes unless operating the type of vehicle indicated, or unless you must turn across the reserved lane in the next half block distance.

- "Transit" or "buses" means the lane is for bus use only.

- "Bikes" means the lane is reserved for bicycles.

- "HOV" - High Occupancy Vehicle lanes are reserved for car pools and vehicles with more than one person in them. Signs say how many people must be in the vehicle as well as the days and hours to which the reserved use applies. For example, "HOV 2" means there must be at least two people in the vehicle for you to legally drive in that lane.

7. Changing Lanes

Changing lanes on a multi-lane highway or interstate should never be done without thinking and looking. Absent-minded lane changing is extremely dangerous. Common sense, alertness, and courtesy are all essential to your safety and the safety of other drivers. Use the following steps to help you make safe lane changes:

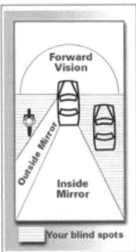

- Pay attention to clearance space ahead and behind your vehicle.

- Check your rearview mirrors.

- Signal your intention to change lanes.

- Look over your shoulder in the direction you will be moving.

- Look behind you to both sides again.

- CHECK YOUR BLIND SPOTS. As shown to the right the driver in front cannot see the motorcycle or other car just by checking his mirrors. He would need to physically turn his head and look over his shoulder in each direction to see those vehicles next to him.

- Change lanes gradually and carefully.

- Do not cruise in the blind spots of any vehicles ahead of you.

When a driver ahead of you (in your lane or the lane next to you) signals a lane change, slow down and leave space for the change. Do NOT speed up or change lanes yourself until the other driver has completed his intended movement. Otherwise you could interfere with his lane change and contribute to a dangerous situation or accident.

PASSING OTHER VEHICLES

Passing another vehicle is a normal part of driving, but it can be very dangerous. Collisions resulting from improper passing are often fatal since the impact is greater in this type of accident. Before you attempt a pass, be sure you have enough room to complete the maneuver. If you have to cut back to your lane too soon, you risk sideswiping the vehicle you are passing. If you do not cut back to your lane soon enough, you risk a head-on collision.

 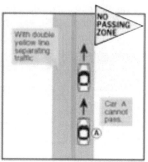

It is equally important to know when NOT to pass as well as when to pass. The decision of whether or not to pass is influenced by the knowledge, judgment, attitude and behavior of the driver. BE PATIENT. Study and learn the following passing rules well and practice them each time you pass another vehicle.

1. **Passing on the Left** — requires the following safety precautions:
   - Know the speed and acceleration ability of your vehicle, and be able to estimate the speed of the vehicle you are passing as well as that of any oncoming traffic. As a rule, if you see any sign of an oncoming vehicle, it is too close for you to risk a pass. When in doubt, stay in your lane.
   - Stay well back of the vehicle you want to pass to allow yourself a better view of the road ahead. Check well ahead for a NO-PASSING ZONE and on-coming vehicles.
   - When overtaking and passing another vehicle traveling in the same direction on a two-lane road in the USA, you should pass only to the left of the vehicle.
   - Signal you move to the left and check your rearview and side-view mirrors before you change lanes.
   - Do NOT swing out across the center line for a look, if you need to do this to see you are either following too closely or attempting to pass in an area where your sight distance is too limited to pass safely.

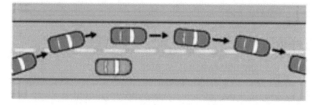

- Check your blind spot for any vehicle that may be starting a pass around your vehicle.
- Move to the left (oncoming traffic lane) ONLY when it is safe to do so. Pass on the left at a safe distance and do not return to the right lane until safely clear of the over-taken vehicle. (See diagram above)
- Complete your pass as soon as possible. When you can see the entire vehicle you passed in your rearview mirror, signal right and return to your lane. Be sure to cancel the signal light so that you are not driving with your right turn signal flashing.
- As a general rule it is NOT SAFE to pass more than one vehicle at a time, although it is not illegal in Tennessee to pass multiple vehicles. It is recommended that you not even consider passing multiple vehicles unless you:
  A. are on a straight, level roadway where your vision of oncoming traffic is excellent
  B. can complete the pass of all vehicles and be safely returned to the right lane before coming within 100 feet of the no passing markings (solid yellow line, signs, etc.) and/or any oncoming vehicles approaching from the opposite direction.
- Take extra precautions during inclement weather and twilight hours. Some oncoming vehicles may not be easily visible at these times, especially if they aren't using their headlights as required.
- Whenever possible try to avoid passing at night, unless you are familiar with the roadway on which you are traveling. It is more difficult at night to see where the passing zone ends and if you aren't familiar with the roadway a slight hill/incline or curve in the road ahead could prove deadly.

2. **Passing on the Right:** The driver of a vehicle may overtake and pass upon the right of another vehicle only under the following conditions:
   - When the vehicle overtaken has signaled to make or is about to make a left turn. *Never pass on the left of a driver who has signaled a left turn.*
   - Upon a street or highway with unobstructed pavement, not occupied by parked vehicles, and such paved roadway is of sufficient width for two or more lines of moving vehicles in each direction.
   - Upon a one-way street, or upon any roadway on which traffic is restricted to one direction of movement, where the roadway is free from obstruction and such road is of sufficient paved width for two or more lanes of moving vehicles.
   - You may never legally pass on the right by driving off the pavement or main portion of the highway. Use extra care

when you pass on the right; other drivers do not expect to be passed on the right if they are not traveling on a multi-lane roadway.

- Do NOT pass on the right using a bike lane or parking lane at any location, nor in the emergency lane within sight of a traffic light or stop sign. This situation often happens at intersections when vehicles are stopped for a red light: *A vehicle attempts to pass on the right and one of the cars ahead starts to make a right turn when the light changes resulting in a crash. The person passing on the right will be "at fault" because the vehicle turning right was properly traveling within the marked lane of traffic.*

- The driver of a vehicle may overtake and pass another vehicle on the right only under conditions permitting such movement in safety. **In no event shall such movement be made by driving off the pavement or** *main-traveled portion of the roadway.*

3. **No Passing:** It is not always safe to pass. Make certain the way is clear. Give the proper signal before changing lanes. Tap your horn when necessary to avoid surprising the driver ahead. Avoid cutting in too quickly if you must return to your original lane. Remember you may NOT cross the center line to pass under the following conditions:

- Do not pass when approaching any road-way intersection or railroad crossing, when approaching any narrow bridge, viaduct or tunnel, or where there is an oncoming car.

Intersections

- Do not cross the solid yellow line in your lane.

- You should always stay to the right of the center whenever the solid yellow line is on your side of the center lane marking.

Railroads

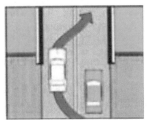

Bridges / Tunnels

- Do not pass unless the pass may be completed without interfering with the safety of the oncoming vehicle and before the solid yellow line reappears in your traffic lane.

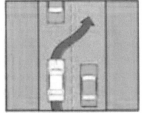

Oncoming Traffic

Hills

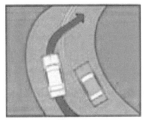

Curves

- Do not pass a school bus or church bus when the flashing lights are operating and the stop arm is extended.

- Do not pass when approaching a hill or curve.

- Do not pass a car that has stopped for pedestrians in a marked or unmarked crosswalk. Passing in this type of situation is a frequent cause of death to pedestrians, especially if the passing vehicle is traveling at a high rate of speed.

Safety Tip: when stopping for a crosswalk on a multi-lane road, you should stop about 30 feet before the crosswalk so you don't block visibility of the crossing pedestrians to a driver in the other lane(s).

- Do not pass on the right shoulder of the highway. Other drivers will not expect you to be there and may pull off the road or turn right without looking.

- The end of a "no-passing zone" does not mean it is safe to pass. It means there is increased visibility ahead. It is still up to YOU to determine if it is safe to pass after considering all the conditions discussed above.

- The solid yellow line marked on the pavement in a "no-passing zone" indicates that you may NOT cross the centerline to pass. You are allowed to turn across the centerline if you are making a left turn into or coming out of an alley, intersection, private road or driveway while in the "no-passing zone".

- Do not "weave" in and out of traffic by repeatedly passing on the left, then back to the right and then passing again on the left, etc. Weaving from lane to lane in an attempt to move faster than the flow of traffic is the sign of an immature driver and is extremely dangerous.

4. **Being Passed by Another Vehicle:** When another driver tries to pass you, there are many chances for a collision. The other driver may cut in too sharply, you may be changing lanes, or the other driver may be forced back into your lane if he/she has misjudged the distance of oncoming traffic. Keep everyone safe - help the other driver pass you safely by:

- Staying in your lane, and moving to the right if being passed on the left.

- Maintaining you speed, DO NOT speed up to keep the other driver from passing.

- Checking oncoming traffic and adjusting your speed to let the other driver move back into the right lane as soon as possible.

- Slowing down if you observe a car approaching from the other direction while you are being passed. By slowing down you will allow the passing driver more space to pull back into the right lane in front of you before meeting the oncoming vehicle.

5. Passing Trucks and Buses

"It amazes me when a car cuts in front of me and then slows down! Don't they realize I can't stop an 80,000 pound truck the way they can stop a 3,000 pound car?" This statement is heard often from truck and bus drivers regarding the actions of drivers of passenger vehicles passing them on the highway.

In addition to following the guidelines for passing any vehicle, to safely pass a large truck or bus there are additional rules you must learn:

- Complete your pass as quickly as possible - do not stay alongside the truck or bus. This is a common misunderstanding. Staying beside the truck or bus does NOT "let the driver know you are there". Instead, it puts you in the driver's blindspot! If you are traveling alongside a truck or bus and can look over and see any portion of the tractor from the driver/passenger door back to fifth wheel area where the trailer is connected you are most likely in the driver's blindspot.

- An excellent point to remember is that if YOU can't see the side mirrors on the truck or bus you are following then HE CAN'T SEE YOU. This also means that all you can see is the back doors of the truck or bus and not a good view of the traffic situations on the road ahead. You are following too closely and greatly increasing your chance of a rear-end collision with the truck or bus.

- Maintain your speed. NEVER pull in front of a truck or bus (or any type of vehicle) and slow down. This takes away the safety cushion of the driver you have just passed and presents a potentially dangerous situation if you must stop suddenly.

- Keep in mind the terrain you're traveling on when passing. On a level highway, it generally takes longer to pass a truck or bus than a car. On an upgrade, these heavier vehicles often lose speed, making it easier to pass. On a down grade, their momentum will cause them to go faster, so you may need to increase your speed to pass. Remember it is illegal to exceed the speed posted speed limit even when passing other vehicles.

- There is also no need to refrain from passing a truck pulling multiple trailers. Motorists should treat these trucks as they would any other commercial vehicle and follow the same

rules for sharing the road. (See Chapter 14 for more on "Sharing the Road with Trucks".)

BACKING AND PARKING

1. Backing

In general, never back a vehicle in any travel lane with the exception of backing into a parallel parking space. Drivers do not expect a vehicle to be backing towards them and may not realize it until it is too late. If you must back your vehicle, look carefully and move slowly.

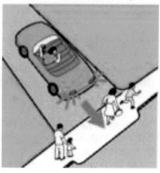

Backing is more difficult for new drivers than traveling forward because the vehicle itself blocks your field of vision, and it's harder to control speed and direction. You will need a lot of practice to learn to maintain absolute control of the vehicle. Although a small part of the driving tests, backing is the maneuver that most often causes new drivers to fail their skills test.

- Backing is dangerous because it is hard for you to see behind your car. Here are some rules you should follow whenever you have to back your car:

  A. Check behind your vehicle BEFORE you get behind the wheel. Children or small objects are hard to see from the driver's seat.

  B. Before backing look to the front, both sides and the rear. Place your arm on the back of the seat and turn around so that you can look directly through the rear window. Do not depend solely on your mirrors. Avoid opening the door and sticking your head out to see - this is dangerous.

  C. Back slowly and gradually. Your car is much harder to control and stop while you are backing. Continue to look to all sides of the vehicle for hazards while backing.

- It is illegal to back into an intersection from a driveway. A driver must take care when backing to see that such movements can be done with reasonable safety and are not interfering with other traffic.

- Backing out of a parking space requires special caution and attention by drivers. You must be aware of the movements of any cars or pedestrians near or approaching your vehicle. Be sure to look both directions before and during the backing maneuver out of the parking space. Be prepared to stop quickly should any hazard appear.

- If you miss your turn or exit, do NOT back up, but go on to the next turn or exit or where you can safely and legally turn around. It is illegal to back up on the interstate.

- Do not stop in the travel lanes for any reason (lost or

confused directions, vehicle breakdown, or letting out a passenger). Keep moving until you can safely pull your vehicle off the roadway.

2. Parking

Drivers are responsible for making sure that their vehicle is not a hazard when it is parked. Whenever you park, be sure it is in a place that is far enough from any travel lane to avoid interfering with traffic and easily visible to vehicles approaching from either direction.

Routine Parking Regulations: The following are some routine rules regulating parking vehicles that you should become familiar with:

- Always park in a designated area if possible.

- When parking adjacent to a roadway outside of city limits, all four wheels must be off the pavement, if possible. In any event you must ensure that you leave at least 18 feet of road width for other traffic to pass your parked vehicle, and your vehicle must be visible for at least 200 feet in either direction.

- Signs or yellow painted curbs usually mark a **"NO PARKING ZONE"** in cities and towns.

- Double parking is prohibited by law.

- It is against the law to leave the engine running in a parked unattended vehicle.

- Remove ignition keys from parked, unattended vehicle. It is a good safety habit to lock the doors of your vehicle when it is left parked unattended.

- **When parking on a hill follow these rules:**

  A. On a downhill with a curb: turn the front wheels toward the curb (right) and set the parking brake. If your car rolls it will roll into the curb and not the roadway.

  B. On an uphill with a curb: turn the front wheels away from curb (left), this way if your car starts to roll back it will roll into the curb and stop, instead of rolling into traffic.

  C. On a downhill without a curb: turn the front wheels toward the edge of the roadway (right). Again this will prevent the vehicle from rolling into traffic if the brake fails.

  D. On an uphill without a curb: Turn the front wheels toward the edge of the roadway (right). This will allow your car to roll away from the center of the road in the event the brakes fail.

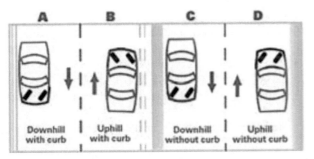

- A driver must look, signal and yield the right-of-way when coming out of a parking place.

- Always set your parking brake when you park. Leave the vehicle in gear if it has a manual transmission or in "park" if it has an automatic transmission.

- The "hazard", or four-way flashing directional lights may be displayed during the hours of darkness when a vehicle is disabled or otherwise presents a traffic hazard.

3. No Parking Zones

There are many areas where you cannot park. **It is illegal to park:**

- In front of a public or private driveway.

- Within an intersection.

- Within 15 feet of a fire hydrant.

- Within 20 feet of a crosswalk or upon the crosswalk marked area.

- Within 20 feet of a fire station driveway on the same side of the street or on the other side of the street within 75 feet of the fire station driveway.

- Within 30 feet of a traffic signal, stop sign or any other traffic control device.

- Within 50 feet of a railroad crossing.

- On a sidewalk.

- Upon any bridge or within a tunnel.

- In a parking space clearly identified by an official sign or pavement markings indicating the space is reserved for use by a physically handicapped person.

- On the traffic side of another parked vehicle (double parked).

- On the shoulder of any interstate (except for an emergency situation).

- Where official signs prohibit stopping or standing.

- Other parking restrictions may be indicated by painted curbs. A painted curb means that you must follow special rules to park there. The colors on the curbs mean:

WHITE
Stop only long enough to pick up or drop off passengers.

YELLOW
Stop only long enough to load or unload. Stay with your car.

RED
Do not stop, stand or park in this space under any conditions.

4. Parallel Parking

Your ability to judge distances while controlling the speed of your vehicle is the key to completing this parking maneuver. When parallel parking, be sure to continually check for oncoming traffic conditions. Parallel parking is a true test of the driver's ability to handling "multi-tasking"

STEP 1: Check traffic behind you , signal, stop even with the car in front of the open parallel space you are going to park in. Your  rear bumper should be even with the bumper of the other parked car and you should ensure that you do not get your vehicle any closer than 2 feet from the other vehicle.

STEP 2: Turn you head to the right and look over your shoulder at the space you are going to back into, also scan frequently back  to the front observing your distance from the other parked car. Begin backing very slowly, turning your steering wheel sharply to the right until your car is at about 45-degree angle with the street. As your front passenger side door passes the rear bumper of the other car quickly straighten your front wheels and slowly continue to back straight.

STEP 3: When your front bumper is even with the other car's back bumper, turn your wheels sharply and rapidly to the left as far  as necessary. It is extremely important that you remember to continually check the space around your vehicle while making this maneuver. You need to be especially aware of traffic on the road and the distances between your vehicle and the other parked cars. This task requires

STEP 4: Turn your steering wheel sharply to the right and slowly pull forward toward the curb.  Continue adjusting slowly and gradually until you car is centered in the parking space.

Upon completion of your parallel parking maneuver you vehicle should be no further away from the curb than 18 inches. As you prepared to exit the vehicle be sure to check the traffic before you open the driver side door. Get out of the vehicle on the curb side if you can. If you have to use the street side, wait till any traffic has passed, get out quickly and shut the door as soon as you can. Move to the curb or sidewalk quickly for your safety.

5. Emergency Parking (Disabled Vehicles)

In the event it becomes necessary for you to leave your vehicle parked on a highway or street, follow these rules:
- Park your vehicle with all four wheels off the traveled portion of the highway if possible. Otherwise pull onto the shoulder of the road as far away from traffic as possible. If there is a curb, pull as close to the curb as possible.

- If you cannot move the vehicle off the highway raise the hood or tie a handkerchief on the left door handle or antenna to warn other motorists.

- Turn on your car's emergency flasher lights. Set your parking brake, shift into park or leave the vehicle in gear,

and turn off the engine. Lock your vehicle

- A stopped car on the Interstate (even on the shoulder) is extremely dangerous. Do not stop on an Interstate highway except for an emergency.

- Walking on the Interstate is both illegal and dangerous. Except for extreme emergency cases, you should remain in your broken down vehicle until a State Trooper, other police officer, emergency service vehicle, or a good Samaritan stops to offer assistance.

6. Handicap Parking Spaces

The handicap parking symbol, which appears on reserved parking signs, placards and license plates, is the international symbol of access for persons with physical disability. Parking spaces marked with this symbol are only to be used by vehicles displaying a valid placard or license plate with this symbol, and only when transporting the person who was issued the placard or plate.

It is illegal for anyone else to park in these spaces. If you improperly park in these designated spaces you will be committing a misdemeanor punishable by a $100 dollar fine and your vehicle could be subject to being towed.

7. Parking Meters

Many public parking spaces are regulated by coin-fed parking meters. Meter regulations are usually in effect during posted days and hours. In most areas, a maximum time limit for parking in those spaces is also posted. If you exceed the limit or fail to pay the meter fee, you may be issued a parking ticket and your vehicle may be towed.

8. Angle Parking

Angle parking is often used in parking lots, shopping centers, and sometimes at curbs.
When you enter an angle parking space on your right:
- Watch for traffic both ahead and behind.

- Signal and begin slowing down.

- Make sure the rear of your car will clear the parked cars.
- Steer sharply into the parking space, then straighten the wheels, centering your car in the parking space.

- Shift to Park or reverse if driving a standard transmission vehicle and apply the parking brake.

Before backing out of an angle parking space:
- Walk around to make sure nothing is in your way.

- Move your car back slowly because it is hard to see oncoming traffic. Be sure traffic is clear in the lane where you are backing.

- Maintain a cautious speed so that you can yield if necessary to pedestrians or oncoming vehicles.

- When you can see past the tops of cars parked next to you, stop and look again. Look back and to each side for other drivers.

- Remember that the front of your car will swing opposite to the direction of your turn.

- Back slowly while turning until your left front wheel passes the rear bumper of the car parked on the left.

- Straighten the wheels as your car comes back into the lane for traffic.

Interstate Highway Driving Is Different!

Traffic on Interstates usually moves more safely and efficiently because access is controlled. There are no stop signs, no railroad crossings and no traffic lights. Interstates usually have few steep hills or sharp curves to limit your view of the road ahead. Limited access or controlled access means that you enter or leave the roadway only at entrances and exits, called interchanges, without ever crossing the path of other traffic. Interstates and divided highways have largely removed the chance of head-on collisions but driving on our Interstates is very different.

Interstates, require good driving skills and habits for you to safely get where you are going. Safe use of the Interstates demands a complete awareness of a higher speed type of driving and constant alertness by the driver.

Before Driving on the Interstate

Plan your trip in advance so that you know your entrance, direction , and exit. Make sure that you and your car are in good condition. Check your gas gauge before getting on the Interstate. In rural areas if may be many miles between exits and you could risk running out of gas before getting to a location where you could refuel. If you cannot or do not wish to drive at or above the minimum speed limit, do not use the Interstate.

Entering the Interstate

In most driving situations, you slow down or stop before you enter a busy road, but when entering an Interstate you do the opposite. You must use the merging or acceleration lane to speed up and merge with fast-moving traffic already on the Interstate.

Good judgment and good timing are necessary to merge smoothly with the fast-moving traffic. Upon entering the Interstate on-ramp, stay to the right and increase your speed in the acceleration lane/entrance ramp. Use the ramp to reach Interstate speed in order to allow your car to merge into the travel lane when the way is clear. Be sure to give the proper left turn signal to indicate your need to enter the traffic lane. Drivers already on the Interstate should, for their own safety, make allowance for those vehicles attempting to enter. However it is your responsibility to yield the right-of-way to other cars on the Interstate.

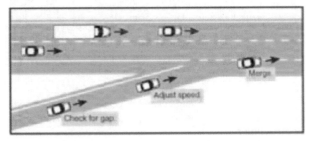

Unnecessary stopping on Interstate on-ramps causes many rear-end collisions and also obstructs the even flow of traffic. Do not drive to the end of the ramp and stop or you will not have enough room to get up to the speed of the Interstate traffic. Drivers behind you will not expect you to stop and if they are watching the traffic on the main road for their space to merge you could easily be hit from the rear. If you have to wait for space to enter an Interstate, slow down on the ramp so that you will still have some room to speed up before you have to merge. Heavy traffic conditions sometimes create a "slowdown" at an entrance ramp, but unless it is absolutely unavoidable, it is best to keep your vehicle moving at least at some slow pace.

LANE ADDED   **MERGING TRAFFIC**

Do you know what the difference in the two signs above is? Both appear to be telling you that traffic is coming into the main road from the right. However there is an IMPORTANT difference.

- The "lane added" sign means that there is a new right lane added to the Interstate/roadway for the incoming traffic. The on-ramp becomes a new lane and the entering traffic does not need to merge immediately. Traffic on the Interstate should avoid making lane changes to the right at this location as the entering traffic will not be expecting vehicles to move into their travel path.
- The regular 'merge' sign means that the traffic coming from the right is going to need to merge into the existing right hand traffic lane and drivers on the Interstate should be aware and cautious of this incoming traffic.

Driving on the Interstate

Interstates usually have several lanes of traffic traveling in the same direction. On these roads, you should leave the extreme left lane for faster traffic. If you drive at an even speed, you will have less need to change lanes. Remember, lane-hopping any time is dangerous, annoys other drivers, increases the risk of a collision, often contributes to "road rage" and very seldom saves the driver any significant amount of travel time.

Keep your vehicle in the middle of your traffic lane. You may change lanes when necessary, but don't weave in and out of traffic. Do not travel alongside other vehicles at the same speed or you risk being in the other driver's blind spots. Change speed and/or lanes to avoid these situations. Avoid cars moving in packs and keep a safe space cushion around your vehicle for emergency maneuvers. If you are going to exit the Interstate move to the right lane as early as possible to avoid hasty lane changes which could result in a dangerous situation or traffic accident.

Stay at least 2-seconds behind vehicles in front of you and increase this space to a minimum of 4-seconds in bad weather, night driving and on higher speed rural sections of the Interstate. Scan the roadway ahead, try to watch 15-20 seconds in front of your vehicle for cars braking, entering or exiting. There are times, especially in major cities, when Interstates get jammed by heavy traffic or tie-ups caused by collisions during rush hour traffic. Be alert for any hint that traffic on the Interstate ahead is not moving at a normal pace. Otherwise, you might have to slam on your brakes to avoid a rear-end crash with the vehicle ahead. If you spot a tie-up that will cause you to slow down or stop, lightly tap your brake pedal several times to alert drivers behind you.

"Traffic Flow" and Speed Control on the Interstate

Speeds traveled on rural Interstates are higher than on other roads. There also are fewer stop-and-go situations. Try to keep pace with traffic on the road, but **don't be lured into exceeding the posted speed to "stay with the flow of the traffic"**.

Do maintain a constant speed and keep a safe pace with other traffic. Do not speed up and slow down unnecessarily. Drive between the minimum (45 M.P.H.) and the maximum (55-70 M.P.H.) speed limits. Driving too slowly is against the law because it's dangerous. A slowpoke on an Interstate can be just as reckless as a speeder. Remember, if you drive at a speed below the flow of traffic, you must use the right lane and if the minimum speed is too high for your comfort you should use a different roadway.

If you are traveling in the left lane and someone comes up behind you at a faster speed, move one lane to your right. Do not tie up traffic in the left lane. Courteous and safe driving practices require that drivers in any lane, except the right lane used for slower traffic, should be prepared to move to another lane to allow faster traffic to pass.

By the same token these practices teach that drivers in the right lane should adjust their speed to allow others to enter the Interstate safely. Be alert to merging traffic signs. When it is safe to do so, you should either slow down or move to another lane to allow space for on-ramp traffic to merge safely. Remember, trucks and buses entering the Interstate may need extra time to adjust to traffic patterns. Be cooperative and give them extra time and space to adjust to the traffic flow.

Leaving the Interstate

Interchanges may be different and it is important to watch for advance directional signs. Choose the right exit, and be sure you are in the proper lane well before you turn off the Interstate. The heavier the traffic the earlier you should move into the proper lane. Exit signs are usually placed at least one (1) mile ahead of the exit turn-off.

To leave the Interstate, signal your intention to change lanes, and move to the lane nearest the exit/off-ramp. Maintain your speed until you enter the deceleration lane, which is usually outlined by a series of amber reflectors, and reduce speed to the exit ramp posted speed. Speed should be reduced further on the exit ramp. You should have your vehicle slowed to the posted limit for the roadway you are exiting onto.

The paved shoulder of the Interstate should not be used for vehicular travel except for deceleration when marked for this purpose or for emergency purposes.

Remember, it is illegal to back up or make a U-turn on Interstate highways. If you miss your exit you must proceed to the next exit.

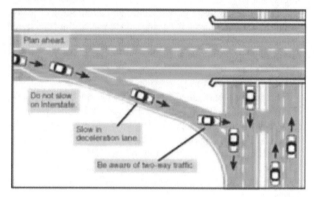

Interchanges

It is also very important to know how to maneuver on the different types of interchanges. Two common types of interchanges are the DIAMOND and the CLOVERLEAF, which are diagrammed and explained below. There are various other types of interchanges and methods of turning may vary from one to the other. When approaching any type of interchange, heed signs that will tell you how to make the turn you want to make.

Diamond Interchange

Traffic using the interstate may gain access to the intersecting roadway by taking the signed exit ramp, proceeding to the cross roadway and obeying the traffic sign or signal at the intersection. Turns may then be made to the right or left as at any ordinary intersection.

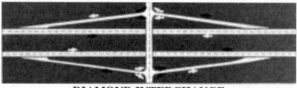

DIAMOND INTERCHANGE

With a diamond interchange, the proper exit ramp will always be encountered before passing over or under the intersecting roadway.

Traffic using the cross roadway may enter the interstate by making either a left or right turn onto the appropriate entrance ramp. THE RIGHT TURN entrance ramp will always be encountered BEFORE crossing over or under the interstate. The LEFT TURN entrance ramp will always be encountered AFTER crossing over or under the interstate.

NEVER MAKE A RIGHT TURN onto a ramp AFTER crossing the interstate lanes.

NEVER MAKE A LEFT TURN onto a ramp BEFORE crossing the interstate lanes.

Cloverleaf Interchange

At a cloverleaf interchange, all turns are right turns.

TO TURN RIGHT...You take the right turn before you get to the overpass.

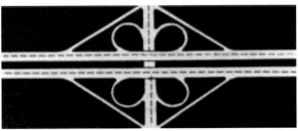

CLOVERLEAF INTERCHANGE

TO TURN LEFT...You take the right turn just after the overpass. The road will carry you around to join the crossroad and you will be going in the same direction as if you had turned left at an ordinary intersection. The advantage of such an interchange is that you do not have to cross the path of traffic to make a turn.

"Weaving" Interchange

One of the most hazardous lane management situations occurs when Interstate traffic is both exiting and entering at the same area. This weaving of vehicles trying to get on or off the highway at the same time requires the complete attention of all drivers and quick reactions for a safe maneuver. A weaving section takes maximum cooperation. It can't work without sharing and sensible, courteous social interaction on the part of every driver. Signs and lane markings do their part. Safe drivers have to do the rest.

You should follow the routine procedures for entering the Interstate as those used at normal on-ramps, however you must be aware that vehicles already on the Interstate may be moving right to enter the exit ramp. This will require both you and the other driver to yield and share the interchange in a equal "give and take" manner. If drivers aren't paying proper attention to the directional signs and lane design this movement of exiting traffic can create the potential for a serious accident. You must use extreme caution when utilizing these type of interchanges.

Fight Interstate Hypnosis

Continuous Interstate driving can become monotonous. A condition of drowsiness or unawareness can be brought about by reduced activity and steady sounds of wind, engine, and tire hum. This is known as Interstate hypnosis. **All drivers should be aware of its danger and of the methods for fighting it.** Use the following tips to help you recognize and avoid this condition:

- **Keep shifting your eyes.** When driving, look well ahead but avoid staring. Get into the habit of shifting your eyes left and right and of checking your rearview mirror. If you sit and stare straight ahead, you can almost put yourself to sleep.

- **Quit driving when you are drowsy.** Drowsiness is the first step in falling asleep.

- **Keep your car's interior as cool as possible.**

- **As a further protection, stop and refresh yourself at regular intervals.** Take a break and get out of the car at least every 2 hours or every 100 miles or so. Even if you are feeling well you should stop, get out of your car and walk around, allow your muscles to relax.

- It is safest for yourself and others if you **do not drive more than 8 hours per day.**

Special Interstate Driving Instructions

1. On the Interstate, you may **NOT:**
   - Drive over or across any dividing section or separation (only emergency vehicles and highway maintenance crews may cross an Interstate median legally).
   - Make a left turn or a U-turn except through an opening provided and marked for such turns.
   - Change lanes without signaling.
   - Drive in the blind spot of other drivers. Traveling in a position where the driver ahead of you cannot see your vehicle can be dangerous. Either stay behind or go around. Do NOT follow to the side.
   - Drive onto the Interstate except through an opening provided for such entrance.
   - Park or stop on the Interstate except at areas especially provided. Parking on the shoulder of the Interstate is prohibited except in cases of emergency.
   - Back up if you miss an exit - You must go to the next exit.

2. Always remember these tips for safe Interstate driving:
   - Drive in a dependable and predictable manner
   - Be a safe and courteous driver.
   - Always signal your intentions well in advance.
   - Keep you attention constantly on your driving.
   - Make frequent traffic checks by looking in your rearview and side-view mirrors often.
   - Keep a safe following distance between your car and the vehicle you are following.
   - Check instruments often for speed and fuel supply.
   - Keep pace with traffic but don't speed illegally just because other drivers are speeding.
   - Stay in the right lane if traveling slower than the other traffic.
   - Be alert to merging traffic signs and vehicles entering the Interstate.
   - When safe to do so, move to another lane to allow on-ramp traffic to enter the Interstate.

3. Special situations to be aware of include:
- **Be prepared for the unexpected!** - When driving on an Interstate highway, look out for pedestrians who may have had a vehicle breakdown, or animals that may be on the roadway. It is not an impossibility for vehicles to be traveling in the wrong direction on an Interstate!
- **Lane Wandering** - Weaving and wandering are dangerous. Keep to the right unless overtaking or passing. Watch mirrors, and signal before changing lanes. Don't cut back until it is safe. Stay aware of surrounding traffic conditions.
- **Maintain Safe Distance** - Following too closely is the cause of many multiple-car collisions. Higher Interstate speeds increase danger, and require greater distances between cars.
- **Night Driving** - Darkness increases driving dangers. On the basis of mileage driven, night driving is far more dangerous than day driving. Fatigue and sharply reduced vision are primarily responsible for this greater danger. It is also true that drinking drivers are more likely to be on the road at night.

Dynamic Message Signs

Dynamic Message Signs are being installed along Tennessee interstates in urban areas to provide traffic information to motorists. These signs advise motorists of traffic incidents or construction ahead so they can consider alternate routes.

Only real-time information about incidents, traffic, roadwork, weather or pavement conditions that could have an effect on driver safety and traffic flow shall be displayed on the DMS. Exceptions to this are messages that may occasionally be displayed:
- advance notification of roadwork requiring lane closures
- advance notification of special events that will adversely affect travel either because of added traffic generated or the requirement to close streets or highways.

Occasional messages associated with Amber Alerts or other Public Safety issues are also displayed. Otherwise, signs will be blank. For more information visit: www.tdot.state.tn.us

Dealing with Traffic Congestion

Chronic traffic congestion is fast becoming the Tennessee commuter's biggest headache, but even small changes in driving habits could provide fast relief. Several driving behaviors that contribute to traffic congestion include:
- *Rubbernecking* - perhaps the most frustrating of behaviors. Slowing down to look at accidents or virtually anything else out of the ordinary, is one of the worst congestion offenders.
- *Tailgating* - following too closely is common on Tennessee interstates, accounting for innumerable accidents which in turn clog major routes often for hours.
- *Unnecessary Lane Changes* - although it produces virtually NO improvement in arrival or travel times, many motorists insist on weaving in and out of interstate lanes dangerously, which at best slows down all traffic and at worst causes many accidents.
- *Inattention* - drivers can commonly be seen eating, grooming in the rearview mirror, talking on a cellular telephone, and even reading the newspaper as they drive to work.

Drivers who do not watch the fuel gauge or maintain their vehicles properly can also cause traffic congestion. These vehicles can malfunction or stall on the interstate or other streets causing bottlenecks and major slow downs in traffic flow.

If you will learn to avoid these "bad behaviors" and keep them from becoming your average driving habits, you will go along way toward helping to keep traffic congestion under control in Tennessee.

Vehicle Breakdowns, Accidents and Emergency Stopping on Interstate Highways

If you have vehicle trouble, move to the right shoulder or emergency stopping area as soon as you can. Turn on your emergency flashers to warn other traffic. If you need help, raise your hood and tie a white cloth to the hood or radio antenna. If possible, it is better to stay in or near your vehicle on the side away from traffic. Walking along the Interstate is dangerous. Keep children away from traffic.

If you stay with your vehicle, a police patrol will stop to help you when they come by if they are not on another call. If you are within one of the major metropolitan areas of Tennessee (Memphis, Nashville, Chattanooga or Knoxville) you may also receive assistance from one of the Tennessee Department of Transportation's Incident Response Units (HELP Truck). These units patrol specific routes on the major Interstates in these cities. The HELP operators have the authority to "remove or cause

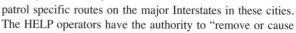

to be removed" any vehicle that is an "obstruction or hazard to traffic". The HELP operators are trained to deal with incident scenes, and you should always follow their instructions same as those of other police or traffic control personnel. (You can find more information on the HELP program at the TDOT website: www.tdot.state.tn.us)

Move It For Safety

If you are involved in a traffic accident on the Interstate, Tennessee law now allows you to move the vehicle to help prevent blocking the traffic flow. If the vehicle is still driveable and there are NO SERIOUS PERSONAL INJURIES or deaths you may pull the vehicle(s) to the emergency lane and await the arrival of a trooper or police officer to the accident scene. Never attempt to move a seriously injured accident victim unless directed to do so by the proper emergency personnel. Also never disturb an accident scene in any manner when a fatality is involved. Under Tennessee law you must not leave the scene of any type of crash, but, while remaining at the scene, you should not "unnecessarily block traffic".

The Tennessee Department of Transportation has placed signs along the state's interstate system reminding motorists to move their damaged vehicles to the shoulder if no serious injury has occurred.

*THP - In the event of a highway emergency, your free cellular phone call connects you directly to a Tennessee Highway Patrol Dispatcher for assistance. Simply dial: ***-T-H-P** (or *847)

Interstate Travel Tips

Plan your trip in advance. Use a map and decide exactly where to get on and off the interstate.

Check your car's gasoline gauge and get fuel if you do not have enough for your trip. Also check for water and oil needs. Higher speeds generate more heat. Because there are no service stations located directly on Interstates, you are in serious trouble if you run out of gasoline or have a breakdown.

Make sure your car is in good mechanical condition; that your tires, including spare, are properly inflated, have good treads and are free of breaks.

If you have car trouble, pull completely off the traveled portion of the road. Be especially cautious at night since there is a danger of being hit from the rear.

To signal for assistance on the Interstate, tie a white handkerchief or scarf to the left door handle or radio antennae or raise the hood of the car. To signal after dark, turn on your inside dome light and/or set out flares or portable warning signals. Wait for help. Do not walk along the Interstate.

Suggested Safety and Emergency Equipment

Often, we don't think about what we need in traveling situations until we encounter an emergency. In case of a flat tire, vehicle breakdown or other roadside emergency on any road, you should have the following items in your car:

- Spare tire in excellent condition (be sure to have it checked each time you have your tires rotated).
- Jack and tire iron
- Tire Pressure Gauge
- Can of sealant for small leaks in tire(s)
- Flash light, portable radio and spare batteries
- Car Owner's Manual
- Insurance information and car registration
- Paper, pen or pencil
- Three fuses or reflectors for night-time emergencies.
- First Aid Kit
- Fire Extinguisher
- Jumper cables
- Spare bottle of windshield washer fluid.
- Empty gas can and an unopened can of motor oil
- Toolbox with screwdrivers, wrenches, small hammer, scissors, duct tape, etc.
- Bottled water and some simple non-perishable snack foods. (water is especially prudent to carry when traveling during hot summer weather)
- Emergency phone numbers of family, friends and auto club or insurance agent.
- Cellular phone
- During winter travel also carry:
  - a blanket,
  - small portable heater.
  - window scraper for iced over windows.,
  - snow tires or tire chains

SPECIAL DRIVING TECHNIQUES

> **Here's a short test:** Most accidents happen_____
> a.) in clear weather   b.) in snow   c.) in rain   d.) in fog

If you picked anything but (a), you're wrong – pretty days can be deadly too! While adverse weather conditions certainly create dangerous driving situations, the purpose of this chapter is to provide you with a focus on techniques that will help you to avoid accidents in any weather.

AVOIDING COLLISIONS

When it looks like a collision may happen, many drivers panic and fail to act. In some cases they do act, but do something that does not help to reduce the chance of the collision. There almost always is something you can do to avoid the crash, or reduce the results of the crash. In avoiding a collision, drivers have three options:

   1. Stop   **2. Turn**   **3. Speed Up**

The following section will give you vital information relating to these three reactions.

1. Stopping Quickly

Many newer vehicles have ABS (Antilock Braking Systems). Be sure to read the vehicle owner's manual on how to use the ABS. Also for general details of braking with ABS refer to Chapter 8 of this manual. The ABS system will allow you to stop without skidding. In general, if you need to stop quickly:

With ABS - If you have an antilock braking system and you need to stop quickly:
- ❑ Press on the brake pedal as hard as you can and keep pressing on it firmly.
- ❑ You might feel the brake pedal pushing back when the ABS is working. Do NOT let up on the brake pedal. The ABS system will only work with the brake pedal pushed down firmly.

In emergency or slippery conditions with ABS, wheels don't lock; car remains stable and is steerable.

In emergency or slippery conditions without ABS, all wheels lock; car begins to skid and is not steerable.

Without ABS - If you must stop quickly and you do NOT have an antilock braking system:
- ❑ Apply the brakes as hard as you can without locking them. You can cause the vehicle to go into a skid if you brake too hard.
- ❑ If the brakes lock-up, you will feel the vehicle start to skid. Quickly let up on the brake pedal.
- ❑ As soon as the vehicle stops skidding, push down on the brake pedal again. Keep doing this until the vehicle has stopped.

2. Turning Quickly

In most cases, you can turn the vehicle quicker than you can stop it. *Evasive steering:* If you are unable to stop in time to avoid a collision, try to steer around the vehicle or object. You should consider turning in order to avoid a collision. Use your brakes only if necessary.

To be able to turn quickly you need to hold the steering wheel correctly. Make sure you have a good grip with both hands on the steering wheel. For most turns, especially quick turns, you must have your hands on opposite sides of the wheel. It is best to have your hands at about the 3 o'clock and 9 o'clock positions. This will keep your wrists and forearms out of the main impact area of the air bag located in the steering wheel should you become involved in a collision.

To make quick evasive turns to the left:
- **Turn the steering wheel to the left as far as necessary to avoid the obstacle or vehicle.** *Hand position = right hand (3 o'clock) swings left toward the 9 o'clock position as far as needed. Left hand moves toward bottom (6 o'clock) to help steady your grip on the wheel.*
- **As you clear the hazard, turn the steering wheel back to the right as far as necessary to get back into your lane.** *Hand position = left hand (9 o'clock) swings right back toward the 3 o'clock position as far as needed. Right hand now moves toward the bottom (6 o'clock) to steady your grip.*
- **As you return to your lane, turn the steering wheel left just enough to straighten the vehicle's path of travel.** *Hand position = returning to the basic driving position of left @ 9 o'clock and right @ 3 o'clock.*

To make quick evasive turns to the right, use the same procedures above, except turn the steering wheel in the opposite direction at each step.

Once you have turned the vehicle away from the road hazard or changed lanes, you must be ready to keep the vehicle under control. Some drivers steer away from one collision only to end up in another. ***Always steer in the direction you want the vehicle to go.***

- ❑ *With ABS* - One aspect of having ABS, is that you can turn your vehicle while braking without skidding. (See illustration at right >) This is very helpful if you must turn to swerve, stop or slow down quickly.
- ❑ *Without ABS* - If you do not have ABS, you must use a different procedure to turn quickly. As you are braking you will need to let up on the brake pedal and then turn the steering wheel. Braking will slow the vehicle some, and it puts more weight on the front tires and this allows for a quicker turn. Do not continue braking if you feel the front wheels "lock-up", or turn so sharply that the vehicle can only plow ahead. Another consideration is that generally it is better to turn off the road then to crash head-on into another vehicle.

3. Speeding Up

Sometimes it is best or necessary to speed up to avoid a collision. This may happen when another vehicle is about to hit you from the side or from behind and there is room to the front of your vehicle to get out of danger. Be sure to slow down once the danger has passed. Also remember to always keep at least a two second (or more) space cushion between you car and the vehicle ahead in order to have this type of emergency out available.

WINTER DRIVING

The three big errors of most drivers in snow and ice are:
- To over-power and spin the wheels
- To over-brake and slide the wheels
- To over-steer and skid the front wheels

Reduced visibility requires that you make every effort to keep the windshield and all glass clear of snow and ice. The heater-defroster should be in good condition. Windshield wiper blades should work particularly well. Keep the inside of the windshield and door glasses clean.
- Carry a high quality ice scraper with a brush for removing snow, frost, and ice from your vehicle's windows, headlights, brake lights, turn signals and outside mirrors. Clear snow, ice or frost from ALL windows before driving.

A good outside rearview mirror is of great help, particularly if the back window glass tends to fog over. To help others see you, always use headlights when visibility is restricted by atmospheric or other weather conditions.

Effect of Temperature on Starting and Stopping Traction-
Wet ice at 30 degrees offers about one-half the traction that is to be had at 25 degrees. If the temperature is 25-30 degrees, ice-covered roads are certain to be slippery. If the temperature is down to 10-15 degrees, there will be a noticeable increase in traction.

Inadequate Traction to Go - Overpowering and spinning the wheels creates heat directly under the tires, raises the temperature, and reduces the available traction. Start your car slowly and avoid spinning wheels when moving your car on ice or snow. Keep your speed steady and slow – but not too slow. In deeper snow, it's often necessary to use the car's momentum to keep moving. Have good treads on front wheels to improve steering ability. Snow tires are helpful for winter driving.

Reduced Ability to Stop and Loss of Steering - Low traction also makes stopping difficult. When traveling at 20 M.P.H., low traction can increase stopping distance to 200 feet or more. Use brakes cautiously. Abrupt braking can cause brake lock-up, which causes you to lose steering control.

Braking on Ice and Snow – The most efficient technique for braking under these conditions is to use "threshold" or "squeeze braking" together with de-clutching (manual shift) or shifting to neutral (automatic transmission). Squeeze braking is accomplished by applying the brakes firmly, to a point just short of lock up, and then easing off the brake pedal slightly (not completely), if the wheels should lock. Re-apply the brakes to a point just short of lock up and hold. Do NOT pump the brake pedal, just apply steady pressure. This will give you the best combination of braking effort and directional control.

ABS – Antilock brakes are designed to overcome a loss of steering control. To make antilock brakes work correctly, or work at all, you should apply constant, firm pressure to the pedal. During an emergency stop, push the brake pedal all the way to the floor, if necessary, even in wet or icy conditions.

Ice on Roads and Bridges – Where Not Expected: The sunny side of a hill may be wet, the shady side covered with thin ice. Usually, signs indicate that ice forms on bridges sooner than on the adjoining roads. In such instances, the car ahead of you may have crossed the icy part of the road and stopped. But a long patch of ice behind his car can easily cause you to skid into him.

Ice and Snow Made Slippery by Traffic – On streets and highways where there is considerable stop- and- go traffic, it does not take long after a storm before the snow packs hard and becomes extremely slippery because of many sliding and spinning wheels. To some extent, steering to one side or the other of the packed section will help avoid the slickest surface.

However, great caution should be used when driving on ice and snow.

Hailstorms/Sleet – find shelter by driving under an overpass or bridge.

Skids

"If Your Wheels Don't Roll - You Don't Have Control"

Skids are caused when the tires can no longer grip the road. Any road that is safe under normal conditions can be dangerous when it is wet or has snow or ice on it. High speeds under normal conditions also increase the possibility of a skid if you must turn or stop suddenly.

Skids are caused by drivers traveling too fast for conditions. If your vehicle begins to skid:

- Stay off the brake. Until the vehicle slows, your brakes will not work and could cause you to skid more.
- Steer. Turn the steering wheel in the direction you want your car to go. As soon as the vehicle begins to straighten out, turn the steering wheel back the other way. If you do not do so , your vehicle may swing around in the other direction and you could start a new skid.
- Continue to steer. Continue to correct your steering, left and right, until the vehicle is again moving down the road under your control.

The best advice is to do everything you can to avoid ever

skidding in the first place. Be aware of weather conditions and slow down well in advance of stopping point when driving on ice or packed snow. During thawing and freezing weather, be alert for slippery areas on bridges and in sheltered areas.

Regaining Control of your Vehicle when the wheels have gotten off the paved roadway:

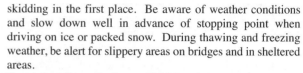

1. Stop feeding the gas. Lift you foot off the gas pedal but do NOT suddenly apply the brake.
2. Maintain a firm grip on the steering wheel, but do NOT jerk the wheel back toward the pavement suddenly.
3. Brake lightly and briefly. Do NOT slam on the brakes or hold the brake pedal down. You want to gradually slow the vehicle.
4. Maintain car control. Keep steering the vehicle straight trying to keep the other wheels from getting off the pavement.
5. Do NOT attempt to steer back onto the pavement until there are no cars in your immediate vicinity.
6. Once oncoming traffic is clear and you have slowed the speed of your vehicle you can turn back onto the pavement sharply.

DRIVING IN RAIN, FOG AND OTHER SEVERE WEATHER CONDITIONS

Wet pavement can be as treacherous as icy pavements, so always reduce your speed in wet weather. You will need additional distance for stopping, and you may skid on quick turns.

Slow down at the first sign of rain on the road. The pavement is particularly treacherous when it first begins to rain. Accumulations of dirt and oil will mix with the water, and create a greasy film on the highway. This is when most roads are the most slippery. The road is slippery and it will not give your tires the grip they need so you must drive more slowly than on a dry road.

HYDROPLANING: Slow down when there is a lot of water on the road. In a heavy rain, your tires can lose all contact with the road at about 50 M.P.H. Your car will then be riding on water or "hydroplaning". A slight change of direction or a gust of wind could throw your car into a skid or spin. If you vehicle starts to hydroplane, slow down gradually by letting up on the gas – don't suddenly apply the brakes.

When hydroplaning occurs there is a loss of the traction needed to steer and brake safely. Stopping distances may be tripled and steering control may be reduced or lost. How soon hydroplaning begins depends on speed, tire inflation, water depth (even a half-inch or less), road surface, and tire tread. Hydroplaning is more common at higher speeds, although tires can hydroplane under certain conditions at ANY speed. This is one reason you must always be extra cautious when driving in rainy weather.

Both rain and fog create vision problems as well as vehicle control problems. Keep your windshield wipers in good condition, and  wait a few seconds after rain starts before you turn them on. There should be enough water on the windshield for the wipers to clear it, not smear it with dust and grime.

Use the defroster or air conditioner to keep windows and mirrors clear. If you drive in fog, reduce speed to make up for the reduced visibility. Use headlights on low beam so the light will be on the road where you need it. In fog or mist, never put your headlights on high beam because the light will be reflected back into your eyes.

RAIN: Drivers often must change driving habits to adjust to poor driving conditions caused by weather. Rainy weather calls for:
- Slower speed.
- Greater stopping distances.
- Driving with headlights on low beam.
- Use of wipers, defroster as needed for maximum vision.
- An early signal for all turns or lane changes.
- Braking well in advance of a stop to warn following drivers of your intentions.

FOG: The best advice for driving in fog is "DON'T". If you must travel in fog you should:
- Drive with lights on low beam. Never drive with just your parking or fog lights.
- Reduce your speed.
- Avoid crossing traffic unless absolutely necessary.
- Listen for traffic (keep radio off or turned down low and do NOT use cell phone while driving in fog).
- Use wipers and defroster as needed for maximum vision.
- Be patient! Stay to the right. Avoid passing.
- Unless absolutely necessary, do not stop on any roadway. However, if you can't see the road's edge, pull off as far to the right as possible – well out of the traffic lane – and turn on your emergency flashers.
- If your car stalls or is disabled, move away from the vehicle to avoid personal injury.
- Consider postponing your trip until the fog clears.
- Adhere to warning devices in fog-prone areas.

WHEN DRIVING THROUGH DENSE FOG, HEAVY RAIN OR SNOW DURING THE DAYTIME, TURN ON YOU LOW BEAM HEADLIGHTS.

This gives you better visibility and alerts oncoming cars to your presence, it is also a requirement of Tennessee law. Have good operating windshield wipers so that they do an effective job.

Slippery When Wet
Some road surfaces are more slippery than others when wet. These roads usually have warning signs. Here are some clues to help you spot slippery roads:
- On cold, wet days, shade from trees or buildings can hide spots of ice. These areas freeze first and dry out last.
- Bridges and overpasses can also hide spots of ice. They tend to freeze before the rest of the road does.
- If it starts to rain on a hot day, pavement can be very slippery for the first few minutes. Heat causes oil in the asphalt to come to the surface and this makes the road extremely slippery until the oil washes off.
- Close to the freezing point, the road is icy and may be more slippery than at colder temperatures.

If your vehicle gets stuck in mud or snow:
- Shift to low gear and keep the front wheels straight.
- Gently step on the gas pedal.
- Avoid spinning the wheels. Drive forward as far as possible.
- Shift to reverse and slowly back up as far as possible. Don't spin the wheels.
- Shift to low gear again and drive forward.
- Repeat forward - backward rocking until the car rolls free.
- Put boards or tree branches under the tires in deep mud or snow. Never do this when the tires are spinning or when the driver has the vehicle "in gear".

Most people think of tire chains as a tool only for winter driving. However you may avoid getting stuck if you always carry chains in your vehicle. Drive as far as possible to the right side of the roadway before installing your chains. Put them on the tires before driving in snow OR mud.

HIGH WATER AND FLOODING DANGERS

Each year, more deaths occur due to flooding than from any other thunderstorm related hazard. Many of these casualties are a result of careless or unsuspecting motorists who attempt to navigate flooded roads. Most people fail to realize the force and power of water. For example, only six inches of fast-moving-flood water can knock a person off their feet.

Does a heavy vehicle equal safety in flood situations? **NO!** Nearly half of all flash flood fatalities are vehicle-related. Many of the deaths occur in vehicles as they are swept downstream. Many believe their 3,000 to 5,000 pound vehicle will remain in contact with the road surface...that it is too heavy to float. Think about that for a minute. Aircraft carriers float don't they? Vehicles (and ships) float because of buoyancy. **In fact, most cars can be swept away in 18 to 24 inches of moving water.** Trucks and SUVs are not much better with only an additional six to twelve inches of clearance. In moving water, all that is needed is for a vehicle to become buoyant *enough* to allow the water's force to push it sideways, even while the wheels remain in contact with the pavement. Once swept downstream, a vehicle will often roll to one side or perhaps flip over entirely. The driver then has only a few seconds to escape. Many drivers panic as soon as the vehicle submerges and are found later with their seat belt intact.

The solution is simple. **TURN AROUND, DON'T DROWN**™. Stay out of the flooded roadway. The water may be much deeper than it appears as the road beds may be washed out. Also, respect "road Closed" barriers posted to warn you of the danger. Keep these following safety rules in mind when driving in severe weather:

- Avoid flooded areas or those with rapid water flow. Do NOT attempt to cross a flowing stream. **As little as six to twelve inches of water may cause you to lose control of your vehicle and *two feet of water will carry most cars away*.**

- In your vehicle look out for flooding at highway dips, low spots and around bridges.

- Flooded roads could have significant damage hidden by the water. NEVER drive through floodwaters or on flooded roads. If your vehicle stalls, leave it immediately and seek higher ground.

- Do not camp or park your vehicle along streams and washes, particularly when threatening weather conditions exist.

- Be especially cautious at night when it is harder to recognize flood dangers.

More information on flood safety is available through the National Weather Service at www.noaa.gov/floods.htm.

Severe Thunderstorms - listen to your car radio and be alert. If you spot a tornado, DON'T try to outrun it. Get out of the car, find shelter in a ditch or low-lying area and lie face down to protect yourself from flying debris.

Wind - Strong winds, especially crosswinds, can make it more difficult for you to control your vehicle. Wind is very dangerous if you are driving a camper or large recreational vehicle, or it you are towing a trailer. Lightweight vehicles are also more difficult to control in strong winds.

- To gain more control over vehicles in a strong wind, slow down.

- If you are approaching an open space after driving in a protected area, be alert for crosswinds that will push you to the side or middle of the roadway.

- If you are pulling a trailer, the wind may cause your vehicle to sway. Be ready to make necessary steering corrections.

- When you meet large trucks or buses, you may also have to make steering corrections because of the gusts of wind these vehicles create. When a truck or bus is passing you on the left, move as far as possible to the right of your lane and slow down. If you are pulling a trailer, wind currents from these larger vehicles can cause your vehicle to jackknife. As the large vehicle passes, accelerate slowly to keep your trailer pulling in a straight path.

- If you are driving into a strong head wind (wind blowing toward your vehicle), you may need to accelerate more, and steering will be more difficult.

- A strong tailwind (wind blowing from behind your vehicle) will increase your speed, so you will have to decelerate and begin braking earlier to stop.

Sun Glare - Bright sunlight in the early morning or late afternoon creates a glare when driving into the sun. Wearing sunglasses, keeping windows clean and using the vehicle's sun visors, can reduce glare. If the sun is behind you, oncoming drivers may have the glare problem. Be aware that they may not be able to see your turn signals or your car.

NIGHT DRIVING

Night driving presents a serious danger, especially on poorly lighted highways and country roads. The distance that you can see clearly is greatly reduced. Dark colored animals, dark vehicles or objects on the roadside, or people walking or riding bikes and dressed in dark clothing will be harder to see.

The chances of a serious crash are much greater at night, even though traffic is not as heavy as during the day. Drivers who do not adjust to light conditions are part of the night safety problem.

- **Three to four times more deaths occur while driving at night, than driving during the day.**

- **90% of a driver's reaction time depends on vision. Depth perception, color recognition, and peripheral vision are impaired after dark.**

- **More fatal crashes take place on Friday and Saturday nights than on any other day of the week. In addition to the darkness, alcohol plays a part in more than half of all these deaths.**

DRIVE SLOWER AT NIGHT

The basic rule for safe night driving is this: ***NEVER OUTRUN YOUR HEADLIGHTS***. Your stopping distance 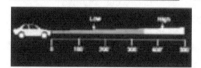 should always be less than your sight distance. You should reduce you speed at night and adjust to the road and weather conditions. Adjust your speed so you can stop within the distance you can see. You should consider how powerful your lights are and how responsive your brakes are. As soon as you see pedestrians, animals, or objects on the road in front of you, you must be able to stop before you hit them. If you are overdriving your lights, you will not be able to stop in time.

The law requires headlights that will enable you to see

clearly any person on the highway at least two hundred (200) feet ahead of your car. Since the effectiveness of headlights diminishes greatly as the distance increases, headlights must be in good order to meet this requirement. They must also be accurately aimed, with clean lenses and a clean windshield inside and out.

Driving at night is considerably more hazardous and difficult than daytime driving. Remember that your range of visibility is limited by your headlights. It is doubtful that you can identify the position, distance and nature of an object within the few seconds it takes for your vehicle to travel several hundred feet. To cope with oncoming traffic during the hours of darkness you should:

- Develop the ability to glance well in front of your headlight beams, looking for dark shapes on the roadway.

- Glance periodically to the right and left to determine the location of the edge of the pavement and oncoming vehicles

- Avoid looking directly into oncoming headlights as this can cause momentary blindness from the glare.

- When an oncoming vehicle does not dim its lights, avoid the glare by watching the right edge of the road and using the white line or road edge as a steering guide.

- Avoid flashing your high beams to warn the other driver as it might serve as a distraction and interfere with their driving resulting in a collision.

- ***Don't wear sunglasses or colored glasses when driving at night or on dark days***. Colored lenses cause your eyes to adjust even more slowly and can reduce you vision.

Glare and Glare Recovery

The glare from the headlights of oncoming vehicles causes the pupil of the eye to contract. After the vehicle has passed it takes an interval of time for the pupil to readjust to the less intense light. This is called glare recovery time. During this recovery period you are virtually driving blind. Glare recovery  time is not based on visual acuity and varies from person to person. The problem is generally more acute in older drivers and those in poor physical condition.

Prepare to Fight Glare: Even before you hit the road, prepare yourself and your vehicle for combating the bright lights ahead. Clean your headlights and keep all glass clean and clear. Scratched eyeglasses or contact lenses also make glare worse. For maximum glare prevention, keep every surface between your eyes and the road as clear as possible – including both sides of your windshield and your eyeglasses.

Remember to drive safely and defensively you must adhere to the proper requirements of dimming you lights at night when:
- Meeting or overtaking vehicles within 500 feet.
- Driving in cities and towns always use your low beams
- On curves or turns to the right avoid "blasting" and oncoming car with your high beams.

Clean the windows (inside and out) at least once a month to get rid of haze – more often if you or others smoke in the car.

Remember that even moderate drinking may reduce a driver's vision as well as reaction time. Both prescription medicines and nonprescription medicines may affect driving, read label warnings carefully.

Aim Your Headlights Correctly:

Your properly aligned headlights will help you see the road better, and will help other drivers to avoid glare.

Lights that shine up or out excessively do NOT help you see objects in the roadway. They do however contribute to glare and blinding the vision of drivers in vehicles you are meeting or following.

Check you vehicle owner's manual on how to align the lights for your car or have them aligned by a mechanic at a reputable garage or car dealership.

Parking At Night

When parking at night, never leave your headlights on, even if you plan on to be parked for a brief period of time. They are just as likely to blind approaching drivers when your car is stationary as they are when it is moving. They may also confuse approaching drivers as to the exact position of the road. The danger is increased if you are parked on the wrong side of the roadway. Whenever you park on or along a highway at night, leave your emergency and parking lights on.

COLLISIONS WITH ANIMALS

While animal-vehicle collisions can happen any time of the year and with any type of animal (opossum, rabbit, squirrel, dogs, etc.). Fall is the peak season for deer-car accidents. That's mainly because autumn is both mating season and hunting season, so deer are more active and more likely to roam beyond their normal territory.

Many of these collisions happen at night but they can occur any time of day. Collisions with deer are generally the most dangerous and costly accidents involving animals. No foolproof way has been found to keep deer or other wild animals off highways and away from vehicles.

You can avoid an unplanned meeting with a deer or other

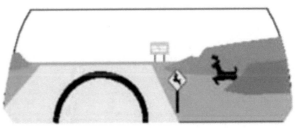

type animal if you:
- Are aware of your surroundings. Pay attention to "deer crossing" signs. Look well down the road and far off to each side. At night, use your high-beam lights if possible to illuminate the road's edges. Be especially watchful in areas near woods and water. If you see one deer, there may be several others nearby.

- Be particularly alert at dusk and dawn, when these animals venture out to feed. Scan the sides of the road to watch for the reflection of your vehicle headlights in the eyes of deer.

- If you see a deer, or other animal on or near the roadway and think you have time to avoid hitting it, reduce your speed, tap your brakes to warn other drives, and sound your horn. Deer tend to fixate on headlights, so flashing them may cause the animal to freeze in the road. If there's no vehicle close behind you, brake hard but don't lock wheels causing a skid.

- If a collision seems inevitable, don't swerve to avoid the animal; your risk of personal injury may be greater if you do. Keep your vehicle under control and on the roadway when you hit the animal.

- Report the accident to the police if it involves a large animal such as a deer or farm animal. If the animal is a domestic pet and homes are nearby you should try to notify the pet's owner if possible.

- Always obey the speed limit and wear your safety belt.

DEFENSIVE DRIVING & OTHER PRECAUTIONS

The purpose of this chapter is to provide you with a discussion of the principles of Defensive Driving, and advice on safety precautions to help you avoid being a Distracted Driver and other precautions that will help you deal with potential life threatening situations including "Road Rage".

DEFENSIVE DRIVING

If every driver always obeyed the rules, and always behaved in a sensible way, driving would be simpler and safer. Unfortunately, this ideal situation does not exist. Instead we frequently encounter drivers who behave unpredictably or recklessly, and other highway users, such as pedestrians and bicyclists, who ignore the rules that apply to them.

> *"Defensive Driving" means being constantly aware of the driving conditions, planning ahead, anticipating dangers and taking the right action so as not to come in contact with any obstacle or other vehicle.*

To protect yourself, you must learn to drive defensively. This means anticipating errors by others and preparing to compensate for their mistakes. In addition, you must always behave in a correct and sensible fashion yourself so that you do not confuse other drivers.

All of us want to avoid collisions that result in personal injury or even death. But, even when there is no personal injury, a collision means inconvenience and auto repair costs. It may also result in a court appearance and fines, as well as increased insurance rates. You have a great financial stake in your own good driving record. *Driving defensively will help protect your life and your driving record*.

> **Courtesy and consideration toward others are the most important driving attitudes you can develop. *They are the key to safe driving*.**

Concentration and Alertness Are Important Elements

Concentration is one of the most important elements of safe and defensive driving. You must develop the habit of keeping your mind on driving. The driver's seat is no place for daydreaming, site-seeing or distracting conversations.

Drive Alert — The defensive driving rules are simple and easy to follow. If you follow them, you should be able to avoid getting yourself into difficult situations. The rules are:

- Use your rearview mirrors. Constantly check the traffic behind you. Always check mirrors before changing lanes.
- Stay out of another driver's blind spot(s). Do not travel in a position where the driver ahead of you cannot observe your vehicle in his mirrors; he might pull out in front of you to pass a car.
- Expect the other driver to do the WRONG thing, and have a plan of action prepared to counter his error.

Drive Cautiously

Remember to always use the two-second rule. Periodically test your following distance by picking out a stationary object on the roadway ahead and doing the "1,001, 1,002" count. Remember if you reach that point before counting to 1,002 you are following too closely. If this is the case, slow down in order to lengthen your following distance. Remember on high-speed interstates, when following large commercial trucks or buses and in inclement weather or limited visibility conditions it is safest to increase this following distance to at least 3 to 4 seconds.

Foresight

In driving terms, foresight means being able to size up traffic situations as quickly as possible and being prepared to take corrective action. Safe driving requires exercising good judgment and recognizing the proper choices to make in any given traffic situation.

- Suppose you are driving down a steep hill; you apply your brake, but your vehicle does not decrease in speed.

    Should you pump the brake? – or – Shift to a lower gear?
    Apply the emergency brake? – or – Run into something?

- Perhaps you see a driver traveling in the wrong direction on a one-way street you are driving on.

    Should you honk the horn? – or – Stop?
    Flash your lights? – or – Move to another lane?

Any of these choices could be the right thing to do. It all depends on how you evaluate your driving situation and the existing conditions. Information in this chapter of the manual will give you tips on safe ways to evaluate and respond to these and similar roadway situations

> *As a driver you will be constantly making decisions every mile you drive. There is a right way to make these decisions. It is known as defensive driving.*

Driving Space or "Safety Cushion"

Sharing Space – You must always share the road with others. The more distance you keep between yourself and everyone else, the more time you have to react. This space is like a "safety cushion". The more you have, the safer you will be. This section describes how to make sure you have enough space around you when you drive.

Try to maintain a safety cushion to the front, rear and each side of your vehicle at all times in order to provide and area of escape or prevention should an emergency occur.

Always drive in such a manner that you are able to control the space (safety cushion or zone) between your vehicle and others. At times this may mean slowing or increasing your speed (within lawful limits only).

1. SPACE AHEAD: Rear-end crashes are very common. Rear-end crashes are caused by drivers following too closely (tailgating) to be able to stop before hitting the vehicle ahead when it suddenly slows or stops. The best way to maintain this safety cushion is to follow the basic 2-Second Rule. Also leave extra space when approaching railroad crossings or when stopped behind another vehicle on a hill or curve.

2. SPACE BEHIND: It is not always easy to manage the space behind your vehicle. However, you can help keep a driver behind you at a safe distance by keeping a steady speed and using turn signals in advance when you have to slow down or turn. Every now and then you may find yourself being followed too closely or being "tailgated" by another driver. If there is a right lane, move over to the right. If there is no right lane, wait until the road ahead is clear and passing is legal, then slowly reduce your speed. This will encourage the tailgater to drive around you. Never slow down quickly to discourage a tailgater. All that does is increase your risk of being hit from behind.

3. SPACE TO BOTH SIDES: You need space on both sides of your vehicle to have room to turn or change lanes. Avoid driving in blind spots of other vehicles. When meeting oncoming vehicles on a two-lane road stay slightly to the right of your lane so as not to "crowd" the centerline. Be courteous and move to the left lane on multi-lane roads when other vehicles are trying to merge into traffic. Keep extra space between your vehicle and parked cars, pedestrians and bicyclists (especially children) on the roadside. Two key rules about space to the side includes:

- "*Split the difference*" – between two hazards. For example, steer a middle course between oncoming traffic and parked vehicles. However, if one is more dangerous than the other, leave a little more space on the most dangerous side. If the oncoming vehicle is a semi-truck, leave a more room on the side that the truck will pass on instead of the side with the parked cars.
- "*Take potential hazards one at a time*." For example, if you are overtaking a bicyclist and an oncoming vehicle is approaching, slow down, let the vehicle pass first so that you can then safely move to the left to give room to the bicycle.

MERGING DEFENSIVELY: A minimum four-second gap is needed whenever you change lanes, enter a roadway or when your lane merges with another traffic lane. If you need to cross several lanes, *take them one at a time*. **NEVER cut across multiple lanes**, it can tie up traffic and even cause you to have a collision or create a crash between other vehicles trying to avoid your sudden and unsafe maneuver.

HANDLING INTERSECTIONS DEFENSIVELY: When you cross traffic, you need a large enough gap to get all the way across the road. **DO NOT BLOCK INTERSECTIONS** or get caught with a portion of your vehicle left in a traffic lane with approaching vehicles. Make sure you can safely complete the cross or entering maneuver before you begin.

PASSING DEFENSIVELY: Whenever signs or road markings permit you to pass, you will have to judge whether you have enough room to safely pass. Do NOT count on having enough time to pass several vehicles at once. Be safe. As a general rule pass only one vehicle at a time. Remember passing does NOT entitle you to exceed the speed limit. At 55 M.P.H. you will need about ten (10) seconds to complete the pass of a single vehicle. That means you need a ten-second gap in oncoming traffic and sight distance to pass. You must judge whether you will have enough space to safely pass.

- **Safely Finishing the Pass**: Do NOT pass unless you have enough space to return to the driving lane. Do NOT count on other drivers to make room for you. You will need enough room between your vehicle and the other vehicle ("space behind") to safely return to the driving lane. It's safest not to return to the driving lane until you can see both headlights of the vehicle you just passed in the rearview mirror.

ALLOW SPACE FOR DANGEROUS SITUATIONS OR PROBLEM DRIVERS YOU MAY ENCOUNTER

- *People who cannot see you*: Anyone who cannot see you may enter your path without knowing you are there. Such as:
  - Drivers at intersections or driveways where their view is blocked by buildings, trees or other vehicles.
  - Pedestrians with umbrellas in front of their faces or with their hats pulled down
  - Blind pedestrians with white cane or guide dogs.
- *People who may be distracted*: Even when others can see you, allow extra room if you think they may be distracted such as:
  - Delivery persons
  - Drivers who are not paying attention to their driving (talking on cell phones, looking at maps, arguing with passengers or trying to take care of children in the car).
- *People who may be confused*: People who are confused may cause an unsafe situation such as:
  - Tourists or persons driving cars with out-of-state license plates (especially at complicated intersections).
  - Drivers looking for street signs or house numbers..
- Drivers in trouble: If another driver makes a mistake (a driver who passes you when they do not have enough room, for example), do NOT make it worse. Slow down and let them safely return to the driving lane. Other situations include:
  - If another driver needs to suddenly change lanes, slow down and let them merge.
  - A driver who is about to be forced into your lane by another merging vehicle, lane closed due to construction, bicyclists, pedestrians or children on the roadside, etc.

These gestures will keep traffic moving smoothly and safely.

Scanning the Road and Traffic for Defensive Reactions

Most of what you do as a defensive driver is in response to what you SEE while driving. When driving, we gather 90% of the information about the road and our surroundings through our eyes. Scanning means looking at the entire scene for anything that might come into your path. As you scan the road, avoid a fixed stare. Keep your eyes moving and learn to read the road. Look ahead, to the sides and behind you.

Scan Ahead – looking ahead will help you see things early and will allow you more time to react. Defensive drivers try to focus their eyes 10 to 15 seconds (about the distance of 1 city block) ahead.

Scan to the Sides – Scan from side to side, checking for directional signs, cars or people that might be in the road by the time you reach them.

Watch for Clues – Look for exhaust smoke, brake or back-up lights and turned wheels on vehicles. Clues like these indicate that the vehicles may pull into your path.

Be Careful in Rural Areas – Watch for hidden intersections and driveways, curves, hills and different road conditions (pavement changing to gravel or dirt road, narrowing road, etc.).

Check Left to Right Before Entering an Intersection – At any intersection, look to the left first, since cars coming from the left will be closer to you. Then look to the right and take one more quick look to the left before you drive through.

Look Behind – Use your rearview mirror to check the traffic behind you frequently, about every 10 seconds. This will alert you if someone is moving up too quickly or tailgating you. Be sure to check the traffic behind you when changing lanes, backing up, slowing down quickly or driving down a long steep hill. But don't keep you eyes off the road ahead for more than a brief look behind.

By knowing the speed and position of traffic on all four sides of your vehicle, you will be better able to make decisions quickly and safely in most situations.

Communicating with other Drivers

Communicating means clearly showing other drivers and pedestrians what you plan to do early enough to avoid a collision. Any time you plan to change directions, use your turn signals – whether you are changing lanes, turning at an intersection, entering an interstate, pulling away from a curb or pulling off to the side of the road. Develop the habit of using your turn signals even when you do not see other vehicles on the road.

Adjusting Speed to Conditions

Slow Speed / Impeding the Traffic Flow – No driver shall drive at such a slow speed as to hold back or block the normal and reasonable flow of traffic.

Speed Control Benefits Everyone – As your speed increases, so does your car's wind resistance, a big factor in gasoline mileage. Most automobiles get about 28% more miles per gallon on the highway at 50 M.P.H. than at 70 and about 21% more at 55 M.P.H. than at 70.

Driving at moderate speeds also:
- Provides you with better stopping and evasive control in emergency situations
- Helps you to maintain the "safety cushion" around your vehicle.

- Reduces the risk of death or serious injury to victims in the event of a crash or other accident.
- Helps to maintain a safer traffic flow, discouraging others from zipping in and out of lanes recklessly.
- Is a key factor in driving safely and defensively.

Compromise

Another important defensive driving skill is compromise. When you cannot separate risks, and you must deal with two or more at the same time, compromise by giving the most room to either the greatest or most likely danger. For example, suppose you are driving on a two-lane roadway with oncoming cars to your left and a child riding a bike to your right. The child is the most likely to move suddenly, so you need a larger space cushion to the right. In this case, moving closer to the centerline is the correct or best compromise.

Knowledge and Experience

Becoming a good defensive driver requires knowledge and experience. The beginning driver should learn through instruction, observation and practice. After you obtain your learner permit, practice starting, stopping and vehicle control in a parking lot or other open area with little traffic. Practice will sharpen your basic skills, as well as build your confidence.

Your knowledge should include recognition of the hazards of driving and how to protect yourself. Skill is more than eye/hand/foot coordination. It is a well-rehearsed driving strategy, which involves anticipation, reaction and the constant changing of the space between your vehicle and other vehicles. You must continually strive for improvement. Improvement can be measured in your elimination of risk-taking, your adherence to speed limits and your ability to take corrective action when necessary.

AVOID BEING A DISTRACTED DRIVER

Distracted Driving Contributes to Many Accidents

Lack of concentration can result in a driver's failure to be observant enough to avoid an accident. Driving an automobile is a full-time job. There have been too many accidents after which the drive said (IF he survived), "I don't know what happened".

Not everything in life is under your control. But driving is! When you're behind the wheel, **YOU control your fate. That's why when you're driving, your one and only focus should be ON DRIVING.**

Did you know that:
- Traffic crashes are often caused by the **WAY** we drive?
- 85% of all reported motor vehicle crashes are caused by **DRIVER MISTAKES**?
- 25% of these police-reported crashes involve some form of **DRIVER INATTENTION**.
- NHTSA reports indicates that inattention caused 68% of rear-end crashes?
- Driver distractions or inattentive driving play a part in one out of every four motor vehicle crashes? That's more than 1.5 MILLION collisions a year – more than 4,300 crashes

each day! This information means that most of these crashes could be totally avoidable.

NOVICE TEEN DRIVERS AT HIGHER RISK: Car crashes are the number one killer of teenagers in America - more than 5,000 teens die each year. Inexperience, risk-taking and driver distractions are some reasons why. Loud music, changing discs and tapes as well as tuning the radio are also potentially deadly distractions when behind the wheel. And  when a teen driver has friends in the car, the risk is even higher - the more passengers, the greater the chance of a serious crash. Here are common teen driver distractions that can be deadly:

- *Friends in other vehicles*: Don't let saying "hi" or other fun and games take your attention off the road. Never try to pass items from one moving vehicle to another.
- *Loud music or headphones*: Hearing what's going on around you is just as important as seeing. It is extremely dangerous to wear headphones or have the volume of your radio so high that it interferes with your "hearing" of traffic conditions, such as other vehicle's warning horns or emergency sirens. In most states it is illegal to wear headphones while driving. _
- *The "show-off" factor*: It may be tempting to go faster, turn sharper or beat another car through an intersection. Many teens fail to realize that they are no longer just "competing for fun" and are now using a 5,000 pound "weapon" in this competition. ***Keep focused on staying safe and staying alive***.

Distraction = More Than Hands and Eyes

Driver distractions are nothing new. They've been a topic of discussion since windshield wipers were introduced in cars during the early 1900s.

What is a distraction? Obviously, drivers are distracted when they take their hands off the wheel or their eyes off the road. Equally troubling, they're also distracted when they take their minds off driving - when they're thinking about things other than the road in front of them and the vehicles around them.

THREE TYPES OF DISTRACTIONS:

1. PHYSICAL – Distractions that cause the driver to take his or her hands off the wheel or their eyes off the road (adjusting the radio, heater or dialing a cell phone).

2. INTELLECTUAL – Activities that take the driver's mind off the road. Such as having an in-depth conversation, mentally preparing for a school test / job project, or thinking about a recent argument with a co-worker or family member.

3. COMBINATION – Some activities take you hands, eyes and mind off the task at hand. An example is reading a map while driving or checking your day planner.

Of course, you have to occasionally glance at your speedometer, fuel and other gauges. But actions like those in the following list can lead to big trouble while you're driving.

Among the most common driving distractions are:
- Adjusting the radio, CD player or climate controls
- Conversing with occupants or tending to kids in the vehicle
- Moving objects in the vehicle (pets, insect, loose items, etc.)
- Using / dialing a wireless phone
- Eating, drinking or smoking while driving
- Personal grooming (make-up, shaving, etc.) behind the wheel
- Attempting to retrieve items from purse, wallet or backseat
- Outside distractions, including:
  o Accidents or other vehicles stopped by police
  o Friends in other vehicles
  o Roadside advertising / New construction (shops, houses, etc.)

How does distraction affect driving performance?

Distraction occurs when a driver is delayed in the recognition of information needed to safely accomplish the driving task, because something within or outside the vehicle draws his attention away from driving. Drivers inadvertently sometimes focus their attention away from the roadway and driving task, thus putting themselves and their families/passengers and other motorists in jeopardy. Additional factors, such as fatigue, weather and traffic conditions, can increase the negative impact of distractions on driving ability.

Safety experts estimate that a driver makes nearly 200 decisions for every mile of driving. If you are mentally solving business, school or family problems while driving, you are adding to the total cognitive workload. Think about it; let's say you're going 60 miles per hour. If you look down for just two seconds to choose a CD or adjust the climate controls, you'll have traveled 176 feet blindly. That's more than _ the length of a football field.

DEVOTE YOUR COMPLETE AND UNDIVIDED ATTENTION TO DRIVING.

Don't get distracted. **Driving is a full time job requiring YOUR full time attention**. When you're behind the wheel, your responsibility is safety:
- To yourself
- To your passengers
- To motorists and others around you

ARE YOU A DISTRACTED DRIVER?

Ask yourself: When driving, do I ever?
- Tune the radio
- Eat, drink or smoke
- Pick something up from the floor or between the seats
- Reach for the glove compartment
- Talk on the cell phone
- Clean the inside of the windshield
- Argue with another passenger

- Comb or brush my hair
- Put on makeup
- Shave or "tie" my necktie
- Daydream or "site see"
- Read a paper, map, book – or – try to write or jot down notes.

If you answered yes to any of the above, you are driving while distracted and are at risk of an accident. Still not sure that you have been guilty of distracted driving? How many of the following things have ever happened to you?
- A passenger in your car screamed or gasped because of something you did or did not do?
- You ran a stop sign or traffic light unintentionally?
- You swerved suddenly to avoid an animal, a car or another highway hazard?
- You slammed on your brakes because you didn't see the car in front of you slowing down or stopping?
- You didn't remember driving from one place to another?
- You drifted in your lane or into another lane of traffic?

These events are clues or signals that you are distracted while driving.

Grooming on the Go is a BIG NO: It is very dangerous to remove a coat or change other articles of clothing while driving. Other activities such as applying makeup, shaving or fixing one's hair while driving are also dangerous. These types of activities can place you in serious danger of a crash.

Eating and Driving Don't Mix: It is not only unsafe, it's messy, and fumbling with napkins, condiments, and beverages means you're not watching the road. Your reaction time is slowed if an emergency arises while you have one hand on the wheel and your other hand around a soft drink you are worried about spilling.

Children, Pets and Passengers: It's hard enough concentrating on the road without the distraction of children, pets and passengers, and adding in just one of those factors can make driving dangerous. Use a pet carrier to limit a pet's ability to roam. Be sure children are safely buckled up, and give them books, games or other items to occupy their time. Teach children the importance of good behavior while in a vehicle.

No matter what the source, drivers who are distracted exhibit the same basic type of behavior. Distractions cause drivers to react more slowly to traffic conditions or events, such as a car stopping to make a left turn or pulling out from a side road. Drivers fail more often to recognize potential hazards such as pedestrians, bicycles or debris in the road. They also decrease their margin of safety, leading them to take risks they might not otherwise take, such as turning left in front of oncoming traffic.

To avoid falling habit to these distractions you must stay focused and pay full attention to the driving task.
- Pre-program radio stations for easy access
- Keep the stereo volume low enough to "hear" traffic
- Limit interaction with passengers and avoid arguments
- Avoid taking your eyes off the road and traffic
- Keep both hands on the wheel

- Plan you trips to allow for rest and meal breaks
- Avoid driver fatigue and don't drive when tired

It's worth repeating that *driving is a full time job*! It requires you full, undivided attention. When you're behind the wheel, your number one responsibility is driving. PERIOD.

FASCINATING FACTS: Fully 62 percent of the crashes involving driver distraction occurred in rural areas.
- RURAL AREA top distractions were driver fatigue, insects, animals, and unrestrained pets.
- URBAN AREA top distractions were rubbernecking, traffic, other vehicles, and cell phones.

Pay attention out there!
Stay focused on the driving. Don't be driven to distraction

The list of driver distractions that contributes to crashes and injuries is long.. The Foundation for Traffic Safety at the American Automobile Association (AAA) videotaped volunteer drivers who didn't know they were being tested for distracted driving. It found that:
- 92%of the drivers fiddled with radios or CD players
- 71% percent ate or drank
- 46 % were involved in personal grooming
- 40% read or even wrote while driving
- Only about one-third used cell phones.

BE SMART WHEN USING CELLULAR PHONES IN CARS

Cellular telephones are everywhere. In an emergency, they can be a lifesaver. In non-emergency situations, they can be a great tool; IF you use the cellular telephone in a safe and responsible manner. However, driving while talking on the telephone can be dangerous to you and other motorists. Cell phones can be a serious source of driver inattention.

Tennessee does not currently have any laws prohibiting the use of cell phones while driving. The Department of Safety and AAA recommends drivers not use their cell phones while driving. However, if using a phone is essential, drivers should follow these safety tips
- Pull over to the side of the road to use your cellular telephone. This is the safest precaution you can take.
- Know your cellular telephone. Get to know your phone and its many features such as speed dial and redial. Take advantage of these features so you won't take your attention off the road.
- Use hands free devices. If available, use a hands free device. *Two hands on the steering wheel is always safer than one*. Using a wireless phone while driving increases your chance of getting into an accident by 400 percent! When you're searching for a number, dialing or talking, you're not watching the road like you should. "Hands-free"

phone features help, but they can't prevent you from becoming involved in a conversation and losing concentration

- Your phone should be within easy reach; this way you can grab it without taking your eyes off the road.
- Don't use the telephone during hazardous conditions. If your driving conditions include heavy traffic or severe weather tell the person that you are driving and will call back. **Remember, your first responsibility is to pay attention to the road**.
- While you are driving, don't take notes or look up phone numbers.
- Be sensible about dialing. If possible, place your calls when you are not moving or before pulling into traffic. However, if you need to dial while driving, dial only a few numbers at a time, check traffic, your mirrors and then continue dialing.
- Don't engage in distracting conversations. *Stressful or emotional conversations don't mix with safe driving*. **This combination can be dangerous because you are not paying attention to your driving**. Tell the person you are talking to you'll call back. Be safe!
- Use your phone to call for help. Dial 9-1-1 for emergency help. This is a free call on your cellular phone. For other non-emergency situations (broken-down vehicle, broken traffic signal, etc.), call roadside assistance or special non-emergency wireless numbers.

NOTE! Research shows that the real distraction is mental because you're talking to someone else outside of your car. Holding the phone and dialing it is just a small part of phone distractions. It is recommended that you do NOT use the phone at all while driving. If you still want to drive and talk on the phone, please try to reduce distractions with tips above. Remember...talking on your phone while driving is not worth killing someone and living with that guilt the rest of your life.

DROWSY DRIVING DANGERS

Sleepiness while driving has become a serious problem and a major traffic hazard. Fatigue and sleepiness seriously impairs driver performance, creating a life threatening combination.

The Facts: According to the National Highway Traffic Safety Administration (NHTSA) every year, falling asleep while driving is responsible for at least 100,000 automobile crashes, 40,000 injuries, and 1,550 fatalities. These crashes most often occur during late night / early morning hours (midnight to six A.M), involve a single vehicle and a sober driver traveling alone, with the car leaving the roadway without any attempt to avoid the crash. Most often these crashes occur on high-speed  roadways. **Drowsy Driving is a problem most people don't stop to think about**.

Fatigue may account for the fact that there are more collisions during evening rush hour traffic than during the comparable morning traffic rush. Drivers going home from work are tired, less alert and slower to react than during the morning rush. Fatigue also can cause a driver to lose his or her temper or make a rash decision.

When most people think about someone being unfit to drive, they usually think of someone drunk or physically unable to drive. In fact, most people are at some time unfit to drive because they are too tired and not alert to changing road and traffic conditions.

Causes of Drowsy Driving

- Sleep loss
- Driving patterns. For example, driving between midnight and six A.M. every night.
- Use of sedating medications.
- Untreated or unrecognized sleeping disorders.
- Use of alcohol.

High-Risk Populations for Drowsy Driving

- Young people between the ages of 16 - 29, especially males.
- Shift workers whose sleep is disrupted by working nights or working long, irregular hours.
- People with untreated sleep apnea and narcolepsy.

Drowsy driving is more common than you think. About one-half of all American adult drivers - approximately 100 million people - admit to driving drowsy in the past year; two in ten say they actually fell asleep behind the wheel. Drowsy driving is more prevalent among males (56% males vs. 45% females), especially young males (16-29 years old).

How to Prevent Drowsy Driving

- Plan ahead to get sufficient sleep before hitting the road. The average person requires about 8 hours of sleep a night.
- Avoid alcohol and medications (over-the-counter and prescribed) that may impair performance. Alcohol interacts with fatigue, increasing its effects - much like drinking on an empty stomach.
- Limit driving between midnight and six A.M.
- If driving on a long trip, schedule regular stops, say every 100 miles or two hours.
- Plan to drive long trips with a companion. Passengers can help look for early warning signs of fatigue or switch drivers when needed.
- Passengers should stay awake to talk to the driver. As soon as a driver becomes sleepy, he or she should stop driving and either let a licensed passenger drive or stop for some sleep before continuing.
- Drink coffee or another source of caffeine. Caffeine can promote *short-term alertness*, but it takes about 30 minutes for it to enter the bloodstream. Blasting a radio, opening a window, or similar "tricks" to stay awake **DO NOT** work.

Having trouble staying awake? Should you take a break?

1. Have you suddenly realized you're tailgating, or drifted from your lane, or onto the shoulder of the roadway?
2. Are you driving on the white lines or have you driven over roadside *rumble strips?
3. Have you had trouble remembering the last few miles driven; missing exits or traffic signs.
4. Are your eyes closing or going out of focus?
5. Have you been yawning, blinking frequently, or head nodding?
6. Are your eyes starting to burn?
7. Have you been shaking your head to stay awake?
8. Did you roll down your window for some fresh air?
9. Do you need caffeine or chocolate to help you stay alert?
10. Are you not able to remember the last warning sign you passed?

If you answer YES to three or more of these questions, you should take a break from your driving. If you are not stopping for the night, find a safe, well-lit area and take a 15-20 minute nap.

---

*What are Rumble Strips?

Rumble Strips are raised or grooved patterns on the road shoulder that provide both and audible warning and physical vibration to alert drivers that they have wandered off the roadway.

Tennessee has been installing rumble strips on all interstate resurfacing projects since 1996. Recent nationwide statistics from the Federal Highway Administration indicate run-off-the-road fatalities comprise almost 1/3 of all fatalities.

Remember that wearing your safety belt is the best way to protect yourself in the event of a crash caused by drowsy driving.

SPECIAL WARNINGS DRIVES SHOULD BE AWARE OF:

Avoid Carbon Monoxide Poisoning

Beware of carbon monoxide poisoning. Vehicle motors give off carbon monoxide which is a deadly gas. You can't see, smell, or taste it, but carbon monoxide gas from your engine can kill you! Carbon monoxide is most likely to leak into your car when the heater is running, when your exhaust system is not working properly, or when you're in heavy traffic and breathing exhaust fumes from other cars. A faulty exhaust system can leak poisonous fumes into the back seat area where children may be sitting or sleeping.

Symptoms of carbon monoxide poisoning:
- You feel drowsy and/or dizzy.

- Skin has a blue color; lips turn blue.
- Lights seem brighter.
- Your forehead tightens.

Pull off the road, park, and turn off the motor. Open your windows. Relax or get out and walk around until you feel better. A child or passenger overcome with carbon monoxide may require artificial respiration or medical attention.

How to avoid carbon monoxide poisoning:
- Have your exhaust system checked regularly by a mechanic
- Be alert for any unusual roar from under the car.
- Do not drive with a defective muffler or exhaust system.
- Never let the engine run in a closed garage.
- Do not leave the motor running and windows closed when you are parked.
- Do not use the heater or air conditioner in a parked vehicle with the windows closed.
- In congested traffic, close the fresh-air vent.
- On the highways in cold weather, open the fresh-air vent.

Warning! When It's Hot Outside, Do Not Leave Children Unattended in a Vehicle.

On a hot summer day, the interior of a car can get dangerously hot. One study found that with the windows up and the temperature outside at 94 degrees, the inside of a car could be 122 degrees in just half and hour, or 132 degrees after a single hour.

An adult or child can develop potentially fatal heat-related health problems inside a parked vehicle when outside temperatures reach 85 degrees. Toddlers and infants are at particular risk because their bodies sweat less, and because unlike most adults, they are unable to get out of a vehicle when they begin to overheat.

Prevent a needless tragedy, and make sure no one leaves small children in a hot vehicle unattended.

Don't forget about family pets. Leaving a family pet in a vehicle during hot weather can also be deadly for the animal.

Be Cautious with Vehicles Equipped with Ignition-Starter Interlock System

Today's vehicles are equipped with ignition interlock systems, that, when used properly, will prevent the theft of an automobile and vehicle rollaway. The U.S. Department of Transportation has passed standards for these systems.

USDOT amended the standard for motor vehicle theft protection and vehicle rollaway, specifically those driving vehicles with automatic transmissions. This rule provided for greater flexibility in designing key-locking and transmission shift locking systems. It permits key removal only when the vehicle's transmission is in "Park" position.

Drivers in an emergency situation on the highway may attempt to turn off the vehicle while it is still in motion, believing they will bring the vehicle to a stop. The basic rule the driver must follow when operating a vehicle with a steering wheel interlock system is: ***never turn the ignition to***

There are various types of Steering Lock Operation:

- **The Transmission Park System**: Park. Shift the transmission into the park position. Turn key to LOCK and remove.
- **The Two-Hand Button System**: Park. This system requires two hands. Depress the button below the steering column. Turn key to LOCK and remove.
- **The Lever System**: Park. Depress the lever located near the ignition. Turn key to LOCK and remove.
- **The One-Hand Button System**: Park. Depress button located near the ignition. Turn key to LOCK and remove.
- **The Push-In System**: Park. Turn key to OFF, push in. Turn key to LOCK and remove.
- **The Turn and Remove System**: Park. Turn key to LOCK and remove.

© 1992 Automobile Safety Foundation

the lock position while the vehicle is in motion. **Your steering wheel will lock as you try to turn the wheel, and you'll lose control of the vehicle.**

AGGRESSIVE DRIVING OR "ROAD RAGE"

Once you get behind the wheel, you have a personal - and legal - responsibility to yourself, your family and friends, and to the other people on the roads to keep a "right attitude" for driving. The RIGHT ATTITUDE can help you, and others, stay safe and alive. Whether you're in a metropolitan area rush hour or driving a deserted rural highway, you should maintain safety consciousness, a cooperative attitude, and a "readiness to respond" to an emergency.

Right Attitudes for the Road -
Alertness, Sharing, Giving, Self-Control

- Give your driving your full attention.
- Obey the law.
- Share the road with others and remember the "Golden Rule"
- Be alert for potential collisions.
- Control your emotions so they don't interfere with your driving.
- Give yourself a cushion of safety and allow others the same.

Road Rage

Aggressive driving - tailgating, honking, fist and hand gestures, yelling, speeding, cutting off other drivers, and more recently, the use of firearms - has become a real danger on America's highways. Drivers taking out their stress and anger on other drivers have been called "the fastest-growing menace on the highway today".

The National Highway Traffic Safety Administration (NHTSA) says about 66% of all traffic fatalities annually are caused by aggressive driving behaviors, such as passing on the right, running red lights and tailgating.

Experts say there may be several reasons why road rage is rising. We are all under more stress. A person who is hostile and frustrated by traffic congestion or problems on the job or at home gets in his car - ready to fight. His car becomes an "ego-enhancer", and he uses it to dominate and intimidate others.

Maybe it's impatience at slowed-down traffic conditions that makes a driver speed and take risks. Some people "take a stand" on the highway and won't let other drivers pass them.

Because road rage is increasing every year, you must learn to protect yourself against aggressive drivers. **If you have a tendency to get irritated and angry behind the wheel, you must learn to change your attitude and your behavior.** Otherwise, you are an accident looking for a place to happen. Law enforcement and insurance companies are getting much tougher on aggressive drivers. They simply cause too many collisions.

Are You an Aggressive Driver?

Do you tend to drive too fast, want to be first, want to teach the bad driver a lesson, or keep that other car from getting by you?

Do you speed up when someone tries to pass you, tailgate people who are going slower than you, weave in and out of traffic lanes or pass cars on the right shoulder?

Do you flash your headlights at vehicles to get them to let you pass, use your car horn when angry or upset with traffic jams or other drivers?

Do you make obscene gestures or glare threateningly at other drivers, yell out your window at pedestrians or other drivers or race for a position on the highway?

NHTSA considers these behaviors to be examples of aggressive driving. So next time, think twice before doing any of these things. You should recognize aggressive

> **BEFORE YOU TURN ON YOUR ENGINE,**
> **TURN OFF YOUR ANGER!**

tendencies in yourself and learn how to overcome behavior that leads to unsafe driving. Otherwise, you may wind up losing your driver license - or worse, losing your life.

What You Can Do To Stay Safe

- "Drive right" and reduce the chance of making another driver lash out.
- Keep away from people who are "driving crazy".
- Avoid eye contact with an aggressive driver.
- Stay cool - keep looking straight ahead and refuse to become part of the problem.
- Don't join in the confrontation, even if it's just honking your horn or glaring back. Just get out of the way. Don't make it worse:
  - Don't make obscene gestures
  - Don't block passing or right-turn lanes.
  - Don't tailgate.
  - Don't use bright lights when following.
  - Don't take more than one parking space.
  - Avoid bumping into another car when you open your car door.

- Drive defensively. Watch out for and avoid drivers who change lanes frequently.
- Give an angry driver plenty of space. If you make a driving error (even accidentally), it is possible the other driver may try and "pick a fight" with you. Put as much distance between your vehicle and the other car as you can.
- Don't cut off other drivers. When you merge, make sure you have enough room and always signal before you merge.
- Lock your doors
- When stopped in traffic, leave enough space to pull out from behind the car you are following.
- Keep your radio/stereo volume down at a reasonable level.
- Limit use of your car phone to urgent or emergency calls only.
- Don't let talking on you car phone distract you.
- Don't travel in the passing lane, and use signals when you do change lanes.
- Don't insist on the right-of-way if another driver challenges you.
- Don't take traffic problems personally. Be polite, even when someone else is rude.
- Don't be tempted to start a fight or carry any sort of weapon. These acts may provoke an assault.
- If a driver follows you, go to a police station or a public place where you can get help. If you are harassed on the road, get the offender's license tag number and report the incident to the authorities.

DON'T GET MAD - GET BETTER!
Suggestions for Avoiding Road Rage:
- Plan ahead - allow up to 50% more time for a trip of any length. Take along a favorite tape or recorded book. Enjoy the trip.

- The competitor who always sees finish lines and goal posts must realize that driving is NOT A GAME to be won. Concentrate on the pleasures of driving and drive yourself healthy.
- Drive relaxed and within the speed limit, passing only when necessary. The change will surprise you.
- Don't take someone else's careless or thoughtless driving personally. Everyone gets distracted and makes mistakes. Remember to relax and "mind your own business" on the road.
- Keep cool.
- Decide to arrive alive and allow other drivers the same advantage.

Make a difference in keeping the roads safe for everyone - Act Responsibly!

YOU CAN'T CONTROL TRAFFIC, BUT YOU CAN CONTROL YOUR REACTION TO IT!

The most dangerous influences on the highway?
- Impatience
- Frustration
- Anger

The most potent precautions on the highway?
- Buckle Up!
- Slow Down!
- Driver Sober!

The best way to stay alive is to keep it under the speed limit, don't drink and drive, and always wear your seat belt. Each and every time. And insist that everyone else in the car is buckled up too. **No Exceptions! Act Responsibility!**

Accidents Don't Just Happen, They Are Caused

The Highway Transportation system is composed of three major elements:

1. **the driver,**
2. **the vehicle, and**
3. **the road**

In most cases where accidents occur, the cause can be attributed to one or more of these elements. ***The majority of accidents relate directly to the driver***. A good driver takes interest and pride in the care and operation of his/her vehicle. The driver knows and observes all traffic laws and respects the rights and safety of others. As a result, such drivers have a much better chance of never becoming involved in a serious traffic accident.

The poor or careless driver all too often neither cares for the vehicle he/she drives, seldom observes traffic laws and has little respect for the rights and safety of others.

As a result of poor driving habits there are approximately 160,000 accidents reported to the Department of Safety annually.

1. THE DRIVER: Be in Shape to Drive

Human error is the single most common cause of traffic crashes. The leading factors in crashes are:

- Excessive Speed
- Lack of Concentration
- Improper Evasive Action

Driving safely is not always easy. In fact, it is one of the most complex things that people do and one of the few things we do regularly that can injure or kill us. It is worth the effort to be a careful driver.

Being a safe driver takes a lot of skill and judgment. This task is even more difficult when you are just learning to drive. Every one of the abilities you have can easily be required to drive safely. If anything happens so you are not up to your full ability, you may not be a safe driver. Your ability to be a safe driver depends on ability to see clearly, not being overly tired, not driving while on drugs, being generally healthy and being emotionally fit to drive. **In other words, being in "shape" to drive safely**.

Your mental and emotional state, as well as your physical condition, affects the way you drive a vehicle. Anger, worry, frustration, fatigue and minor illnesses such as a cold are a few of the temporary conditions that can make you an unsafe driver.

VISION

Good vision is a must for safe driving. You drive based on what you see. If you cannot see clearly, you will have trouble identifying traffic and road conditions, spotting potential trouble or reacting in a timely manner.

Vision is so important that Tennessee requires that you pass a vision test before you get a driver license. This test measures that you have at least 20/40 vision in at least one eye, with or without corrective lenses.

Side Vision — You need to see "out of the corner of your eye". This lets you spot vehicles and other potential trouble on either side of you while you look ahead. Because you cannot focus on things to the side, you also must use your side mirrors and glance to the side if necessary.

Judging Distances and Speeds — Even if you can see clearly, you still may not be able to judge distances or speeds very well. In fact you are not alone, many people have problems judging distances and speeds. It takes a lot of practice to be able to judge both effectively. It is especially important in knowing how far you are from other vehicles and judging safe gaps when merging and when passing on two-lane roads, or when judging the speed of a train before crossing tracks

Night Vision — Many people who can see clearly in the daytime have trouble seeing at night. It is more difficult for everyone to see at night than in the daytime. Some drivers have problems with glare while driving at night, especially with the glare of oncoming headlights. If you have problems seeing at night, don't drive more than is necessary and be very careful when you do drive at night.

Because seeing well is so important to safe driving, you should have your eyes checked every year or two by an eye specialist. You may never know you have poor vision unless your eyes are tested.

When required to wear glasses or contact lenses, remember to:

✓ Always wear them when you drive, even if it is only to run down to the corner. If your driver license says you must wear corrective lenses, and you do not wear them when driving; you could be fined and receive a ticket.

✓ Keep an spare pair of glasses in your vehicle. If your regular glasses are broken or lost, you can use the spare to drive safely.

✓ Avoid using dark glasses or tinted contact lenses at night, they cut down the light you need to see clearly.

HEARING

Hearing can be helpful to safe driving. The sound of horns, a siren or screeching tires can warn you of danger. Hearing problems, like bad eyesight, can come on so slowly that you do not notice it easily. Drivers who know they are deaf or have hearing problems can adjust and still be safe drivers. These drivers learn to rely more on their vision and tend to stay more alert. Studies have shown that the driving records of hearing-impaired drivers are just as good as those drivers with good hearing.

FATIGUE

You cannot drive as safely when you are tired as when you are rested. You do not see as well, nor are you as alert. It takes you more time to make decisions and you do not always make good decisions. You can be more irritable and can get upset more easily. When you are tired you could fall asleep behind the wheel and crash, injuring or killing yourself or others.

Things you can do to help from getting tired on a long trip.
- Try to get a normal night's sleep before you leave.
- Do not leave on a trip if you are already tired. Plan your trips so you can leave when you are rested.
- Do not take any medicine that can make you drowsy.
- Eat lightly. Do not eat a large meal before you leave.
- Take breaks. Stop every hour or so or when you need to. Walk around, get some fresh air and have some water, coffee, soda or juice. The few minutes spent on a rest stop can save your life. Plan for plenty of time to complete your trip safely.
- Try not to drive late at night when you are normally asleep. Your body thinks it is time to go to sleep and will try to do so.
- Never drive if you are sleepy. It is better to stop and sleep for a few hours than to take a chance you can stay awake. If you fail to stay awake it could become a real nightmare.

HEALTH

Many health problems can affect your driving – a bad cold, infection or virus. Even little problems like a stiff neck, a cough or a sore leg can affect your driving. If you are not feeling well and need to go somewhere, let someone else drive.

Some health conditions can be very dangerous:
- **Epilepsy** – So long as it is under medical control, epilepsy generally is not an obstacle to driving. In Tennessee, you may drive if you are under the care of a doctor and have been seizure free for a minimum of six months.
- **Diabetes** – Diabetics who take insulin should not drive when there is any chance of an insulin reaction, blackout, convulsion or shock. Such a situation could result from skipping a meal or from taking the wrong amount of insulin. It also might be a good idea to have someone else drive for you during times when your doctor is adjusting you insulin dosage. If you have diabetes you also should have your eyes checked regularly for possible night blindness or other vision problems.
- **Heart Condition** – People with heart diseases, high blood pressure or circulation problems or those in danger of a blackout, fainting or a heart attack should not get behind the wheel. If you are being treated by a doctor for a heart condition, ask if the condition could affect your driving.

EMOTIONS

Emotions can have a great affect on your driving safely. You may not be able to drive well if you are overly worried, excited, afraid, angry or depressed.

- If you are angry or excited, give yourself time to cool off. If necessary take a short walk, but stay off the road until you have calmed down.
- If you are worried, down or are upset about something, try to keep your mind on your driving. Some find listen to the radio helps.
- If you are impatient, give yourself extra time for your driving trip. Leave a few minutes early. If you have plenty of time, you may not tend to speed or do other things that can get you a traffic ticket or cause a crash. Don't be impatient to wait for a train to cross in front of you. Driving around lowered gates or trying to beat the train can be fatal.

ALCOHOL and DRUGS

Alcohol is involved in about 40% of the traffic collisions in which someone is killed. If you drink alcohol, even a little, your chances of being in a collision are much greater than if you did not drink any alcohol (or drugs). No one can drink alcohol and drive safely, even if you have been driving for many years. **DRIVING SHOULD ALWAYS BE A DRUG AND ALCOHOL FREE ZONE**.

You should fully review Chapter Five of this manual for full details on Tennessee's laws and penalties regarding drinking and driving.

2. THE VEHICLE: Maintenance is a Must

Driving safety starts with the vehicle you are driving. *It is the duty of drivers to make certain that the vehicles they drive are safe to operate.*

A poorly maintained vehicle can break down or cause a collision. If a vehicle is not working well, you might not be able to get out of an emergency situation. A vehicle in good working order can give you an extra safety margin when you need it most.

You should follow the recommendations in your vehicle owner's manual for routine maintenance.

CHECK THE VEHICLE
- ✓ *Braking System* – Only your brakes can stop your vehicle. It is very dangerous if they are not working properly. If they do not seem to be working good, are making a lot of noise, smell funny or the brake pedal goes to the floor, have a mechanic check them.
- ✓ *Lights* – Make sure that turn signals, brake lights, taillights and headlights are operating properly. These should be checked from the outside of the vehicle.
- ✓ *Battery* – Car batteries tend to run down more rapidly in cold or damp weather. A neglected battery may leave you stranded with a vehicle that will not start.
- ✓ *Jumper Cables* – In the event your vehicle's battery becomes run down, jumper cables may help get you started. It is a prudent idea to keep a set of cables in your vehicle. See the vehicle manual for proper use to prevent vehicle damage or personal injury.

✓ **Windshield and Wipers** – Damaged glass in a windshield can easily break in a minor collision or when something hits the windshield. Have a damaged windshield repaired or replaced

Windshield wipers keep the rain and snow off the windshield. Some vehicles also have wipers for rear windows and headlights. Make sure all wipers are in good operation condition. If the blades are not clearing your windshield, replace them.

Windshield washer solution – Non-freezing windshield washer fluid is essential for cleaning the windshield of debris, salt, and grime when driving in inclement weather. Get in the habit of checking the washer fluid level with each gas fill-up and/or adding more solution with each oil change.

It is important that you are able to see clearly through the windows, windshield and even your mirrors. *The following are things you can do to help*:

- Keep the windshield clean. Bright sun or headlights on a dirty windshield make it hard to see. Get in the habit of cleaning the windshield each time you stop to put gas into your vehicle.
- Keep the inside of your windows clean, especially if anyone using the vehicle smokes. Smoking causes a film to build up on the inside of the glass. Carry liquid cleaner and a paper or cloth towel so you can clean you windshield whenever it is necessary.

✓ **Heater / Defroster** – A working heater/defroster keeps the vehicle's windows free of fog and ice and helps maintain comfortable driving conditions.

✓ **Tires** – Worn or bald tires can increase your stopping distance and make turning more difficult when the road is wet. Unbalanced tires and low pressure cause faster tire wear, reduce fuel economy and make the vehicle harder to steer and stop.

Worn tires can cause hydroplaning, and increase the chance of a flat tire. Check the tire pressure often with an air pressure gauge (a good idea is to keep a gauge in your glove box since they are no larger than your average ink pen). Check the vehicle manual or the side of the tires for the proper pressure rate.

Check the tread with a penny. Stick the penny into the thread headfirst. If the tread does not come at least to Lincoln's head (2/32 inch), the tire is illegal and unsafe and you need it replaced. **Don't forget the spare tire**! The spare should be checked and maintained periodically in case it is needed in an emergency.

✓ Steering System – If the steering is not working properly, it is difficult to control the direction you want to go. If the vehicle is hard to turn or does not turn when the steering wheel is first turned, have the steering checked by a mechanic.

- **Never turn your vehicle's ignition to the "lock" position while the vehicle is in motion. This will cause the steering wheel to lock in place and you will lose control of the vehicle.**

✓ **Suspension System** – Your suspension helps you control your vehicle and provides a comfortable ride over varying road surfaces. If the vehicle continues to bounce after a bump or a stop, or is hard to control, you may need new shocks or other suspension parts. Have a mechanic check the vehicle for suspension problems.

✓ **Exhaust System** – The exhaust system helps reduce the noise from the engine, cools the hot gases coming from the engine, and moves them to the rear of the vehicle. *Gases from a leaky exhaust can cause death inside a vehicle in a very short time*.

If you ever start to notice that you and/or your passengers tend to get a sleepy feeling when driving or riding in your car you may have an exhaust leak that needs to be repaired immediately.

Never run the motor in a closed garage. When sitting for prolonged periods in a vehicle with the motor running (idling), open a window to provide fresh air. Some exhaust leaks are easily heard but many are not – **have the system checked periodically**.

✓ **Engine** – A poorly running engine may lose power that is needed for normal driving and emergencies, may not start, gets poor fuel economy, pollutes the air and could stall when you are on the road causing you and other vehicles a traffic problem. Follow the procedures recommended in the owner's manual for maintenance.

✓ **Engine Cooling System** – Antifreeze/coolant level should be checked periodically to ensure proper levels as recommended by your vehicle owner's manual. Improperly maintained levels can result in overheating in warm weather or engine freezing during winter. Be careful to check your radiator ONLY when the vehicle is cool, not immediately after operation.

✓ **Loose Objects** – Make sure that there are no loose objects in the vehicle that could hit someone in the event of a sudden stop or crash. Make sure there are no objects on the floor that could roll under the brake pedal and prevent you from stopping the vehicle. Also check the outside of the vehicle to ensure that there are no loose parts that could come off in traffic and create a safety hazard.

✓ **Horn** – The horn may not seem like it is important for safety, but as a warning device, it could save your life. ONLY use your horn as a warning to others.

✓ **Fuel** – Be sure your vehicle always has at least a half tank of gas before starting any trip of significant length. Running out of gas on the roadway can be dangerous and could cause traffic jams or accidents.

3. THE ROAD: Rules, Conditions & Traffic

A safe and defensive driver never really stops learning "the road". The "road" is a continually evolving portion of the highway transportation system. In order for a driver to develop a thorough understanding of the road you must:

❑ Study and learn the rules of the road. Studying this manual is the first step to accomplishing this task. However good drivers don't just study for a driving test and then never pick up a driving manual again. Good drivers periodically review the manual for the newest law changes and safety information and study the manual for any new state they move to whether or not a test is required to transfer their license to that state.

❑ Be aware of the various road conditions you may encounter when driving. Driving safely means obeying speed limits and adjusting for road conditions. There are various road conditions where you must slow down to be safe. For example, you must slow down for a sharp curve or when the road is rough or damaged

Again the road condition is a topic that you should never expect to stop learning about. In all states, the Department of Transportation is continually improving road designs in attempts to make driving safer. This means that as new ideas are implemented (such as HOV lanes or rumble strips) there will be new conditions regarding the road that drivers will need to become familiar with.

❑ Be prepared for traffic conditions. Traffic is another factor that about the road that is always changing. Chapter 14 of this manual gives you information on sharing the road with various types of traffic including road construction and maintenance vehicles. Traffic conditions vary according to many factors:

- Volume of vehicles
- Types of traffic control devices
- Accidents or work zones
- Road type (interstate, rural, city, etc.)
- Weather conditions
- Speed limits

Vehicles moving in the same direction at the same speed cannot hit one another. Collisions involving multiple vehicles often happen when drivers go faster or slower than other traffic.

Traffic Trouble Spots – Wherever people or traffic gather, your room to maneuver is limited. You need to lower your speed to have time to react in a crowded space. **Some situations where you may need to adjust speed for traffic conditions include**:

- If you see brake lights coming on several vehicles ahead of you.
- Shopping centers, parking lots and downtown areas – these are busy areas with vehicles and people stopping, starting and moving in different directions quickly and randomly.
- Rush hours often have heavy traffic and drivers that always seem to be in a hurry.
- Narrow bridges and tunnels – vehicles approaching each other are closer together.
- Toll Plazas – vehicles are changing lanes and preparing to stop and then speeding up again when leaving the plaza. The number of lanes could change both before and after the plaza.
- Schools, playgrounds and residential streets – these areas often have children present. Always be alert for children crossing the street or running or riding into the street without looking.
- Railroad crossings – you need to make sure that there are no trains coming and that you have room to cross. Some crossings are bumpy so you need to slow down to safely cross.

BEING READY FOR THE DRIVING TASK

Throughout this chapter we have discussed ways to determine that both you and your vehicle are in safe shape for driving. Also we covered the importance of knowing the road and traffic conditions. While all this information is vital for new drivers to develop the knowledge or safe driving; no driver manual can teach you how to operate a vehicle or ensure that you are a safe driver. **Becoming a safe driver requires skills you can only gain through instruction and practice**. As a final review the following tips will help you as you begin to develop safe driving skills while you practice and learn the actual "driving task" with your learner permit or GDL.

- **STARTING**: Check the vehicle owner's manual to determine the proper way to start the vehicle. Make sure the parking brake is on before you start any manual transmission vehicle. Vehicles with manual transmissions must not be in gear and in some newer vehicles the clutch must be depressed before the vehicle will start. For a vehicle that has an automatic transmission, you must ensure that the gearshift selector is in the "PARK" position.

You should always check the position of the seat AND mirrors before you start to drive. Make any necessary adjustments before you move the vehicle.

- PROPER DRIVING POSTURE: You will be driving more effectively, safer and with less fatigue if you are comfortable, your body is well-aligned in your seat, you are the proper distance from the steering wheel, pedals, and if you can use your mirrors to the best advantage.
  - Adjust the seat to a comfortable upright position so you can reach the pedals easily and have good clear vision through the windshield and each side window and all mirrors. DO NOT DRIVE WITH THE SEAT IN A RECLINED OR SEMI-RECLINED POSITION. This is dangerous, reduces your vision and thus your ability to react to emergency situations.
  - You should sit so you can touch the floor below the brake pedal with your feet.
  - Do not move the seat so far forward that you cannot easily steer. You should sit at least 10 to 12 inches from the steering wheel so the air bag will hit you in the chest if there is a collision. Sitting closer could result in serious head or neck injuries from the air bag hitting you in the chin or face.
  - Head restraints are designed to prevent whiplash if you are hit from behind. They should be adjusted so the head restraint contacts the back of your head.
  - Use a solid, firm grip on the steering wheel; you should always drive with BOTH hands on the wheel.
  - Don't drive with you elbow or arm propped on the door or out the window. You don't have full control of the steering wheel and a sideswipe collision could take off your arm.

- **USE SEAT BELTS AND CHILD RESTRAINTS**: Fasten you seat belt (both lap and shoulder if separate belts) and make sure all your passengers are using safety belts or child restraints before you begin driving.
    - You may have to pay a fine if you or your passengers under 16 are not wearing a seat belt or are not secured in a child car seat or booster seat. Refer to Chapter 7 for specific details on Tennessee's seat belt and child protection laws.
- **ADJUST YOUR MIRRORS**: You need to adjust all three of your rear view mirrors so that you get the widest view possible while keeping your blind spots to a minimum. You should wait to adjust your mirrors after you have your seat adjusted correctly, but always before you begin driving.
    - *Interior rearview mirror* – The position for the inside rearview mirror should allow the driver to see fully out of the rear window from the driver's seat. To get the smallest blind spot at the right side of the car, turn you inside mirror so you can see the edge of your right rear window post.
    - *Exterior rearview mirrors* – To eliminate as much "blind spot" area as possible adjust the side-view mirrors just beyond the point where you could see the side of the car on the inside edge of the mirror. With this setup, you almost completely solve the blind spot problem. When you lean slightly backward in your seat, if you see more than a glimpse of the rear corners of your car in your outside mirrors they are turned too far inward and you should adjust them outward.
    - To make sure your mirrors are in the correct position, let a car behind pass you on the left. As it passes out of view in your inside mirror you should see it's front bumper in your outside driver-side mirror.
    - Even with properly adjusted mirrors, always turn your head and check blind spots when you want to turn or change lanes.

- **USING A STANDARD TRANSMISSION**: With a standard or manual transmission, you can control the gear-speed ratio and use your gears, rather than your brakes, to help slow down your car. The following techniques for smooth shifting will help you handle driving vehicles with standard transmissions.
    - Hold the clutch pedal all the way down when starting, shifting gears, and when your speed drops below 10 M.P.H. as you're coming to a stop.
    - Don't "ride the clutch", meaning don't drive with your foot resting on the clutch pedal.
    - Practice to get smooth coordination in using the clutch and accelerator pedals.
    - Don't coast with the gears in neutral (it's illegal) or with the clutch pedal pushed down except when shifting gears.
    - In going down steep hills, place car in a lower gear.

- **USING AN AUTOMATIC TRANSMISSION**: With automatic transmissions the driver usually does not need to change gears. The vehicle is put in "R" for reverse when you want to back-up and in "D" for drive when you want to drive forward. (Some newer cars have an "O" gear selection for overdrive, which is generally for use when driving on interstates or other expressways where there is very little stop, and go traffic.) Most automatic transmissions also have lower gears that will be indicated by an "L", "2", or "1" on the gearshift indicator. These gears are generally not used except for special or emergency situations such as:
    - Driving down steep mountain grades.
    - Slow speed driving on icy or other slippery roads.
    - Emergency deceleration if you have brake failure.

NEVER move your car until you have looked in front, behind and to the side for pedestrians and oncoming traffic. Then, signal and pull into traffic when safe.

The Road Has Many Users

Our streets and highways are becoming more crowded every day. Drivers are not the only people using these roadways. They share the highways with many other users:
- Pedestrians
- Bicyclists
- Motorcyclists and moped riders
- Large trucks and buses
- Even animals

Other people have certain rights and privileges on the highways of which automobile drivers must be aware and must respect. As a driver or user of the road, you need to know and practice the rules for sharing the road safely and defensive driving. You should always be aware of the traffic around you and be prepared for emergency situations. A two-ton automobile can be a dangerous weapon. Use common sense and courtesy with other highway users.

Your responsibility as a defensive driver includes making allowances for and adapting to the other people and vehicles on the road. There are skills and techniques you should use for sharing the road. Knowing what to do and how to do it can help you stay alive and avoid damaging your car or someone else's vehicle or causing bodily injury to other highway users.

SHARING THE ROAD WITH PEDESTRIANS

"Pedestrians" include people walking, skateboarders, in-line or roller skaters, and the disabled who use wheelchairs, walkers, tricycles, or similar supports. As a driver you must recognize the special safety needs of pedestrians. You should be especially alert for young, elderly, disabled and intoxicated pedestrians. They are the most frequent victims in auto-pedestrian collisions.

Generally, pedestrians have the right of way at all intersections. There is a crosswalk at every intersection, even if painted lines and boundaries do not mark the crossing. Crosswalks are intended to encourage people to cross only at certain locations. As you know, some people will cross when and where they want to, regardless of traffic signals, marked crossings, or even their own safety. As the person controlling a potentially dangerous machine, it's your job to "play it safe" where pedestrians are concerned and protect them when you see they may be in danger. Regardless of the rules of the road or right-of-way, the law specifically requires YOU, as a driver, to exercise great care and extreme caution to avoid striking pedestrians.

Your Role as a Driver:

Drivers should not block the crosswalk when stopped at a red light or waiting to make a turn. You also should not stop with a portion of your vehicle overhanging the crosswalk area. Blocking a crosswalk forces pedestrians to go around your car, and puts them in a dangerous situation.
- Be alert to people entering the roadway or crosswalks any place where pedestrian traffic is heavy.
- Be alert to pedestrians to the right of your vehicle and be especially watchful for pedestrians when you are making a right turn.
- You must immediately yield to pedestrians as soon as they step off the curb into the roadway when the pedestrian is on your half of the road/lane or so close to your half of the road that he is in a position of danger.
- Always yield to blind pedestrians carrying a white, metallic, red tipped white cane or using a guide dog.
- Children are often the least predictable pedestrians and the most difficult to see. Take extra care to look out for children in residential areas and at times and places where children are likely to be around. (school zones, playgrounds, parks, near ice cream or snack vendor vehicles/carts, etc.)
- Yield to pedestrians walking on the sidewalk when you're entering or leaving a driveway, public parking garage, alley or parking lot and your path of travel crosses that sidewalk.
- Don't honk your horn, gun your engine, or do anything to rush or scare a pedestrian crossing in front of your car, even if you have the legal right-of-way.

Your Role as a Pedestrian:

Most of us cross streets every day. We take for granted that we can cross without incident, because most of the time we do. But sometimes we aren't so fortunate. Each year 7,000 pedestrians die and 100,000 are injured in traffic accidents. Young children and the elderly are more likely to be killed or injured in a pedestrian crash.

While it is easy to blame drivers, they are not always responsible for these accidents. All too often, pedestrians are the cause of such accidents. These senseless tragedies don't have to happen. You can avoid potential injuries and even death by reviewing the advice for safe street crossing. You too will be a pedestrian on occasion. So learn and obey the common sense rules when the roles are reversed.

When you are a pedestrian, do all you can to make yourself visible and to help drivers prevent crashes.

WALKING

- Pedestrians must walk along sidewalks when available. It is unlawful for pedestrians to walk IN the road where there are sidewalks.

- When there are no sidewalks, always walk on the left side of the road facing traffic (the traffic should be coming toward you), this allows you to see any sudden dangers coming at you. Two or more pedestrians should walk in single file and never side by side of each other.

- Wear or carry something white – do not assume that drivers can see you. At night, remember that it is more difficult for drivers to see you; do everything you can to make yourself visible to drivers – use a flashlight or wear clothing reflectors.

- Be alert and ready to move out of the way in case a driver cannot see you. It is not a good idea to walk or jog along busy roadways while wearing radio headphones or listening to a portable disc player. You may not hear important traffic sounds that would help you avoid potential dangers.

CROSSING

- **Before crossing, stop** at the curb, edge of the road, or corner before proceeding.

- **Look left-right-left,** and if it's clear, begin crossing, looking over your shoulder for turning vehicles.

- Continue to check for approaching traffic while crossing.

- At intersections with traffic lights and pedestrian signals, it's important to follow the signals carefully. Pedestrians may cross on a green traffic signal or when you see the WALK signal, following, again, the basic rules for crossing.

- If you are in the middle of the street and the DON'T WALK signal starts flashing, continue walking. You will have time to complete the crossing.

- Pedestrians may NOT cross on a red or yellow traffic light, or on a red-green (i.e. red for turn(s) while green for straight traffic, or vice versa) combined light, unless facing a WALK signal.

- On a green arrow, whether alone or accompanied by a steady red or yellow, you may enter the road ONLY if you can do so safely without interfering with vehicle traffic.

- The WALK signal and the green traffic light indicate that it's your turn to cross the street, but they do NOT mean it is SAFE to cross. The WALK signal and the GREEN

light mean LOOK, and then, IF it's safe, proceed to cross.

- Although drivers must yield to pedestrians crossing the roadway, pedestrians must not suddenly leave a curb or other safe waiting place and walk into the path of vehicle traffic if it is so close that it is an immediate hazard. Vehicles cannot stop at once!

Remember to make eye contact with drivers to ensure they see you. Don't take a walk signal, a green traffic light, or a driver for granted. Crossing safely is YOUR responsibility. Remember, it's up to you.

Sharing The Road With Bicycles

Bicyclists have the same rights and responsibilities on the streets that drivers do, and in most cases, they must share the lane. Bicycles are required to travel on the right hand side of the road with other traffic. Bicyclists are not allowed to travel facing traffic, since this is far less safe. They must ride as near to the right hand side of the road as practical, while avoiding road hazards that could cause them to swerve into traffic. When you're sharing the road with bicycles, you should always expect the rider to make sudden moves. Trash, minor oil slicks, a pothole or crack in the concrete, a barking dog, a parked car or a car door opening, and other surprises can force a bicycle rider to swerve suddenly in front of you.

Similarly, when cyclists are traveling past parked cars, they tend to move away from the cars, toward the center of the lane. This is to avoid injuring, or being injured by, persons getting out of those cars. In such cases, the bicyclist is operating the bicycle properly. If possible, give the cyclist the entire lane. When road conditions prevent this, pass the cyclist with extreme caution. Cyclists who are not on the extreme right hand side of the lane are not being careless, but are in fact attempting to account for traffic conditions and/or preparing to make a left turn.

Bicycles are hard to see. The riders are exposed and easily injured in a collision. Oncoming bicycle traffic is often overlooked or its speed misjudged.

Safety Tips for Drivers:
- The most common causes of collisions are drivers turning left in front of an oncoming bicycle or turning right, across the path of the bicycle.
- Drivers often fail to pick the bicyclist out of the traffic scene, or inaccurately judge the speed of cyclists making a left turn.
- Drivers overtaking a bicyclist, then making a right turn in front of the cyclist is also a cause of many accidents. Look once, then again, make sure you see the cyclist and know his speed before you turn.
- Merge with bicycle traffic when preparing for a right turn. Don't turn directly across the path of a bicyclist.

- Watch for bicycle riders turning in front of you without looking or signaling, especially if the rider is a child.
- Most bicyclists maintain eye contact with drivers of vehicles around them, particularly when the cyclist or vehicle is making a turn. Before turning, a driver should attempt to gain and maintain eye contact with the bicyclist to ensure a safer turn.

- **Allow plenty of room when passing a bicycle rider.**

  - A driver should NEVER attempt passing between a bicyclist and oncoming vehicles on a two-lane road. Slow down and allow vehicles to pass. Then move to the left to allow plenty of room to pass the rider safely. Leave at least three feet of space between your car and a cyclist when passing.
  - NEVER pass a bicycle if the street is too narrow or you would force the bicyclist too close to parked vehicles. Wait until there is enough room to let you pass safely.
  - If you are about to pass a bicycle on a narrow road and you think the rider doesn't know you're coming, tap your horn gently and briefly as a signal that you're going to pass. Don't blast your horn or otherwise startle or try to intimidate the rider.

- **Residential Areas Are Danger Zones:**

  Bicyclists may ride in the middle of the street and disregard stop signs and traffic signals. BE CAREFUL in all neighborhood areas where children and teenagers might be riding.

  - Children riding bicycles create special problems for drivers. Children are not capable of proper judgment in determining traffic conditions, therefore drivers should be alert to the possibility of erratic movement and sudden changes in direction when children on bicycles are present.
  - Watch out for bikes coming out from driveways or from behind parked cars or other obstructions.
- Bicyclists riding at night present visibility problems for drivers. At night, watch the side of the road for bicyclists. Bicyclists are required to have proper illumination, a front light and rear reflector, but drivers should be aware that bicyclists are not easily seen. Lights from approaching traffic may make them even harder to see at night.
- If you see a bicyclist with a red or orange pennant flag on an antennae attached to the bike, slow down; this is a common symbol to indicate the rider has impaired hearing.

Lane Positions for Bicycles:

Bicycle riders are required to ride as far right in the lane as possible only when a car and a bicycle, side by side, can safely share the lane. Even then, there are certain times when a bicycle can take the full lane. **A bicyclist should be allowed full use of the lane when:**

- The rider is overtaking and passing another vehicle going in the same direction.
- If the lane is marked and signed (as shown at right) for bicycle use only, drivers must NEVER use that lane as a

turning lane, passing lane or for parking.
- The bicyclist is getting in place for a left turn at an intersection or turning left into a private road or driveway.
- There are unsafe conditions in the roadway, such as parked cars, moving vehicles or machinery, fixed obstacles, pedestrians, animals, potholes or debris.
- The lane is too narrow for both a car and a bicycle to safely share the lane. In this case, it is safest to let the bicycle take the full lane.

To learn more specifics on bicycle riding and safety contact:
The League of American Bicyclists
1612 K Street NW, Suite 800
Washington, D.C. 20006
202-822-1333
www.bikeleague.org

SHARING THE ROAD WITH MOTORCYCLES

Research shows that two-thirds of car-motorcycle collisions are caused, not by the motorcyclist, but by the driver, who turned in front of the motorcycle. The drivers didn't see the motorcycles at all or didn't see them until it was too late to avoid the collision.

Why Drivers Don't Always See Motorcyclists

Drivers tend to look for other cars and trucks, not for motorcycles.

The profile of a motorcycle is narrow and the body is short, making it harder to see and making it harder for a driver to estimate the cycle's distance and speed.

Motorcycle riding requires frequent lane movements to adjust to changing road and traffic conditions.

Motorcycles have the right to the use of the full lane. Riders need the lane's full width to respond to and handle hazards such as potholes, shifting traffic blocking their view or blocking them from being seen, and strong winds or blasts of air from passing vehicles. You must never try to share a lane with a motorcycle, and you should always respect the cycle's space and position in traffic.

Driver Tips for Sharing the Road with Motorcycles:
- *Passing* – Pass as you would pass a car, and don't pass too close or too fast, as the blast of air can blow a motorcycle out of control.
- *Left turns* – Always signal your intention to turn. Watch for oncoming motorcycles.
- *Following Distance* – Allow at least a two-second following distance, so the motorcycle rider has enough time to maneuver or stop in an emergency. Both cyclists and drivers are more likely to make bad decisions if there is not enough stopping distance or time to see and react to conditions.
- *Check you Blind Spots when Changing Lanes* –

Motorcyclists riding alongside a lane of cars are often out of the view of the driver. An unsuspecting driver may change lanes and clip or hit a motorcycle.

- *Anticipate Motorcyclists' Maneuvers* – A cyclist will change lane position to prepare for upcoming traffic conditions. Expect and allow room for the rider to adjust to road hazards that you can't see. At intersections, where most collisions and injuries occur, wait until the rider's intentions are absolutely clear (turning or going straight) before you move into the path of travel. Be even more careful in difficult driving conditions – rain, wet roads, ice, and heavy winds – when the motorcyclist's braking and handling abilities are impaired.

- *Pay Extra Attention at Night* – You can easily misjudge distance because the single headlight and single tail light of a motorcycle can blend into the lights of other vehicles. Always dim your headlights as you would for cars and trucks.

- *Drive Aware* – Whenever you are on the road or at an intersection with a motorcycle, use extra caution and care. Learn to watch for the narrow profile.

Hazards that can affect Cyclists' Maneuvers:

Special conditions and situation may cause problems for cyclists (both bicycle and motorcycle), which drivers need to anticipate. Drivers should be aware of these problems, so they can help share the road safely with cyclists. Here are a few examples:

- Bad weather and slippery surfaces cause greater problems for cyclists than for cars. These conditions create stability problems for all vehicles. Allow more following distance for cyclists when the road surface is wet and slippery. Also be alert to the problem of glare that rain and wet surfaces create, especially at night.

- Strong cross winds can move a cycle out of its lane of travel. Areas where this can happen are wide open, long stretches of highways and bridges. Large, fast-moving trucks sometimes create wind blasts which, under certain conditions, can move the cyclist out of his or her path of travel.

- Railroad grade crossings are a particular hazard to cyclists, and will usually cause them to slow down and possibly zigzag to cross the tracks head on.

- Metal or grated bridges cause a cycle to wobble much more than a car. An experienced cyclist slows down and moves to the center of the lane to allow room for handling the uneven surface. An inexperienced cyclist may become startled and try to quickly change direction. Be prepared for either reaction.

Being aware of these situations and consciously looking for cyclists can help you share the road safely with both bicycles and motorcycles.

To learn more about motorcycle safety, pick up a copy of the Tennessee Motorcycle Operator Manual at any Driver License Station. Good information is also available at: www.tennessee.gov/safety/mrep.

SHARING THE ROAD WITH LARGE TRUCKS AND BUSES

You will always be sharing the road with trucks because they haul more freight more miles than any other form of transportation. Trucks are the sole method of delivery and pickup for 77% of America's communities.

A typical tractor-trailer combination, a power unit pulling a loaded semi-trailer hinged to its rear end, may weigh up to 80,000 pounds. Depending on the trailer length, the total length of the combination may exceed 70 feet. On the busiest intercity routes, a driver may encounter double or even triple-trailer combinations sometimes exceeding 100 feet in length.

Trucks that were involved in fatal accidents nationally has decreased by 6% from 1997 to 2001. When driving on the highway you are at a serious disadvantage if involved in a crash with a larger vehicle. In crashes involving large trucks, the occupants of a car, usually the driver, sustain 78% of fatalities.

Many truck-car crashes could be avoided if drivers know about truck (and bus) limitations and how to steer clear of unsafe situations involving large vehicles. Seems obvious, doesn't it? But the fact is that while most people realize that it is more difficult to drive a truck than a car, many don't know exactly what a truck's limitations are in terms of maneuverability, stopping distances, and blind-spots. Remember: Large trucks, recreational vehicles, and buses are not simply big cars. **The bigger they are:**

1. The bigger their blind spots, trucks have deep blind spots in front, behind and on both sides.
2. The longer it takes them to stop, a car traveling at 55 M.P.H. can stop in about 240 feet; however, a truck traveling at that speed takes about 450+ feet to stop.
3. The more room they need to maneuver, such as making right turns. Trucks must swing wide to the left to safely negotiate a right turn. They cannot see cars behind or beside them.
4. The longer it takes an automobile to pass them.
5. As stated above the more likely you are to be the "loser" in a collision.

Truck drivers are always watching for smaller vehicles and working to avoid collisions. There are some techniques that you can use to help them – and yourself – share the road safely and reduce the likelihood of a collision with a large vehicle.

Do NOT enter a roadway in front of a large vehicle, a truck or bus can't slow down or stop as quickly as an automobile. By pulling out in front of these vehicles you could easily cause a rear-end collision.

Avoid driving directly behind a truck or bus. Keep a reasonable distance between your car and the large vehicle ahead; this way you will have a better view of the road to anticipate problems, and you will give yourself room for an emergency "out".

- Do NOT cut abruptly in front of a large vehicle; if you are exiting, it will only take a few extra seconds to slow down and exit behind the truck. Cutting off a large vehicle on the Interstate is particularly dangerous because of the high speeds being traveled.

- When passing a large vehicle do not pull back over into the lane in front of the truck unless you can see the whole front of the vehicle in your rearview mirror. Do NOT slow down once you are in front of the truck.

- Position your vehicle so you are outside the truck driver's "blind spots", and be sure the truck driver can see YOU in the side rearview mirror. **If you can't see the truck's mirror, the driver can't see YOU.** A truck's blind spots are immediately in front, on either side of the car, and up to 200 feet in the rear. A trucker may not be able to see the road directly in front of the cab. If the tractor has a long hood, the trucker may not be able to see the first 10-20 feet in front of the bumper – plenty of room for a car to slip unnoticed into a dangerous position.

- If you're stopped behind a truck on an uphill grade, stay to the left in your lane so the driver can see you. When stopped in a traffic lane, leave extra space in front of your car in case the truck rolls back when it starts to move.

- Pay close attention to the large vehicle's turn signals. Because trucks make wide right turns, they need to swing to the left before turning right – make sure you know which way the vehicle is turning before trying to pass.

- Do not linger beside a large vehicle, because you may not be visible to the driver in the wide area the truck needs for maneuvering a turn.

- When you are near a Commercial Vehicle Weigh Station, avoid driving in the right lane so slow-moving trucks can easily merge back onto the roadway.

- Dim your lights at night. Bright lights reflected in the mirrors can blind the driver.

- In rainy conditions, stay back. Spray and splash back from the rear wheels can cover your windshield with sheets of water, mud and road film.

- Never underestimate the size and speed of approaching trucks or buses. Because of their large size they often appear to be traveling more slowly than their actual speed.

Risky Situations with Large Vehicles

Passing a Large Vehicle: A tractor-trailer or other combination vehicles, takes a longer time and requires more space to get around than passing a car.

- On a two-way road, leave yourself more time and space when passing these large vehicles. Check to your front and rear and move into the passing lane only

if it is clear and you are in a legal passing zone.

- If the truck or bus driver blinks the truck's lights after you pass, it's a signal that you are cleared to pull back in front of the truck. Move back only when you can see the front of the truck in your rearview mirror.

- Remember that on an upgrade or steep hill, a large vehicle usually loses speed.

- Because of their weight, trucks travel faster downhill and you may have to increase your speed to pass a truck on a downhill grade. Complete your pass as quickly as possible and don't stay alongside the truck. After you pass, maintain your speed. Don't pass a truck, then slow down, making the truck driver brake while traveling downhill.

- When a truck passes you, you can help the driver by keeping to the far side of your lane and reducing your speed slightly. NEVER SPEED UP AS A TRUCK OR BUS IS PASSING.

- When you meet a truck/bus coming from the opposite direction, keep as far as possible to the right of the road to avoid being sideswiped and to reduce wind turbulence between vehicles. The turbulence PUSHES vehicles APART, it does NOT suck them together.

The "Right Turn Squeeze": Trucks make wide right turns and often must leave and open space on the right side. Do NOT move into that space or try to pass a truck if it might be making a right turn. If you are between the truck and the curb, the driver may not be able to see you and your car can be crunched or sideswiped by the truck's trailer.

A Truck Backing Up: When a truck is trying to back into a loading dock, there may be no choice except to block the roadway for a short time. Never try to cross behind a truck when it is preparing to back up. This is a high-collision situation because you will be in the driver's blind spots. Give the driver plenty of room and wait patiently for the few minutes it takes to complete the maneuver.

Maintaining a Safety Cushion with Large Vehicles: As stated previously trucks and buses need more maneuvering room and stopping distance than small vehicles. A good safety strategy for car drivers is to leave plenty of space between your car and the larger vehicle, especially in these situations:

If you are driving in front of a truck, keep you speed up so that you maintain a safe distance in front of the truck. Always indicate your intention to turn or change lanes early enough for the driver of the truck or bus to prepare for your maneuver. Avoid sudden moves, slow downs or stops.

Don't cut in front of a truck or bus, or you remove the driver's cushion of safety.

When following a truck or bus, it is a good idea to add more following distance. A safety cushion of at least 3 to 4 seconds is recommended.

If rain or water is standing on the road, spray from a truck passing you, or one you are trying to pass, will seriously reduce your vision. You should move as far away from the truck as you can, while staying in your lane.

Don't drive too close to trucks that are carrying hazardous materials, since they make frequent stops, such as at railroad crossings.

Hills or Mountain Roads: Beware of dangers caused by slower moving trucks or buses on steep hills or mountain roads. Watch for slow moving trucks or buses going both up and down hills. Heavy vehicles cannot maintain speed when climbing hills and must go slowly down hills to stay under control.

Watch for trucks or buses that may be in trouble. Smoking wheels or a high speed can be a sign of brake loss. If you encounter this situation, fall back, and DO NOT pass.

Runaway ramps: These ramps are designed to stop out-of-control trucks or buses going down steep downgrades. Vehicles should never be stopped or parked in these areas.

Learn the "NO ZONES" for large vehicles:

Many motorists falsely assume that trucks and buses can see the road better because they sit twice as high as the driver of a small vehicle. While trucks and buses do enjoy a better forward view and have bigger mirrors, they have serious blind spots into which a small vehicle can disappear from view.

The NO-ZONE represents danger areas around trucks and buses where crashes are more likely to occur.

1. The area approximately up to 20 feet directly in front of a large vehicle is considered a NO-ZONE. When small vehicles cut in too soon after passing or changing lanes, then abruptly slow down, trucks and buses are forced to compensate with very little time of room to spare.

2. Unlike small vehicles, trucks and buses have deep blind spots directly behind them. Avoid following too closely in this NO-ZONE. If you stay in the rear blind spot of a large vehicle, you increase the possibility of a traffic crash. The truck/bus driver cannot see your car, and your view of the traffic ahead will be severely reduced.

3. Large vehicles have much larger blind spots on both sides than cars do. When you drive in these blind spots for any length of time, the vehicle's driver cannot see you. When passing even if the vehicle's driver knows you are there, remaining alongside a large vehicle too long, you make it impossible for the driver to take evasive action if an obstacle appears in the roadway ahead. If the truck or bus driver needs to swerve or change lanes for any reason, a serious crash could occur if any vehicle is in either of these NO-ZONES.

4. Truck and bus drivers often cannot see vehicles directly behind or beside them when they are attempting to safely negotiate a right turn. If you cut in between the truck or bus and the curb or shoulder to the right it greatly increases the possibility of a crash in this "right turn squeeze".

For more details on operating commercial trucks or buses pick up a copy of the Tennessee Commercial Driver License Manual at any Driver License Station. Also more safety information is available through U.S. Department of Transportation at:

www.sharetheroadsafely.org
www.nozone.org
www.fmcsa.dot.gov

— OR —

Tennessee Trucking Association
4531 Trousdale Drive
Nashville, TN 37204
(615) 777-2882
www.tntrucking.org

SHARING THE ROAD WITH TRAINS

Actually, you don't share the road with trains – you stop and let them have the right-of-way! You can stop your car suddenly but a train can't. **Drivers must ALWAYS yield to trains because that's the law.**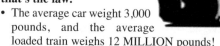

• The average car weight 3,000 pounds, and the average loaded train weighs 12 MILLION pounds!

• A train traveling at 55 M.P.H. takes a full mile to stop.

• You are 30 times more likely to die in a collision with a train than in a crash with a car or even a large truck or bus.

Over half the car/train collisions in America happen at crossroads with lights, bells, or gates; and two-thirds of the crashes happen in full daylight.

Why?

Impatience – Drivers don't want to wait the 30 seconds to 2 minutes average time it takes for the train to pass through the intersection. They try to beat the train. In 1996 across the U.S., over 4,000 cars and trucks were hit at crossings because the trains beat them. More than 1,500 drivers and passengers were hurt and 415 died. Don't let yourself or your family and friends be one of these statistics.

Negligence – When drivers see a railroad crossing sign or warning, they don't respect the potential for danger; they cross the tracks without looking, listening, or stopping. Most of the collisions occur within 25 miles of the driver's home, suggesting that drivers KNEW the tracks were there and they were in the habit of crossing without looking.

If you are on a collision course with a train, only YOU can avoid the collision. The train cannot stop in time or swerve to avoid you.

Stopping For Railroad Crossings

Countless people lose their lives or suffer tragic injuries due to train/vehicle collisions. Invariably, the cause for such collisions is the disregard, and often the willful evasion, of railroad crossing warnings by drivers.

Railroad Crossing Warning Signs: Railroad crossing signs signal a driver to slow down, look, listen and be prepared to stop for a train. These signs include the round yellow railroad ahead crossing sign, the railroad cross-buck sign, pavement markings, and at crossings with significant vehicular traffic, red flashing lights and crossing gates.

ALWAYS EXPECT A TRAIN

Railroad Crossing Stop Signs: If you approach a railroad crossing at which a stop sign is posted, you must come to a complete stop and proceed across the tracks only after looking both ways to make sure a train is not approaching. Never assume the track is not used or a train is not approaching.

Safety Guidelines for Railroad Crossings:

Obey the Warning Signs: Look both ways and **LISTEN**, because you may have to stop. Expect a train on any track at any time. Don't trust a "schedule" because trains can cross at any time. Due to the size of trains, the actual speed of a train can be very deceiving.

Don't Attempt to "Beat the Train": Under no circumstances attempt to race a train to a crossing. If you lose, you will never race again.

Don't Try to "Evade the Gates": Never drive around a crossing gate that has extended down. If the gates are down, stop and stay in place. It's against the law to drive through lowered gates. Don't cross the tracks until the gates are fully raised and the lights have stopped flashing.

When Approaching a Railroad Crossing: Slow down far enough ahead of the crossing to be certain that you can stop when you reach the point where a train could first be seen. Railroad crossings equipped with electric or mechanical signal devices require the operator to bring his vehicle to a complete stop within 50 feet, and no closer than 15 feet from the nearest rail and shall not proceed until he can do so safely.

Avoid Stopping on the Railroad Tracks: Never proceed to cross the tracks unless you can legally clear all tracks without stopping. If you are crossing the tracks and the warning lights begin flashing or the gates start coming down, don't stop. KEEP MOVING! The warning signals will allow enough time for you to finish driving through the crossing before the train arrives. The gate on the far side of the tracks will not block you in. Do NOT try to back up.

If your vehicle stalls on the tracks, all occupants should exit the vehicle immediately and get off the tracks. If a train is coming, get away from the tracks and run toward the direction from which the train is coming (away from the point of impact) as shown in the illustration above. If no train is in sight, post lookouts and try to start the vehicle or push it off

the tracks. If you are alone notify local law enforcement for assistance. Look to see that no train is approaching the crossing and carefully proceed to have the vehicle removed from the tracks.

Your car is replaceable. You aren't!!
No vehicle is worth a human life.

Watch for Additional Trains: Where there is more than one track, a driver waiting for one train to pass must make sure another train is not approaching from the opposite direction. Once the first train has cleared the tracks, caution should be taken that a second train is NOT proceeding in the opposite direction. Don't go across the tracks until you are sure that no other train is coming on another track from either direction.

Watch for Vehicles that Must Stop at Highway- Railway Crossings: School Buses, Passenger Buses and Trucks carrying hazardous materials must stop at all crossings whether signals are activated or not. Never attempt to pass such a stopped vehicle on a two-way road. For safety's sake do NOT pass such stopped vehicles on a multi-lane roadway unless the crossing is clearly marked with signal lights and/or gates that are NOT activated. Otherwise the stopped vehicle in the right lane may block your clear view of the tracks.

Intersection Warning Signs: Some variation of the sign shown at right will be posted prior to intersections or crossroads where railroad tracks cross one of the roadways. Always be alert and pay attention to these signs as they give you advance warning that you may encounter a train if turning onto the road indicated in the sign.

For more information on Railroad Crossing Safety contact:
Federal Railroad Administration
Office of Public Affairs (Stop 5)
1120 Vermont Ave., NW
Washington, DC 20590
www.fra.dot.gov
— or —
Tennessee Operation Lifesaver at: www.tnol.org

SHARING THE ROAD WITH SCHOOL BUSES

School buses are one of the safest forms of transportation in the nation – nearly 2,000 times safer than the family car. Accidents are rare because school districts and the school bus contractors who serve them work hard to train drivers to avoid accidents.

The reality of school bus safety is that more children are hurt outside a bus than inside one. *Children are at the greatest risk when they are getting on or off the school bus.* Most of the children killed in bus related crashes are pedestrians, five to seven years old; they are hit by the bus or by motorists illegally passing a stopped school bus. In fact pedestrian fatalities while loading and unloading school buses accounted for nearly three out of every four fatalities.

The child who bends over to retrieve a dropped school paper, or who walks too closed to the bus while crossing the street, needs to be aware that every yellow school bus is surrounded by a danger zone.

This Danger Zone is the area on all sides of the bus where children are in the most danger of being hit. Children should stay ten feet away from the school bus and NEVER go behind the bus.

In many school districts, children are taught to escape from that zone by taking five giant steps as soon as they leave the bus. If they must cross the street after exiting, they are taught to cross at least five giant steps in front of the bus – and to be sure they're able to be seen by the school bus driver and can maintain eye contact with the driver.

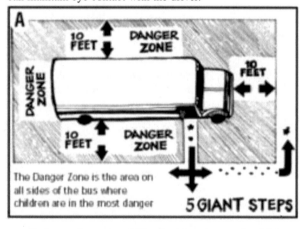

The Danger Zone is the area on all sides of the bus where children are in the most danger

Perhaps the most difficult thing to teach children, especially young children, is not to go back to pick up items they've dropped near the bus, or left on the bus.

Parents and other adults must also do their part. *For instance, most drivers need to learn to share the road with school buses and stop when the bus stops to take on or let off passengers.* If we all do our part – if drivers heed school bus warning lights, bus drivers drive defensively, parents help their children learn to ride safely and children learn to avoid the bus's danger zone – it can be safer still to ride to and from school in that yellow bus.

Safety Tips For Drivers
- Drivers must be familiar with the Danger Zone. Since children are taught to take the "five giant steps" from the school bus for safety, drivers must ensure that they stop far enough from the bus to allow for this needed safety space. **Stay at least 20 feet away from any stopped school bus**.

- **STOP** when the bus's warning lights are flashing, or the stop arm comes out.

- When backing out of a driveway or leaving a garage, **watch out for children** walking to the bus stop or walking or bicycling to school.
- **Slow Down.** Watch for children walking in the street, especially where there is no sidewalk. Watch for children playing and gathering near bus stops.
- **Be Alert.** Children arriving late for the bus may dart into the street without looking for traffic.
- **Obey School Zone Speeds**. Be sure to pay attention to posted speed zones near schools and slow to the proper speed limit when the zone warning lights are flashing and/or during posted hours if not equipped with warning lights.

When driving in neighborhoods and especially in school zones, and near bus stops; **watch out for young people** who may be thinking about getting to school, but may not be thinking about getting there safely or the traffic around them. Every driver should remember the following about elementary school children:

- They become easily distracted and may start across the street without warning.
- They don't understand the dangers of moving vehicles
- They can't judge vehicle speeds or distances.
- They may be blocked from your view by the bus or other objects, shrubs, trees, or parked vehicles.
- MOST IMPORTANTLY, CHILDREN EXPECT VEHICLES TO STOP FOR THEM AT THE SCHOOL BUS STOP. .

For more information on School Zone and School Bus Safety contact:

Tennessee DOS – Pupil Transportation
1148 Foster Avenue
Nashville, TN 37210
(615) 687-2302

SHARING THE ROAD WITH SLOW-MOVING VEHICLES

Be alert for slow-moving vehicles, especially in rural areas. Driving on empty rural highways can be just as dangerous as driving in heavy city traffic. It is easy to relax your attention…and suddenly come upon a dangerous surprise. Animals in the road, farm equipment moving from one field to another, horse drawn vehicles just over the crest of a hill, or a low spot covered with water are not unusual hazards in rural driving.

Stay alert, watch for warning signs, and slow down when approaching curves or hills that block your view of the roadway ahead. The "slow moving vehicle" emblem, a fluorescent or reflective orange triangle, must be displayed on the rear of vehicles drawn by animals, and most farm vehicles and construction equipment. Use caution when

approaching a slow moving vehicle and be sure it is safe before you pass. Be especially alert for:

Farm Machinery: Watch for tractors, combines, and other farm equipment moving across the road and traveling on state highways in rural areas. This type equipment can be very large and wide enough to take up more than one traffic lane. Farm machinery usually does not have turn signals and to make a right turn, operators of farm machinery may first pull wide to the left, then turn to the right. In most cases, these vehicles will be traveling at less than 25 M.P.H. Coming over the top of a hill at 55 M.P.H. to find a large slow-moving tractor in front of you is a frightening and dangerous experience. Expect the unexpected and be prepared to protect yourself and your passengers.

Horse Drawn Carriages: In some areas of Tennessee you may be sharing the road with animal-drawn vehicles. They have the same rights to use the road as a motor vehicle and must follow the same rules of the road. They are subject to heavy damage and injury to the occupants if hit by a car. Warning signs will be posted in areas where you are likely to find animal-drawn vehicles. Be Alert!

Horseback Riders: Horseback riders are subject to, and protected by, the rules of the road. They also must ride single file near the right curb or road edge, or on a usable right shoulder, lane or path. The law requires you to exercise due care when approaching a horse being ridden or led along a road. Areas where horseback riding is common will usually be marked with an advisory sign like the one shown above. You must drive at a reasonable speed, and at a reasonable distance away from the horse. Do NOT sound your horn or "rev" your engine loudly when approaching or passing a horse.

SHARING THE ROAD WITH HIGHWAY WORK ZONES

Work Zone Safety: It's Everybody's Business

Work zones on U.S. highways have become increasingly dangerous places for both workers and travelers, with the death rate approaching two per day. Approximately 40,000 people per year are injured as a result of crashes in work zones. With more than 70,000 work zones in place across America on a given day, highway agencies are realizing that it is not enough to focus on improving the devices used in the work zone areas, but that they must also reach out to the public in order to change the behavior of drivers so that crashes can be prevented.

What is a Work Zone? A work zone is any type of road work that may impede traffic conditions. Many work zones involve lane closures. They may also be on the shoulder or in the median. Moving work zones such as sweepers, line painting trucks, or mowing equipment and workers are also quite common.

Highway work zones are set up according to the type of road and the work to be done on the road. There are a number of events that make up a work zone. They can be long-term projects of short term actions. A work zone can also exist at anytime of the year. The common theme among work zones is the color orange. Work zone materials such as cones, barrels, signs, large vehicles, or orange vests on workers give you an indication that you are either approaching a work zone or are already in a work zone.

What do you do when approaching a Work Zone? Watch for the color orange – it always means: "road work—slow down". All temporary signs in work zones have an orange background and black letters or symbols. These signs will be found on the right side of the road, or on both left and right sides when the roadway is a divided highway, and they will tell you what (one lane traffic, uneven lanes, etc.) and how soon (miles or feet ahead) you will encounter the work zone. Most work zones also have signs 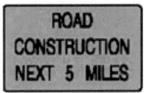 alerting you to reductions in the speed limit through the work zone.

These speed reductions are necessary for the safety of the workers and motorists. The reduced speed limits are clearly posted within the work zone and if there are no reduced speed limit postings, drivers should obey the normal posted speed limit. Under Tennessee law, speed violations that occur in the work zones where the speed has been reduced and where employees of the DOT and/or construction workers are present will result in a fine up to a maximum of $500 dollars.

What should you do when driving through Work Zones?

Signing, traffic control devices, roadway markings, flaggers, and law enforcement officers are used to protect highway workers and to direct drivers safely through work zones or along carefully marked detours.

As a driver you should learn and abide by the following safety tips for driving in work zones:

• *Slow down and pay full attention to the driving situation*! A car traveling 60 M.P.H. travels 88 feet per second. If you see a sign that says "Road Work 1500 Feet", you'll be in that construction zone in 17 seconds!

• **Follow the instructions** on the road work zone warning signs and those given by flaggers.

• **Avoid complacency**. Don't become oblivious to work zone signs when the work is long term or widespread.

• **Be aware** that traffic patterns in work zones can change daily including lane shifts or alternating lane closures.

• **Use extreme caution** when driving through a work zone at night whether workers are present or not.

• **Calm down**. Work zones aren't there to personally inconvenience you. They're there to improve the roads for everyone.

• **Watch the traffic** around you, and be prepared to react to what the traffic is doing. Check the taillights/brake lights of vehicles ahead of you for indications of what is happening on the road ahead. Be ready to respond quickly.

- **Merge as soon as possible**. Motorists can help maintain traffic flow and posted speeds by moving to the appropriate lane at first notice of an approaching work zone.

- **Obey the posted speed limits.** Workers could be present just a few feet away.

- **Adjust you lane position** away from the side workers and equipment when possible.

- **Keep a safe distance** between your vehicle and traffic barriers, trucks, construction equipment and workers. **Don't tailgate!**

- Some work zones – like line painting, road patching and mowing – are mobile. Just because you don't see the workers immediately after you see the warning signs doesn't mean they're not out there. Observe the posted signs until you see the on that says "End Road Work".

- **Use total concentration** when driving through work zones. Pay attention to your surroundings. This is not the time to use the cellular phone, change the radio station, read the paper, apply make-up, shave or fill out the expense report.

- **Avoid road work zones** altogether by using alternate routes, when you can.

- **Expect delays**; plan for them and leave early to reach your destination on time.

BE SAFE! BUCKLE UP!

One of the best safety precautions you can do to protect your life and the lives of you passengers is __ALWAYS WEAR YOUR SEAT BELT.__

Some Final Safety Reminders To Think About:

The color orange is a signal to motorists that a work zone is near. <u>When you see orange, use common sense, caution and concentration as you drive through these areas.</u>

Everyone has a right to a safe workplace. The roads are a construction or maintenance worker's job. <u>One careless mistake by a motorist and a worker could be killed or injured. So could the motorist.</u>

Don't expect the road workers to see you coming. They may be concentrating more on work than on the traffic.

The lives of highway construction workers depend on drivers like you obeying the posted speed limits in work zones.

SEE ORANGE, NOT RED

Work zones are no place for impatience or aggressive driving. After all, they're there to make the roads better and safer for you. The extra seconds or minutes it takes to get through a work zone are a small price to pay for years of safer driving.

For more information on Work Zone Safety visit these websites:

http://safety.fhwa.dot.gov

If you are trying to teach someone else how to drive, **the most important thing you can do is to drive safely yourself**. Though it sounds trite, it is true. Your friend or family member is now watching more carefully than you can ever dream. How do we know? Examiners quite often hear, "Well, that's how my dad/mom does it." Sometimes the young drive is saying this to defend such things as "rolling stops". Luckily, it is also often said with pride, when the applicant is giving a parent credit for their safe driving habits.

Getting a driver license is often referred to as the modern equivalent of a rite of passage to adulthood for the young, new driver – and it's certainly a dangerous one. The driving world they enter is far too intense to tackle without serious preparation.

As a parent (or concerned mentor for a friend) you are the one who cares most about your teenager's driving ability and safety. This chapter will help give you some hints and ideas on ways to participate in the process of educating your teenager (or inexperienced adult) behind the wheel.

Which Comes First, the Book or the Road?

You both will find it helpful to review this handbook, and any other materials you can find before actually letting the new driver get behind the wheel. People under the age of eighteen (18) must have a learner permit for 180 days and qualify under the GDL program before they can be road tested. (See Chapter 3 for full details.) This requirement involves "book learning" before getting on the road and a minimum amount of "supervised on the road learning" before getting a license to drive solo. This is a good principle for people of any age who are just learning to drive.

A SAFE Attitude for Driving and Learning

Attitude determines how the knowledge and skills your teen or new driver learns will be used. It determines whether a driver will be cooperative or competitive in traffic, whether he or she will accept a high level of risk or put into practice the concepts of defensive driving taught by their instructor and covered in Chapter 13 of this manual.

As we mentioned above your biggest contribution to your new driver's safety and effectiveness behind the wheel will be your example. Patience, courtesy, and a willingness to improve will be your best assets. Now is the time to review your own driving habits and offer your teen or new driver the example of courtesy and consideration for other road users. This may do more than anything else to ensure your teen's driving safety.

Verbal Teaching in the "Moving Classroom"

A second helpful thing you can do is to talk out loud while you are driving. Rather than overload the new driver with information and advice while he or she is also trying to simply learn the mechanics of driving, take advantage of

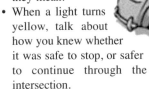

teaching opportunities while you are behind the wheel. These are truly "teachable moments". For example, you can:

- Point out tricky road signs, and ask what they mean.
- When a light turns yellow, talk about how you knew whether it was safe to stop, or safer to continue through the intersection.
- Ask the teen/new driver questions about the traffic behind you or beside you – make them aware that you have to pay attention to traffic all around you, not just in front of you.
- Practice the "two-second" rule by explaining out loud the steps you are taking to gauge your following distance.

Once you start doing this, you will be surprised at all of the wisdom you already have. You may also be surprised when it opens the door for your pupil to offer friendly and constructive criticism of your own driving habits! Since most of us have room for improvement, you will, hopefully, be able to accept with humor any good criticism they have.

Planning Safe and Informative Practice Sessions

It's important to plan practice sessions. Always decide where to go and what you are going to do before setting out. Random driving around during practice sessions can be dangerous. It is all too easy for the novice driver to get into trouble particularly in the early stages. Before venturing into traffic for practice driving be sure that your teen / new driver has good coordination with hands and feet. Until the novice is sure of the pedals, the danger of hitting the wrong pedal in a panic situation is always present.

Nothing substitutes for actual experience on the road. However you will want to have your first lessons concentrate on simply gaining control of the vehicle. Later lessons can build on this, getting increasingly more challenging. Listed below is some ideas for one approach you might choose to follow:

Phase One: Have the new driver practice controlling the car itself. Find someplace safe and away from traffic. A large deserted parking lot is ideal for these initial sessions because it allows the beginner to concentrate fully on the feel of the controls and the response of the car. Start by practicing these basic skills:

- Buckling up, adjusting the seat and mirrors so that all necessary controls are within easy reach.
- Operating the gearshift (and clutch if manual transmission), gas and brake pedals.
- Backing and pulling the car forward.

- Right and Left turns while driving in the parking lot.
- Staying within an imaginary lane.

Phase Two: Take the driver to a quiet residential area and let your new driver practice not only the above skills, but also add:
- Pulling into traffic and navigating simple intersections
- Keeping proper lane position and allowing safe (2-second) following distances.
- Easy lane changes.

Phase Three: After you are satisfied that the basic controls are fairly well mastered, you are now ready to take the new driver into heavier traffic. Again, you will practice all of the above, and add:
- Parallel parking and up / down hill parking
- Navigating multiple turn lane intersections
- U-turns and quick stops (simulating emergency)

Phase Four: When you have confidence the new driver can handle greater challenges, you should guide him or her to practice all the above in the following conditions:
- On high-speed multi-lane highways or interstates
- In various weather conditions
- At night in good weather and bad weather
- City driving or heavy traffic areas

Additional hints to help you as a teacher / mentor:

Stay Alert.: Anticipate problems and always be ready to react to help avoid accidents or other unsafe situations.

Communicate Clearly: Give directions well in advance and try to always use the same terms (don't say accelerator one time and gas pedal the next, for example).

Don't hit the beginner with everything at once: rather than taking the new driver to a multi-lane intersection for their first left turn do this in a calmer traffic area. Remember even a simple right turn involves several steps (checking mirrors, signaling, braking, lane use, braking, turning, etc.) To expect a beginner to follow all of these correctly during the early sessions is asking too much.

Don't get excited during practice sessions: calmly respond to errors as needed. Don't "yell and fuss" over every mistake. This can quickly erode the new driver's confidence and make performance difficult.

Don't overload or distract: Remember everything you say is also a distraction for the drive. Be sparing in your comments and, above all, try to avoid letting the beginner get into situation he or she isn't ready to handle.

Stop and Discuss: Stop as soon as you can, while a major mistake is still fresh in the new driver's memory. Then take time to discuss what happened and what the safest response should be.

Two Reference Tools to Consider

Driving Log: Safety researchers have found that the more supervised miles new drivers have before driving on their own, the fewer accidents they have. This seems like common sense, but is there a magic number of miles you should ride with your student? The University of Michigan's

Transportation Research Institute recommends 3,000 miles.

Each new driver is different, of course, and yours may not need that many miles to be a confident, competent driver. Tennessee's GDL program requires a specific number of hours (50) be driven by minors prior to being eligible to move up to the Intermediate license level. To keep track of these hours we suggest either getting a simple spiral ring notebook to keep in the glove compartment to record your practice sessions – or – you may choose to make copies of the sample log on the next page.

Driving Contracts: The first year of driving is a high-risk period for the beginner. Inexperience combined with a lack of skill means that one in five male 16-year old drivers and about one in ten female 16-year olds will have an accident during their first year of driving. Some of the worst accidents occur at night and with a group of young people in the car. If alcohol or any other kind of impairment is involved the risk in this situation is magnified several times. This is one of the reasons that Tennessee's GDL program places restrictions on these two areas for new teen drivers.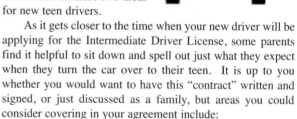

As it gets closer to the time when your new driver will be applying for the Intermediate Driver License, some parents find it helpful to sit down and spell out just what they expect when they turn the car over to their teen. It is up to you whether you would want to have this "contract" written and signed, or just discussed as a family, but areas you could consider covering in your agreement include:
- ✓ Where they may drive (miles, road types, etc.)
- ✓ What hours of the day they may drive
- ✓ The condition the car should be returned (gas in tank, clean, etc.) and the consequences if this is neglected.
- ✓ Who pays for the car's gas and maintenance
- ✓ What amount they will contribute toward auto insurance
- ✓ Responsibility for parking tickets or vehicle damage
- ✓ Consequences for moving violations, including speeding

Safe driving is very much a matter of seeing what needs to be seen and making good decisions, but this is not simple to achieve. Experience and training play a major role in ensuring that a driver's eyes will look in the right places at the right time and that their knowledge of safe and defensive driving will help them make the proper response to the situation.

Being a good defensive driver means more than just being cautious; and mere experience isn't enough either! The good defensive driver has to work at developing good driving techniques. And this work does not end with passing the driver license examination. The novice driver's biggest enemy is the complacency that comes from early success at

Made in the USA
Columbia, SC
29 August 2024

41307211R00061